G0 CBW 156

The international sugar trade

A C HANNAH
DONALD SPENCE

Published in association with the
INTERNATIONAL SUGAR ORGANIZATION

John Wiley & Sons, Inc.

New York • Chichester • Weinheim • Brisbane • Singapore • Toronto

382.4136
H24i

This text is printed on acid-free paper.

Copyright © 1996 by Woodhead Publishing Ltd.
Published 1997 by John Wiley & Sons, Inc., by agreement
with Woodhead Publishing Ltd. *LKP*

All rights reserved. Published simultaneously in Canada.

Reproduction or translation of any part of this work beyond
that permitted by Section 107 or 108 of the 1976 United
States Copyright Act without the permission of the copyright
owner is unlawful. Requests for permission or further
information should be addressed to the Permissions Department,
John Wiley & Sons, Inc., 605 Third Avenue, New York, NY
10158-0012.

This publication is designed to provide accurate and
authoritative information in regard to the subject
matter covered. It is sold with the understanding that
the publisher is not engaged in rendering legal, accounting,
or other professional services. If legal advice or other
expert assistance is required, the services of a competent
professional person should be sought.

Library of Congress Cataloging in Publication Data:
ISBN 0-471-19054-3

Printed in the United States of America

10 9 8 7 6 5 4 3 2 1

Contents

University Libraries
Carnegie Mellon University
Pittsburgh PA 15213-3890

CONTENTS

University Libraries
Carnegie Mellon University
Pittsburgh PA 15213-3890

CONTENTS

Foreword

When Woodhead Publishing invited the International Sugar Organization (ISO) to act as a co-publisher for a book on the international sugar trade, there was not the slightest hesitation to accept. To the contrary, for the ISO as the unique governmental body dedicated to improving conditions on the world sugar market through debate, analysis, special studies and transparent statistics the proposal was very much welcomed because it fitted extremely well into our general philosophy to contribute to better market transparency and to offer more and better services, primarily to our member countries, but also to all other parties involved in sugar matters, such as growers, millers, refiners, traders, consumers and the media.

Since the late 1940s the ISO has been at the forefront of sugar statistics and analysis. In particular *The World Sugar Economy – Structure and Policies* (1963) remains a standard work today, much consulted by researchers and analysts. It was therefore particularly appropriate that the ISO should be associated with this book, which perfectly fits the current philosophy of the Organization.

The book in hand fills a gap because it deals in a condensed and comprehensive way with the challenges and key features of the world sugar economy. This book on the international sugar trade together with the annual ISO Sugar Year Book, the newly published book on ISO World Sugar Statistics 1955–94, our regular publications and studies and our international workshops, seminars and forums, hopefully help to explain the complexity of the world sugar situation and contribute to a better understanding.

Dr Peter Baron
Executive Director
International Sugar Organization

Preface

S ugar is unique. We hope that anyone reading this book will be
convinced of this before reaching the end. In its historical,
political, sociological, economic and geographical aspects sugar
has built up a track record of associations which mark it out as
different from other soft commodities.

Although the title of this book is *The International Sugar Trade,* it
is impossible to describe and analyse sugar trade without first
discussing sugar's history, its production processes and consumption
patterns – trade is the residual. The book is therefore designed to be a
comprehensive account of sugar, the commodity. As such it fills a gap,
not only in the publisher's series, but also for a detailed book covering
all aspects of the world sugar industry. Remarkably, for such a
fascinating subject, the last comparable book was Timoshenko and
Swerling *The World's Sugar – Progress and Policy* published back in
1957 (and still, surprisingly, in print). We have therefore tried, where
possible, to carry the main body of the analysis and statistics back to
the early 1950s to provide some continuity with Timoshenko and
Swerling. A secondary, but important objective was to provide, where
possible, long series which fellow analysts might find useful in their
work.

While trying to avoid overlapping, each chapter is constructed to
be a self-contained essay on the subject matter, so the book can serve
equally as a reference on specific topics as well as an overview of the

world sugar economy. The book is thus aimed at a wide audience, from specialists looking for more background, to traders coming to sugar for the first time, and finally students, non-specialists and laymen in search of an introduction to the fascinating world of sugar. It covers the diversity of production and consumption, the properties and popularity of sugar and also refers to the health issues and alternative sweeteners. The book is co-published with the International Sugar Organization, whose statistics are used, with few exceptions, throughout.

Part I covers the origin, background and production of sugar, and places sugar in its political and sociological context. Part II starts with a review of sugar policies – sugar is the type of commodity around which complex production policies have grown – and goes on to deal with major producers and consumers and substitute products. Part III focuses on the trade itself, including a structural analysis of the world sugar trade, trends in prices and trading techniques. Part IV deals with future trends, and the appendices cover important issues such as sugar and health, sugar and the environment, the Brazilian fuel alcohol programme and international sugar agreements.

The authors would like to acknowledge with gratitude the contribution of Mireille Neri, of the ISO Secretariat, who prepared the charts and the larger tables, and Victoria Greatorex, also of the ISO Secretariat, who prepared the manuscript.

A C Hannah
Donald Spence

Origins, background and production

1

A brief history

Production

The evolution of sugar into the nutritious and plentiful plant of today took a long time. It is now widely assumed that the natural home of sugar cane is the Polynesian islands of the South Pacific where it is believed to have existed as long ago as 2000 BC. It was well known in India a thousand years later and in Persia around 500 BC. One of Alexander the Great's generals came across it in Persia and called it 'the reed which makes honey without bees'. From around 100 BC it was introduced into China and other Far Eastern countries and by AD 100 the art of sugar making was well advanced throughout those areas.

Hitherto, the only source of sweetness was from honey; bees are often found amongst the hieroglyphics that surround Egyptian tombs, signifying that the person, when alive, kept them.

Later, the armies of the prophet Mohammed also found sugar in Persia whilst waging a holy war designed to convert the whole world to Islam in about AD 630. It was quickly introduced to all the surrounding countries within the prophet's sphere of influence and spread to the north coast of Africa, eventually reaching the western end of the Mediterranean.

At this time it was known as the Persian reed and the production of sugar from it was very primitive. It involved a blindfold and tethered mule or ox walking in a circle, driving a vertical grinding mill to crush the cane. The juice was then evaporated, by boiling, to leave a mixture of crystals and syrup. It did not keep very long and could not be stored. This method is still used in parts of India and elsewhere.

Almost five hundred years later, in 1100, the first samples of the Persian reed reached Britain, brought back by the returning Crusaders. However, it was not until the early fourteenth century that it started arriving in sufficient quantities to be widely available. The first regular trade in sugar to Britain began in 1319 when some Venetian traders started regular shipments. Shipments were erratic and it was also very expensive and therefore out of the reach of all but the richest. One of the earliest mentions of sugar in Britain was in 1226, when the Mayor of Winchester held a banquet for King Henry III. The Mayor was charged to provide 'three pounds of Alexandrian sugar, if so much is to be found'.[1]

By about 1500, sugar cane had become widely known, extensively cultivated and actively traded south of the 35th parallel. Often grown as a garden plant, it was also used as a medicine. The Dutch East India Company began shipments from Java and nearby countries to Europe from about 1615.

Sugar cane was first introduced to the New World by Christopher Columbus who took some Canary Islands plants on his second voyage in 1493. It quickly flourished all over the Caribbean, which was known as the Spanish Main at that time. After Britain's acquisition of the Caribbean in the middle of the seventeenth century, the industry continued to grow and sugar soon became an important export to Britain. There was a large demand for it since, up to then, the quality of the sugar in Britain was very bad; most of it came from Morocco and it was frequently unusable. This severely restricted consumption growth and led to widespread complaints to the government. Approximate growth of cane production in the Caribbean area and Brazil is shown in Table 1.1.

By 1700, things had greatly improved; both Britain and France were actively encouraging the planting of new stronger variations and strains of cane from both the Mediterranean and the Far East.

The cultivation of sugar cane is labour-intensive and the experiment of shipping British agricultural labourers to the Caribbean to work in the fields was not a success. The climate proved too much for them. Spanish and Portuguese workers absconded and set up shops and so the only answer to the labour shortage was indented labour from West Africa. These slaves were shipped in their thousands to the West Indies in the most appalling conditions, although, to be fair, the sailors at that time were only marginally better off.

A flourishing three-way trade developed with textiles, toys, etc,

---

1 Hugill A, *Sugar and All That – A History of Tate and Lyle*, Century, London, 1978.

Table 1.1 Approximate growth of cane production in the Caribbean area and Brazil, tonnes

	1750	**1770**	**1790**
Cuba	NK	NK	17 000
Jamaica	25 000	40 000	61 000
St Dominique (Haiti)	30 000	60 000	80 000
Leeward Islands	20 000	20 000	20 000
Windward Islands	NK	21 000	30 000
Brazil	20 000	20 000	21 000
Suriname	8 000	6 000	9 500
British Guiana	NK	3 500	NK

Note: Totals are approximate and have been rounded. NK = not known. *Sources: Noel Deerr, ISO.*

being shipped to West Africa and bartered for slaves and gold dust and taken to the West Indies, from where sugar and rum was shipped to Europe. The success of this trade essentially altered the pattern of production around the Mediterranean. Apart from Egypt and parts of Spain, it had disappeared completely by the end of the eighteenth century.

Between 1690 and 1790, some 12 million tonnes of sugar cane were shipped to Europe from the Western hemisphere but by the end of the eighteenth century the Napoleonic wars again altered the situation considerably. The superiority of the Royal Navy successfully blockaded all European ports, effectively preventing any goods from reaching them. By now, the consumption of sugar was widespread and the cost had fallen to such an extent that it was within the grasp of virtually everyone. The wars, however, quickly reversed that trend and the shortages prompted a public outcry. Cane sugar production in 1800 is shown in Table 1.2.

Shortages led to the arrival of sugarbeet. About 50 years earlier in 1748, a German scientist, Andreas Sigismund Marggraf became the first person to discover the presence of sugar in the red and white beet plants. Not being a businessman, Marggraf failed to recognize the commercial implications of his discovery and it was left to Franz Carl Achard to follow it up. By 1799 Achard's experiments had advanced sufficiently to persuade King Frederick William III to build, at his own expense, a beet factory in Silesia, which opened in 1801. Europe's first commercial sugarbeet factory had been built two years earlier in Bohemia in Austria-Hungary.

But this, too, failed for lack of business acumen. However, by this time, several others had started up and were actively engaged in production. It had also spread to other countries, notably France,

Table 1.2 Cane sugar production in 1800, tonnes

India	12 000	Leeward Islands	17 000
China	NK	Windward Islands	24 000
Java	6 000	Mexico	16 000
Mauritius	3 000	Brazil	21 000
Cuba	29 000	Peru	7 500
Jamaica	71 000	Suriname	7 500

where, by 1811, thanks to official action and encouragement, a thriving industry had been established. Napoleon decreed that French farmers grow sugarbeet and by 1813 there were over 300 factories in operation, providing some 7.7 million lb of sugar. However, the Treaty of Paris in 1814 reopened French ports to colonial sugar, causing the temporary collapse of the industry throughout most of Europe. Nevertheless, it revived from about 1830 and by 1850 there were thriving industries in France, Germany, Russia and Austria–Hungary, see Table 1.3.

Table 1.3 Beet sugar production 1840–80, 000 tonnes

	1840	1850	1860	1870	1880
Austria–Hungary	4	17	77	213	533
France	30	76	101	282	331
Germany	14	53	127	263	594
Russia	NK	13	26	125	304

Note: NK = not known. *Sources: Noel Deerr, ISO.*

In Britain, however, attitudes were somewhat different. Powerful vested interests both at home and abroad were extremely hostile to any advancement in beet technology as they saw it as a threat to the extremely lucrative livelihood they were enjoying. Despite this hostility, two Quakers opened a beet factory in Essex in 1830 and a second one started up six years later.

Being fervent anti-slavers and taking advantage of the growing anti-slavery movement, these pioneers labelled their product: 'Home-grown sugar – not made by slaves'. However, they could not compete with colonial suppliers and both ventures soon ended in failure. Apart from one brief attempt in 1870, no further developments occurred until 1912 when beet cultivation was perceived to be a sensible precaution in the light of a deteriorating European situation. Britain's first commercial beet factory opened in Norfolk in that year. In 1914, Britain depended upon continental suppliers for three-quarters of total sugar consumption.

Sugar production was one of the oldest industries of the old Russian Empire, emerging at the beginning of the nineteenth century. By the time of Napoleon's invasion in 1812, there were four beet plants in the country. By the middle of the century, the main centre of activity shifted to the Ukraine where over three-quarters of the beet crop was then grown. This continued until the revolution. A smaller centre developed in the black-soil region further north.

Yields were lower than in the rest of Europe and fluctuated widely despite the fact that extraction rates were similar. Yields increased 25% in the period immediately preceding World War I. The agrarian revolution of 1917–20 completely devastated the industry, destroying the large estates on which it was based.

Before World War I, production exceeded two million tonnes but by 1921–22 it had fallen to a mere 57 000 tonnes and did not recover to pre-war levels until the 1930s. In the 1920s and 1930s the industry expanded to the eastern region of the USSR, as far as the climate allowed. Sugarbeet cultivation under irrigation was also introduced in the warm but dry regions of Central Asia and Transcaucasia. During this time, Ukraine's share of the market fell from its peak of 84% in 1921 to less than 70% by 1935.

At the end of the eighteenth century, with Florida, Louisiana and Texas under Spanish rule, there was no sugar production in the USA. After a hesitant start in the early 1800s, a disastrous fall in the price of sugar and a substantial rise in the price of cotton caused farmers to switch to the latter. However, it soon revived and, by 1853, production passed the 200 000 tonne mark. At the start of the Civil War, production had reached 240 000 tonnes, but by the end of it, in 1864, had fallen to only 5000, largely due to the desertion and impressing into the army of the slaves needed to cultivate the cane. This was quickly followed by the emancipation of slaves in the southern states, so recovery was very slow. Output in 1880 was still less than half the level of 1854.

As was the case in Europe, the US beet industry suffered a slow start and it did not become permanently established until 1890, when the Alameda Sugar Company of California was formed.

Throughout the nineteenth century, the development of cane sugar industries in Africa and Oceania, as well as in the Western hemisphere, was a continuous process, evolving steadily, adapting to technical innovations and combating the competition from beet. In the Western hemisphere, the development of Cuba at this time was one of rapid economic progress and sugar production grew from 29 000 tonnes in 1800, to over 700 000 tonnes in 1868. Possessing the first steam engine in a cane sugar factory, 25 mills were steam-driven by 1808. Technology in Cuba at this time was way ahead of that in Europe. Slavery was not finally abolished in Cuba until 1886 which, latterly, gave the country a competitive advantage over other producers. If it had not been for the endless rebellion and riots by the slave population and the general antagonism towards the Spanish colonial regime, progress might easily have been considerably greater. The emancipation of slaves throughout the region presented further challenges to producers in the nineteenth century. One of these was the inequality of duties and quotas on sugar from countries not controlled by Britain.

In Africa, cane production continued to flourish in Egypt throughout the nineteenth century. It was introduced into Natal in 1847 when the first seeds arrived from Mauritius. After a slow start, production reached 12 000 tonnes by 1880. Meanwhile in Mauritius, development gathered momentum from 1825 when duty disadvantages had been eliminated. Production quickly reached 33 000 tonnes and averaged 115 000 tonnes per year by the end of the century.

Despite its geographical proximity to the Polynesian islands of the South Pacific, sugar cane is not indigenous to Australia and it was not until 1822 that sugar was first produced in New South Wales. By 1859, production had started in Queensland and total Australian production had reached 16 000 tonnes in 1880.

Important changes also occurred in Asia during the nineteenth century with Java and the Philippines playing major parts in world trade. China also remained an important producer but attempts in other countries, such as Malaya and Ceylon (now Sri Lanka), only resulted in small quantities for domestic consumption.

India did not start to produce sugar until 1923 but quickly made up for lost time, expanding rapidly to reach the 1 million tonne level in only 12 years. Production was not affected by World War II and reached 3 million tonnes by 1963 and 13.8 million in 1992.

Nevertheless, the nineteenth century was a period of great change and technological advance for the sugar industry and by about 1880, the basic technical development was complete. World production in 1800 totalled 245 000 tonnes and by 1880 it had reached 3 832 000 tonnes, see Table 1.4. This figure does not include non-centrifugal sugar which 30 years earlier was the only type produced. The centrifuge was the last of the inventions connected with the industry and today's suspended type was first used in Hawaii in 1867. Non-centrifugal sugar denotes that produced by primitive methods; very little of which, if any, reaches the international trade. In 1800, cane was the only sugar produced but 80 years later, beet had gained just under half the total of world production. In 1885, beet overtook cane

Table 1.4 Total world sugar production from 1800, 000 tonnes, raw value

Year	Total	% cane	Year	Total	% cane
1800	245	100	1950	29 160	63
1830	572	100	1960	49 011	60
1860	1725	80	1970	72 896	60
1870	2723	63	1980	84 539	61
1880	3832	52	1990	110 894	63
1890	5716	39	1991	112 100	66
1900	8385	34	1992	117 564	67
1910	12 705	48	1993	112 377	64
1920	12 382	73	1994	110 288	69
1930	24 615	63	1995	116 000*	70
1940	27 075	60			

*Estimate
Sources: Noel Deerr, ISO.

production and reached over 50% of the total by 1915, falling to about a quarter in 1919 and thereafter recovering to around 40% from 1930 to 1960. Today the ratio is approximately 30% beet and 70% cane.

Up to the outbreak of World War I, the expansion of the sugar industry continued at an increasing pace. World output increased to more than 16 million tonnes, 7.7 million of which was European beet.

European beet output was significantly boosted by the system of sugar bounties that prevailed from around 1850 until their abolition in 1903. Bounties were in operation in Germany, France, Austria-Hungary, Russia, Belgium and the Netherlands and, although different in each country, had the same final effect – the large-scale dumping of sugar and a ruinous decline in prices, from 25s 6d per hundredweight in 1872 to 7s 3d in 1902.

By the end of World War I, world production had fallen to just over 12 million tonnes but, due to greatly improved prices, had recovered to reach over 25 million tonnes by 1930. Cane-producing countries were well prepared to take advantage of this situation and their improved cultivation techniques and new higher-yielding varieties were chiefly responsible for the increase in output. By the mid-1920s, however, this increased production began to exceed consumption, and prices started to fall. This fall continued through the Depression of the 1930s and resulted in a fall in production until 1935 when both recovered significantly. World production reached a peak of 27 million tonnes in 1939 but by 1945/46 it had fallen back to 18.2 million, only 1.5 million tonnes above the previous peak of 16.7 million tonnes in 1913/14.

It was during the inter-war period that various preferential arrangements and international agreements were formed. These were designed to improve the value of sugar during times of low prices but that, coupled with increasing competition from cane producers, caused many beet producers to resort to protectionist measures in the form of import duties and subsidies. The implication of these preferential arrangements and international agreements are discussed in Chapter 4.

Since World War II, the industry has continued to expand. From 18.2 million tonnes in 1945/46, world production reached 55 million tonnes 15 years later, 100 million in 1981/82 and over 115 million in 1991/92.

Consumption

The growth of sugar consumption throughout its history is subject to great inequalities and a dearth of reliable statistics. Indeed, it was not until 1950 that consumption statistics became even remotely accurate. Prior to that, the only guide was from production figures which, since there was never any surplus, were also the assumed consumption figures.

When, in about 1000 AD, sugar was coming into common use, it was only just becoming known in Europe and remained a luxury confined to the very rich for another 500 years. After about 1500 AD quantities increased considerably and consumption grew accordingly.

In the first decade of the eighteenth century, per capita consumption in the UK was estimated to have been around 2 kg, and to have reached 8 kg by 1800 and 39 kg by 1900. In that year, it was estimated at 32 kg in the USA. However, when measured in terms of production versus population, world consumption in 1900 was just 5 kg per capita, see Table 1.5.

Using this method, it reached around 12 kg by 1930 before falling in the Great Depression. Following the severe decline in production during World War II, that figure was not exceeded until 1951, reaching 17.5 kg by 1962.

World figures, though, are misleading and hide great geographical disparities. European consumption, for instance, grew from 19 kg per capita in the 1930s, to 34.5 kg by 1962.

During the 1970s and 1980s, however, further growth in consumption was seriously restricted by various health scares and a vociferous anti-sugar lobby that claimed that it caused cancer and heart disease. The medical properties of sugar are discussed in

Table 1.5 World per capita sugar consumption from 1900, kg, raw value

1900	5.1
1910	7.0
1920	7.3
1930	12.3
1940	11.9
1950	11.9
1960	16.1
1970	19.9
1980	20.2
1990	20.6
1994	20.4

Source: ISO.

Chapter 8 but, in fact, there is no conclusive proof that it is harmful. Indeed, there is now a strong school of thought that considers it to be positively beneficial in moderation.

Nevertheless, partly as a result of these attacks, per capita consumption is now little changed from 30 years ago, although it peaked in the early 1980s. European consumption reached 43 kg per capita in 1987, but totalled only 36.2 kg per capita in 1993, while world consumption has remained fairly steady, at around 20 kg per capita for the past 20 years.

The potential for further growth in consumption is enormous, particularly in Asia and Africa, where in some countries it is less than 3 kg per head per year. Even in 1993, China's consumption was only 6.4 kg per head per year; it is not unreasonable, bearing the international average in mind, for that figure to more than double which would make an enormous impact on the statistical picture. However, at present, the Chinese get their energy needs from rice. Table 1.6 shows growth figures for sugar consumption; Tables 1.7 and 1.8 list highest and lowest sugar consumers in 1993.

Trade

Sugar was traded in the east ever since it came into common use, around AD 1000. As production spread westwards to Persia and the eastern Mediterranean, the trade slowly developed in those areas.

From the eleventh to the thirteenth centuries, Egypt was the major source of sugar for Europe, via the ports of Genoa and Venice.

Table 1.6 Growth of per capita sugar consumption

	Pre-World War II	1962	1993
USSR/FSU	11.2	37.9	37.7
UK	48.4	54.2	37.5
France	28.1	41.2	37.5
Germany	26.9	32.2	37.5
Netherlands	30.9	46.3	37.5
Belgium/Luxembourg	29.3	36.7	37.5
Spain	12.4	19.6	37.5
Portugal	10.0	18.2	37.5
Denmark	55.3	56.8	37.5
Greece	11.1	14.1	37.5
Austria	26.5	43.1	51.7
Sweden	49.3	45.7	44.4
Switzerland	41.0	48.1	45.4
Poland	11.8	32.8	43.9
Czechoslovakia	26.6	41.3	42.5
Hungary	11.2	30.2	37.1
Canada	44.3	45.6	40.0
USA	47.0	47.9	31.7
Argentina	32.2	39.2	35.8
Brazil	17.1	37.3	47.6
Chile	25.8	36.2	44.1
Peru	12.0	25.3	30.1
Venezuela	5.4	34.3	34.8
China	1.0	2.8	6.4
Hong Kong	14.3	22.3	26.4
India	3.2	6.4	14.6
Indonesia	4.6	5.9	14.3
Iran	6.4	18.9	25.8
Japan	12.3	16.9	21.5
Pakistan	3.1	3.5	22.6
Singapore	35.9	47.6	73.2
Thailand	4.3	4.2	23.3
Africa	5.1	10.8	13.2
Australia	53.1	54.0	50.9
New Zealand	50.2	51.7	53.6

Table 1.7 World's highest consumers in 1993, kg per capita per annum

1 Gibraltar	77.5	5 Costa Rica	60.5
2 Swaziland	77.0	6 Fiji	60.2
3 Singapore	73.2	7 Iceland	57.7
4 Cuba	73.1	8 Israel	57.1

Source: ISO.

Table 1.8 World's lowest consumers in 1993, kg per capita per annum

1 Central African Republic	1.1	5 Nepal	1.9
2 Myanmar	1.2	6 Guinea-Bissau	1.9
3 Rwanda	1.5	7 Burundi	2.0
4 Kampuchea	1.6	8 Laos	2.2

Source: ISO.

Even after the decline of Egypt as a supplier and the emergence of Tripoli, Sicily and Cyprus, these European ports continued to prosper. In the fifteenth century, thriving refining industries developed there to supply the very rich of Central and Northern Europe.

By the sixteenth century, Turkish warmongering eroded the importance of these producing areas as output dropped due to the fighting. Lands further west were quick to fill the gap and Madeira, the Canary Islands and the Iberian peninsula became important producers. Logistical problems prevented Venice from continuing as the refining centre of Europe as it became quicker and more practical to ship the sugar from Lisbon northwards to Antwerp. North-west Europe and Britain were becoming increasingly important consumers by this time, and Antwerp quickly became the chief sugar trading and processing centre of Europe.

However, Antwerp's dominance was short-lived for, in 1576, the town was sacked and from then until about 1660 Amsterdam took over. During the first half of the seventeenth century, supplies from both Java and the New World competed with those nearer to home and all were shipped to Amsterdam which had a virtual monopoly of the trade at that time.

From 1660, when Britain passed its Navigation Acts, the sugar trade became more protectionist. The situation thereafter changed completely; trade with the British and French colonies became restricted to their mother countries. Sugar production in the colonies was expanding rapidly and refining industries in both Britain and France were quickly established. These were soon protected by tariff legislation.

Amsterdam remained the chief port for distribution to the rest of Europe but its importance diminished as competition from Hamburg (at that time, a free city) eventually overtook it as the chief supplier to Central and North-eastern Europe.

During the eighteenth and nineteenth centuries, restrictions were greatly reduced and the trade became more of a free-for-all as sugar could be carried in almost any ship to almost any port. During this time, different countries became significant exporters and the trade expanded. Exports from Cuba and the Dominican Republic greatly increased and the Philippines, Mauritius and Hawaii emerged as significant exporters.

Towards the end of the nineteenth century, Europe became an exporter of beet sugar which led to even fiercer competition for the European markets and, to a lesser extent, the North American ones also.

The adoption of a free trade policy by Britain opened up the market to cheap foreign supplies of sugar which, thanks to the bounty system prevailing in Europe, caused a steady decline in prices. This also had an adverse affect on conditions in the British sugar colonies and undermined the competitiveness of cane producers.

At the end of the nineteenth century, however, trade as measured by total exports only amounted to around 6 million tonnes. After 1900, it expanded steadily; indeed, between 1900 and 1993, the volume quintupled to around 30 million tonnes. During this time, production grew from 10 million to 112 million tonnes so the share of the market held by exports declined from around 60% to around 21% today.

Progress, however, was not smooth; from 1900 to 1914, exports gradually increased. During World War I, they remained constant while production declined and it was not until about 1925 that a recovery started. Exports' share of world production fell from 70% to 62% between 1920 and 1930. Then came the Great Depression, again heralding a sharp decline in activity. After 1936, recovery started and by 1940, exports were averaging 11.9 million tonnes, only marginally higher than 15 years earlier, although the share fell to 47%.

World War II saw a further decline in the trade as exports fell to 7.1 million tonnes in 1942, the lowest since 1909. The 1941–45 average of exports was 8.6 million tonnes, 37% of production. Post-war recovery and expansion of trade was rapid and exports quickly passed 10 million tonnes in 1947 reaching 14 million in 1951 and 28 million in 1977, close to the present average.

Europe is the biggest exporter in the mid-1990s, with around 29% of the market followed by the fast expanding Asian producers which account for a further 21%. Central America has 18%, South America 14% and Oceania 13%.

2

Cultivation

Cane

Sugar, in some form or other occurs in all green plants, but commercial sugar, or sucrose, is stored most abundantly in cane and beet plants. Sugar cane is a grass of the genus *Saccharum* which grows in the tropics, roughly between latitudes 35 °N and 35 °S. In certain places it grows outside that belt, but it is usually found within the area where palm trees grow. It overlaps beet only in a few sub-tropical areas such as Southern Spain and Portugal.

Cane is a perennial plant which requires a hot and moist environment. A water-retaining soil is essential, as is strong sunlight with temperatures above 20 °C. It grows from the ratoon (bud) that forms on stubble from the previous harvest and reaches around five metres in height. New plantings are not often necessary and occur only every six to ten years. The stalk is hard and yellow with a few red and green spots; at the top, the green leaves are stiff in the middle, while the lower ones drop rather in the manner of palms. Inside the stalk are tubular channels, through which water and minerals in the soil are drawn up to the green leaves where photosynthesis takes place. The sugar is then carried back down and stored in the thick stalk. Cane is the most efficient collector of solar energy in the plant kingdom.

There is a multitude of commercially-produced varieties of sugar cane, all derived from their wild origins. Under natural conditions its growth is both rapid and prolific and the higher the temperature, the higher the sugar component of the canes. Excessive ratooning – the production of successive crops from stubble without fresh planting –

can affect yields, although it is very time- and labour-saving and results in a shorter growing period, due to the fact that the root system is already intact. High prices, labour surpluses and land shortages reduce the tendency for ratooning. The abundance of land in Cuba encourages a high degree of ratooning and the consequent low yields go a long way towards explaining the parlous state of the crop in the mid-1990s.

Commercially-grown crops are now largely free of insect pests and diseases. Chemicals and pesticides are widely used and most varieties are strongly resistant to infection. The threat of any epidemic disease to the plant has been greatly reduced in recent years. A cane is around 75% water, 14% sugar and 10% bagasse – the residual fibre which is used mainly as boiler fuel for the processing factory.

Prolonged periods of dry weather are needed for harvesting; mechanical methods are now widespread in most producing areas, apart from some countries, such as Mauritius, where the terrain makes this very difficult, if not impossible. In India, too, some areas where sugar is crushed to make gur or jaggery, a coarse brown sugar, are still primitively farmed. A pair of bullocks is yoked to a shaft and walked round and round in a circle. A young boy walks behind them making encouraging noises and occasionally hitting them to stop them falling asleep at their monotonous task. The green juice that is squeezed out of the cane is then heated in an open black pan by an oven that is fuelled by the crushed cane. Even the water used to wash out the pan after each boiling is recycled – it is given to the cattle to drink.

Sugar content declines rapidly after harvest, so swift removal to a mill is essential to enable the speedy extraction of the juice to take place. Processing mills are never far from the fields or plantations.

Beet

Beet is limited exclusively to temperate zones and is cultivated under a wide range of natural conditions. Temperature and rainfall are important factors in determining a crop's yield so the uncertain weather in temperate zones produces some wide variations from year to year. Therefore if a deficiency in one area is not compensated by a surplus in another, final outturns can be adversely affected.

The beet is a biennial plant requiring two seasons to produce seed. However, where grown for sugar production, it is harvested after the first growth – generally about six to eight months after planting. Good beet soils need high water-retaining properties but must not be so retentive as to impede growth, cultivation and harvesting. They must also be deep enough to allow the roots to develop. A typical beet is about 76% water and 16% sugar.

Sugarbeet is usually rotated one year in three or four with wheat and barley. It is more expensive to produce than cane but its advantage lies in its integration into the farming systems of the temperate zones. It also provides the farmer with a ready-made feed crop from the beet's tops and leaves. European Union (EU) subsidies through the Common Agricultural Policy (CAP) ensure the continued prosperity of beet farmers.

Sugarbeet is normally sown during March or early April and harvested mid-September to mid-December. Processing can go on until the following February. Insecticides and chemical weedkillers efficiently control weeds, pests and insects that attack the crop. One disease of particular concern to sugarbeet is rhizomania; it is a soil-borne disease that destroys the root and can reduce yields by as much as 50%. Research into this problem continues apace and it is hoped that a variety that is resistant to the virus responsible for rhizomania will be available by the turn of the century.

Harvesting and topping are now completely mechanized; sugar content does not deteriorate as rapidly as cane after harvesting but some loss is experienced during storage. Beet processing factories these days are fewer and situated further from the fields than formerly. Beets are consequently stored in frost-protected clamps on the edges of the fields to await transportation to the processing factories. Conditions for cost-effective harvesting usually deteriorate as autumn progresses and severe frosts can also damage the crop. Farmers therefore aim to have the clamps formed by mid-December. These clamps are a familiar sight in the landscape of Eastern England and Northern France at that time of year. The only beet areas in the Southern hemisphere are in Chile and Uruguay.

Processing

The transformation of both cane and beet into raw sugar is essentially the same. In both cases processing needs to be done as quickly as possible to gain optimum yields and sugar content, which is why the factories are often situated close to the fields.

Cane is shredded and beet is sliced and the juice is extracted. The bagasse and pulp are removed for fuel and animal feed. The juice is heated, lime is added and, after filtering, the juice is concentrated by evaporation. This thickened juice is boiled in steam-heated pans under vacuum, producing a mix of crystals (raw sugar) and syrup (molasses). These are separated by spinning in centrifugal machines. Molasses is converted into rum and baker's yeast as well as cattle food and industrial alcohol. The raw sugar, at this stage, is unfit for human consumption, unless specially treated and cleaned, but is ready for refining.

Centrifugal and non-centrifugal sugars are terms now commonly used to distinguish between modern sugars and those produced by more primitive methods.

Refining

Unlike processing, refining is usually carried out near areas of consumption rather than production. The raw sugar that reaches the refinery contains many impurities and is covered with a coating of molasses; the refining process is designed to remove these and produce a product that is over 99.95% pure sucrose. It contains no artificial colourings, preservatives or flavourings of any kind. Refined products obtained from cane and beet are identical.

The first step in sugar refining is affination, the mingling of the raw sugar with a heavy syrup to form a softened mixture that is spun in a centrifuge while sprays of hot water wash off the syrup coating. Clarification is achieved by phosphatation or carbonation which produces a chalk precipitate which traps impurities. This chalky substance, containing the impurities, is removed by pressure filtration – through diatomaceous earth after phosphatation or through calcium carbonate after carbonation. This also helps in colour and poly-saccharide removal.

The liquor emerging is clear and sparkling but still an amber or yellow colour, so it is passed over a decolorizing agent such as resin to remove it and all soluble impurities and other extraneous matter. The liquor itself then becomes clear and colourless and is ready for crystallization.

The liquor is then boiled under vacuum in large enclosed pans and, when it reaches the right thickness, crystallization is started by adding a controlled quantity of very small crystals to it. When these have grown to the required size they are separated in centrifugal machines and then dried in granulators. Four crystallizations are usually performed in series and the crystals from each stage yield about 50%. Sugars from the fourth operation, together with other low-purity liquors are sent through the system again or used to produce a range of other sugars and syrups where colour is not so important.

Different sizes of crystals are produced by variations in boiling technique and duration and these are graded either granulated, finest granulated or caster sugar. Icing sugar is made by pulverizing crystals in a mill and cube sugar by compressing moistened crystals in moulds before drying. To icing sugar, which is also known as powdered or confectioner's sugar, is added a small amount of corn starch or calcium phosphate to prevent caking.

CHAPTER

3

Sugar in its political and sociological context

More than just a sweetener

R eaders should already be convinced that sugar is a special product, with strong social, political, geographical and emotional attributes. How has sugar come to be the product that we know today? The purpose of this chapter is to place sugar in its social and political context.

Sugar performs many roles, but the two that stand out are as a sweetener and as a source of energy (calories). Sweetness is a very basic taste to the human palate, with a strong emotive quality. Sweetness is pleasurable and is first encountered early in life in breast milk (through lactose). Before 1650 the main sources of sweetness were honey and fruit. Up to that time sugar had been known (in Western Europe since the Dark Ages) as a rare spice, used to change the taste of food but not sweeten it in the modern sense.

As a source of energy sugar remains important. Table 3.1 shows energy content of 1990 world food output and it can be seen that in 1990 sugar was the fourth largest provider of calories. Sugar retains its fourth place in spite of declining per capita consumption in some industrialized countries. In developing countries sugar is still used as *both* a sweetener and an energy source, and is particularly important in some areas, e.g. Central and South America, with per capita consumption levels of 44 kg and 43 kg, respectively, in 1994.

Table 3.1   Energy content of 1990 world food output

	Production, million tonnes	Energy content, million calories
Wheat	601.7	2 413
Rice	521.7	1 847
Cassava	150.8	530
Sugar	123.4	460
Meat	176.6	387
Milk	537.8	349
Oilseeds	75.4	313
Fruit and vegetables	795.9	235
Pulses	58.8	200
Potatoes	268.1	165
Other	345.4	409

Source: Waggoner.

How did sugar reach this position in the world's diet? The history of sugar has already been discussed, but following Mintz,[1] we will look briefly at the development of sugar in Britain, a path which was paralleled in other developed, industrial countries.

In Britain in 1650, when most of the population was rural, the diet of the mass of the population was meagre and unpalatable, based around cereals supplemented, when available, by wild animals and domestic chickens. Wealthy people knew sugar as a spice and a luxury. From the mid-seventeenth century Britain began to acquire and develop colonies in the Caribbean, and sugar cultivation and production became the major plantation crop, especially in Barbados and Jamaica. The supply of sugar to Britain by the colonies increased a hundredfold from 1660 to 1750.

Sugar consumption among the labouring classes began in the eighteenth century with sugar as a sweetener associated with three other exotic imports – tea, coffee and chocolate. Since these were not at first sweetened and were bitter to taste, the wealthy early users had started to add sugar. By the time tea drinking became common, it was served hot and sweet. Of the three beverages, tea was the one to be drunk universally because it was cheaper to produce and a little went a long way. Among the poorer classes tea was also used to moisten bread – which was often stale – and to make it more palatable. Sugar was used on porridge (as sugar or treacle) again to make a relatively tasteless food palatable. By the mid-eighteenth century the quantities

---

1 Mintz SW, *Sweetness and Power – The Place of Sugar in Modern History*, Viking, New York, 1985.

21

of tea (and sugar) imported were so high and the price had fallen so much that it reached the point where tea, and its condiment sugar, had penetrated fully the working class market. By the mid-nineteenth century, when import duties were lifted, sugar had begun to take on a further role as an energy provider. Jams, jellies and puddings, all using sugar, became common amongst the labouring classes now urbanized by the Industrial Revolution.

The evolution of sugar consumption in Britain can therefore be summarized as follows:

- 1650–1750: Sugar is a spice, a luxury, available only to the upper classes, a symbol of wealth and power.
- 1750–1850: Sugar enters the working class diet, mainly as a sweetener. Process is accelerated by the Industrial Revolution.
- 1850–1950: The addition of jams, jellies and puddings adds the energy providing dimension, and sugar becomes a necessity. By 1900, sugar is providing one sixth of calorie intake.

Sugar was at first a symbol of colonial power, encompassing plantations, slavery, wealth (early capitalism) and the exploitation of the colony by the metropolitan power. Its demographic effect on the world must not be underestimated. The importation of slaves, largely for sugar plantations, has created large African populations in the Caribbean, USA and Central and South America whose social conditions and rights remain an issue today.

Sugar was transformed by the spread of its consumption and the Industrial Revolution into a means of power over the working class – keeping tea and sugar cheap and readily available kept the workers well enough fed to work hard.

Sugar and international politics

In addition to the international influence of sugar during the colonial era, sugar trade problems have been addressed at an inter-governmental level since the nineteenth century.

Concerned at the increase in bounty fed exports from continental Europe the governments of Belgium, France, Holland and the UK signed the Paris Sugar Convention in 1864. They agreed to suppress protective duties and bounties so as to put sugar production and trade on an equal footing. The convention failed, partly because of the technical difficulties of determining with accuracy the refining quality of different sugars. All subsequent international conventions of 1875, 1877 and 1888 were not ratified. By the end of the nineteenth century, however, the European beet sugar industries had matured and governments had grown tired of escalating subsidies. The UK was concerned that subsidized imports could affect its domestic refining industry and colonial suppliers. There was sufficient agreement between exporters and importers for the Brussels Convention to be signed in 1902 by the governments of Austria, Belgium, France, Germany, Hungary, Italy, Holland, Norway, Spain, Sweden and the UK. Except for Russia, all the major beet sugar exporters were represented. To equalize conditions of competition between beet and cane sugar the participants agreed to eliminate all direct and indirect production and import subsidies on sugar, to bar entry to or impose countervailing duties on sugar imports from countries granting bounties and to limit surtaxes. Russia became a member in 1907 and the convention was renewed in 1908 and 1912. It was annulled in 1920 after World War I rendered it inoperative.

After World War I sugar trade became dominated by relatively cheaper cane sugar. (European beet production had been severely disrupted by the war.) Large investments, from the turn of the century, in Cuba, Puerto Rico, Hawaii, the Philippines, Java, Japanese-occupied Taiwan and other tropical areas had initiated a phase of rapid expansion in the cane sugar industry, which continued up to 1930. The advantages of cheap land, low cost labour, large scale processing techniques and new cane varieties fuelled this expansion. Good crops in 1924/25, 1927/28 and 1928/29 brought low prices and efforts to find an international regulatory solution. However, the Tarafa Action of 1927/28 and the Chadbourne Agreement of 1931 which resulted, were not inter-governmental agreements but were made largely at an industry level. Neither succeeded and calls for a broader, more binding approach led to the negotiation of the 1937 International Sugar Agreement (ISA) under the auspices of the League of Nations. The price objective was defined in 1937 as 'a reasonable price, not exceeding the cost of production, including a reasonable profit of efficient producers'. The main instrument was the regulation of exports through adjustable quotas, supplemented by provisions concerning stocks. The agreement was the first to make the distinction between the free market and preferential markets. Needless to say, the 1937 ISA was never able to establish itself because of the imminent World War II.

ISAs since World War II, will be discussed in Chapter 9. In addition, the post-war era furnishes many examples of the international geopolitical significance of sugar.

The Cuban Revolution of 1959 is a good example of sugar being used as an instrument of international power politics. In an effort to cripple the Cuban economy, the USA banned imports from Cuba, hitherto its main supplier. In response, the USSR undertook to import most of Cuba's surplus, although the full quantity was not required for domestic consumption. Refining and exporting the surplus over domestic requirements, the USSR became a major exporter of white sugar, helping to drive down world prices in the late 1960s. This whole period caused immense problems in the world sugar market as the world's largest trade flow (Cuba–USA) was disrupted and diverted to a completely different destination.

Another major post-war political event, the break-up of the USSR in 1991, similarly had a direct effect on the world's sugar market. The flow of sugar from Cuba to the Former Soviet Union (FSU) was steeply curtailed. In this case the brunt was borne by Cuba itself with the loss of the subsidized market causing production problems which led to a concomitant fall in output. But some recovery in Cuba is virtually assured with foreign investment in the industry supplying missing essential inputs and there is no doubt that this will put pressure on the world sugar market in the second half of the 1990s.

The world sugar economy today

4

National policies

Why national policies have evolved

I t is important to discuss national sugar policies because of the role they have played over decades, even centuries, in shaping some of the interactions of the international sugar trade.

One of the principal reasons for the development and refinement of national policies will be discussed in more detail in Chapter 5: the significantly higher cost of production of sugar made from beet than sugar made from cane. Currently the cost of production of beet sugar is estimated to be 70% higher than that of cane sugar; historically the margin has been higher. From the upsurge in beet sugar production in the second half of the nineteenth century through to the rapid increases in production in the EC following the 1974 world sugar price boom, the production of beet sugar has required protection from cheaper cane sugar imports involving not only co-ordinated national policies but also the support of border controls. Since sugar beet is a temperate crop widely grown in developed countries, sugar policies have tended to reach their greatest complexity and have had their greatest impact, nationally and internationally, in these countries.

The higher production costs associated with developed countries have not been confined to beet. Since sugar production in general is relatively labour and land intensive, and these factors of production are more expensive in developed countries, cane sugar, in spite of being intrinsically cheaper to produce (principally because it comes with its own 'free' energy source – bagasse) has also required a high level of protection in one developed producer – the USA. The other major developed cane producer, Australia, has avoided the need for protection in recent times by the development of highly efficient, relatively large (by international standards) one-family production units and the full mechanization of the most labour intensive part of production, the harvest.

Another associated reason that national sugar policies have become commonplace is the widespread nature of sugar production and the consequent large number of exporters and importers. Of all the commonly traded commodities, it is sugar that brings the interests of developing country exporters most into conflict with those of developed country farmers. Therefore, in a mirror image of the protectionist policies generally adopted in developed countries, many developing countries have also evolved strict national policies in an attempt to safeguard their interests.

The perceived need for national policies, and to some extent their dynamics, has been greatly influenced by the characteristics of the international sugar market, in particular the exceptional volatility of international sugar prices. (The reasons for and the dynamics of the volatility of world sugar prices will be discussed in more detail in chapters 7 and 9.) For importers who produce sugar the alternation of extremes of high and low prices has, in turn, made imports extremely expensive thus encouraging measures to develop their domestic sugar industries, and then threatened their sugar industries with a flood of cheap imports. Exporters have been faced with the problems of stop–go situations: short periods of high returns followed by long periods when they were exporting sugar for much less than its cost of production. The interaction between domestic policies and the international sugar market partly explains the wide spread of such policies. A good example of this interaction is provided by the 12 years from 1974 to 1985. In 1974 the world sugar price peaked at US cents 64/lb (more than ten times the cost of efficient production). The response of the EC, then a net importer, was to increase significantly support prices and production quotas. In the USA production of an alternative, domestically cheaper sweetener, High Fructose Corn Syrup (HFCS or isoglucose), was encouraged. World prices, of course, fell rapidly as production increased and consumption levelled off in response to boom prices and by 1978 had fallen below US 8 cents/lb. In response to the low prices and some climatic problems world production fell in 1979/80 and prices again rose sharply to peak at 47 cents/lb in 1980. The EC again raised support prices. A surge in world production in 1981/82 brought prices crashing down to the point that in 1982 the USA, where consumption had fallen due to the growth in HFCS production, introduced import quotas to protect the domestic industry from cheap imports. By 1985 world prices had fallen below 3 cents/lb. Thus, the extreme volatility of world prices between 1974 and 1985 had caused the EC to raise the level of support and protection for its sugar industry, massively increasing production and exports. Also, in the USA the growth of HFCS cut consumption and the protective policy instrument adopted, import quotas, drastically cut US imports. Consequently, a massive world surplus built up in the early to mid-1980s and world prices remained depressed until 1988.

As can be seen from this example the relationship between policy and price is quite complex and dynamic, sometimes with policy driving price and sometimes vice versa. Some analysts ascribe to policy the leading role: 'The dynamic that these national policies created in the world sugar economy contributed greatly to the 1974 and 1980 price booms, and culminated in the sugar depression of the mid 1980s when the world price fell below 3 cents per pound.' (Early and Westfall). However, although the sugar depression of the mid-1980s was largely the result of policy changes in the EC and USA, those policy changes had themselves resulted from the high world prices of 1974 and 1980. And why stop the analysis in 1985? Both EC and US policies remained intact in 1990, when world stocks had fallen to hitherto critical levels and world prices began to rise. Yet in 1990 world prices peaked at only 16 cents/lb. Why such a low price peak, if US and EC policies were still in place and they really had contributed to the 1974 and 1980 booms? The reason for the modified price behaviour in 1990 lies elsewhere, in the changing structure of the market. In 1974, and to a lesser extent 1980, the import market was dominated by low price elasticity developed countries; by 1990, higher price elasticity developing countries had replaced them as the dominant force. These countries' response to rising prices is to buy less, relieving market pressure and lowering price peaks.

Although the developed/developing, beet/cane divide explains much of the development and refinement of national sugar policies, other goals can be pursued. Income redistribution, normally through the price system, from consumers to producers, can be one of these. Underlying income redistribution can be more fundamental goals such as preventing the depopulation of rural areas and self-sufficiency in food production. Another goal can be economic development, and sugar, because of its high labour requirement and its industrial content, is particularly suited to this. Although, internationally, expanding production to promote development may appear uneconomic (depending on the actual level of the world sugar price), domestically it may make sense in relation to other feasible uses of land and labour. The attractions are increased employment at both farm and industrial level, spin off industrial development (processing molasses, surplus bagasse) and import saving. Generation of revenue can be another objective, but its relevance is more historical; nowadays taxes, duties, tariffs and levies are more likely to be a direct tool of protection or used to redistribute income, usually from consumers to producers.

Policy instruments

Border measures

Border measures are the most important method of control because incoming supplies can be controlled and domestic prices can be differentiated from prevailing international prices. The most common form of border controls are tariffs and quotas, sometimes used together. Sugar imported within the quota limit may be landed at the domestic price or the international price plus a tariff. Since 1990 the USA has employed a combination of tariffs and quotas whereby sugar imported within the quota limit pays a small or nominal tariff and sugar imported beyond the limit pays a high, prohibitive tariff – the tariff rate quota (TRQ). Up until 1995 the EU used a variable levy to protect domestic production. The variable levy was set monthly at a value which resulted in the world price plus the variable levy (the import price) always exceeding the domestic support price (the intervention price). Other border measures include import and export licensing.

Domestic production measures

There are many variations of domestic production support measures ranging from guaranteed prices, whether direct or indirect through intervention (EU) or a loan rate (USA), through to production quotas; subsidies on production, inputs or credit; deficiency payments; and export subsidies.

Domestic consumption measures

In developed countries most domestic policies are geared to protecting and supporting producers and are paid for by consumers or taxpayers. In some developing countries, however, it is the consumer that is protected. The main instruments used are price controls or rationing systems that provide the consumer with a minimum quantity at a lower price.

Measuring subsidies

A complete analysis of all subsidies, direct and indirect, is a difficult task, but during the General Agreement on Tariffs and Trade (GATT) Uruguay Round negotiations 1987–95 techniques were developed to enable international comparisons to be made. The producer subsidy equivalent (PSE) expresses in monetary terms all government measures which aid or tax producers divided by domestic production. A positive value means that the producer is receiving aid, a negative value that the producer is, in effect, taxed. A consumer subsidy equivalent (CSE) can be calculated in a similar way, taking account of whether domestic prices are above or below the world price. A positive value for the CSE indicates that consumers are being subsidized, a negative value that prices are higher than they should be.

Table 4.1 shows PSEs for a selected group of producing countries, while Table 4.2 shows CSEs for a selected group of consuming countries.

National policies in some important countries

Developed countries

EU

Since its inception in the 1960s the sugar regime of the CAP has been subject to a great deal of fine tuning and has become entrenched to the extent that the EU, despite its relatively high cost of production (since it produces largely beet sugar – see Chapter 5 for a discussion of the relative production costs of beet and cane sugar), has become a major exporter of sugar and is the largest free market exporter.

The EU sugar regime works by holding the internal domestic price of sugar at a sufficiently high level to afford adequate returns for

Table 4.1   Producer subsidy equivalents for sugar, US$/tonne

	1985	1986	1987	1988	1989	1990
Australia	20	17	22	19	26	27
Chile	–	–	150	113	112	106
Colombia	91	88	86	25	–26	–27
EC	110	164	181	55	14	–
Egypt	–77	–55	–176	–205	–332	–27
Jamaica	28	–21	–31	–72	–94	–
Japan	719	986	966	912	748	795
Kenya	97	96	63	63	–9	–
Nigeria	–262	–221	73	73	106	–
Poland	16	–31	–91	–136	331	–
South Africa	21	51	48	12	–62	–
USA	200	217	183	153	133	178
USSR	–	221	248	152	74	73

Source: USDA.

Table 4.2   Consumer subsidy equivalents for sugar, US$/tonne

	1985	1986	1987	1988	1989	1990
Canada	–23	–22	–23	–24	–22	–20
China	–335	–216	–180	–319	–264	–137
EC	–454	–570	–605	–398	–322	–
Jamaica	–85	–54	–91	–4	77	–
Japan	–523	–709	–831	–719	–491	–589
Korea	–427	–393	–406	–461	–256	–268
Nigeria	269	235	–66	–69	–118	–
Poland	–67	–64	–92	–71	–	–
South Africa	–66	–53	–68	–99	–17	–
USA	–303	–328	–275	–219	–186	–262
USSR	–	–138	–147	–81	–19	–20

Source: USDA.

growing sugar in even the less efficient production areas. This is done through the mechanism of *intervention*. The intervention price is set by the EU Commission and is the price at which the Commission will buy all sugar produced in the EU and place it into intervention stocks. Thus any domestic sugar *user* must pay at least the intervention price to obtain supplies. Recourse to cheap imports is not possible because the intervention mechanism is backed up by variable levies on imports, set monthly at the difference between the world sugar price and the intervention price plus a margin. Imports for consumption are thus effectively prohibited.

Production is controlled through a set of national production quotas, which are divided into 'A' quotas, on which a production levy

Table 4.3 A and B quotas in EU countries, 1995/96, tonnes, raw value

Member States	Basic quantities A quota, t	1995/96 B quota, t	Total A & B
Germany*	2 867 078	882 188	3 749 266
France	3 256 532	875 908	4 132 440
(share of DOM	473 915**	50 652	524 567)
Italy	1 434 787	269 838	1 704 625
Netherlands	750 002	197 827	947 829
Belgium/Luxembourg	739 133	158 696	897 829
United Kingdom	1 130 438	113 044	1 243 482
Denmark	356 523	105 032	461 555
Ireland	197 827	19 783	217 610
Greece	315 218	31 522	346 740
Spain	1 043 482	43 478	1 086 960
Portugal	69 170	6 917	76 087
(share of Azores	9 882	988	10 870)
Austria	344 054	80 306	424 360
Sweden	365 614	36 561	402 175
Finland	145 036	14 503	159 539
EU–15	13 014 894	2 835 603	15 850 497

Note: p = preliminary. *Including former GDR; basic quantities 1995/96: A quota 704 027 tonnes, B quota 216 628 tonnes. **According to Regulation (EEC) No. 1785/81 the A quota of the DOM amounts to 506 523 t, of which France has the right to carry over 32 609 t to the mainland A quota and has done so since 1981/82.

of 2% must be paid, and additional 'B' quotas on which a production levy of 39.5% must be paid. Table 4.3 lists A and B quotas in EU countries for 1995/96. A quotas currently amount to 12.4 million tonnes and B quotas to 2.7 million tonnes, giving a total for the EU of 15.1 million tonnes, compared to EU consumption in 1994 of 13.4 million tonnes; an exportable surplus from *domestic production under quota* of 1.7 million tonnes. However, production beyond quota levels is permitted. This so-called C sugar must be exported outside the EU at the world price in the year of production or carried over to the next year to be set against the A quota in that year. Typically, the EU produces annually between 1.5 and 2.5 million tonnes of C sugar, mainly in France and Germany. This level of C sugar production can be partly explained by cross-subsidization from A and B returns, so that the marginal cost of C sugar is close to zero, and the world price of sugar, much lower than the intervention price less the levies, becomes attractive. Currently the EU intervention price is around 38 cents/lb ($838/tonne) for white sugar compared to a world white sugar price varying normally between 13–20 cents/lb ($287–$400/tonne).

The revenue obtained from the production levies on A and B quota sugar are used partly to subsidize exports of A and B quota sugar. Export restitutions, set weekly, are obtainable, making up the difference between the world price and the intervention price. In a normal year around half of the revenue needed to subsidize exports is obtained from the production levies. The balance comes from the general budget and is the equivalent of restitutions that would be payable on the 1.4 million tonnes of preferential imports made annually by the EU under the terms of the Lomé Convention. This part of the payment of export subsidies (restitutions) is considered as development aid, which explains why it is drawn from the general budget.

The final piece in the EU policy jigsaw is the preferential imports from African, Caribbean and Pacific (ACP) countries, amounting to approximately 1.4 million tonnes annually. The sugar protocol of the Lomé Convention was essentially a successor to the Commonwealth Sugar Agreement (CSA) and dates from the formal accession of the UK to the EC in 1975. Country specific quotas of raw sugar are allowed into the EU for refining (see Table 4.4) and receive the raw equivalent of the white sugar intervention prices (again, substantially above the world raw sugar price). Although the main recipient, the UK, uses the sugar to meet the deficit of domestic production in consumption, the protocol effectively raises availability, and therefore EU export potential, by 1.4 million tonnes. Hence the provision of the export restitutions at the white sugar equivalent of 1.4 million tonnes from the general budget is termed as 'development aid'.

An additional agreement exists with India, originally covering 25 000 tonnes (white sugar value). The quantity was reduced to zero from 1 July 1982, but since 1 July 1983 stands at 10 000 tonnes.

Table 4.4 ACP import quotas under the Lomé Convention, tonnes, raw value

Barbados	54 687	St Christopher and Nevis	16 947
Belize	43 858	Suriname	0
Fiji	179 726	Swaziland	128 093
Guyana	173 272	Tanzania	11 072
Ivory Coast	11 072	Trinidad and Tobago	47 556
Jamaica	129 018	Uganda	0
Kenya	0	Zimbabwe	32 853
Madagascar	11 695		
Malawi	22 635	Total	1 407 287
Mauritius	533 731		
PR Congo	11 072	ACP states	1 294 700

Source: Zuckerwirtschaft.

Table 4.5 EU free market availability in a normal year, million tonnes, raw value

A and B quota exports	1.7
C sugar exports	2.0
Lomé equivalent exports	1.4
Total	5.1

Source: ISO.

Taking into account all the sources of sugar available to the EU in a 'normal' year there is a free market availability of approximately 5.1 million tonnes, making the EU consistently the world's largest free market exporter (see Table 4.5). Finally, to prevent effective competition from cheaper substitutes, the EU imposes restrictive production quotas on HFCS. These quotas, strictly enforced, have effectively prevented the growth of more than an incipient HFCS industry in the EU.

The 1994 GATT Uruguay Round agreement on agriculture has forced some relatively minor adjustments on the CAP sugar regime, as follows:

- The variable levy on imports has been replaced with a tariff, reducible by 15% progressively up to end-2000. However, the initial tariff has been set high enough for the end-2000 reduced tariff plus the world price to be still at or around the current intervention prices,[1] *unless* the world price falls substantially in which case safeguard clauses apply.
- The volume of subsidized exports must be reduced by 21% and the value by 36% from the 1986–90 average by end-2000. Effectively this will reduce the volume of EU subsidized exports by 340 000 tonnes by end-2000.
- The minimum market access commitment (3% of domestic consumption provided by imports rising to 5% by end-2000) is taken care of by the Lomé Convention imports from ACP countries.
- Production quotas and production levies on A and B quota sugar remain unchanged.
- Most subsidies to the Italian sugar industry will be phased out

---

1 The base tariff (1994/95) was set at 424 ECU/tonne (31 cents/lb on $683/tonne) for white sugar and 424 ECU/tonne (25 cents/lb on $550/tonne) for raw sugar. After the required reduction of 15% by end-2000 the tariff will be 419 ECU/tonne) for raw sugar. Assuming end-2000 world prices of 15 cents/lb for white sugar and 12 cents/lb for raw sugar, the world sugar price plus the tariff would be 40 cents/lb for raw sugar – well above the current intervention price of 28 cents/lb for white sugar.

during the World Trade Organization (WTO) agreement transition period (1995–2000).

The basic EU sugar regime has remained substantially unchanged since the 1960s apart from the introduction of production levies in response to falling world prices in the early 1980s and the replacement of the variable levy by a tariff in 1995 in accordance with the Uruguay Round agreement on agriculture. Like most developed country sugar policies it has interacted with changes in the world sugar market, for example the raising of intervention prices following the 1974 and 1980 world sugar price booms and the raising of production quotas after the 1974 world sugar price boom which had far reaching effects, in addition to the introduction of production levies mentioned above. The provision of a stable price regime, which more than compensated for the cost of production disadvantage associated with being a beet sugar producer, converted the EC from a net importer in the early 1970s in to the world's largest free market net exporter in the 1980s and 1990s. Estimates of harm done to markets, in terms of depression of prices, are fraught with difficulty in welfare terms because low world prices bring welfare gains to importers, but there can be no doubt that the substantial increase in EC production in the late 1970s–early 1980s contributed strongly, along with the substantial cut in US imports, to the depressed world sugar prices of the mid-1980s.

USA

The US system of support for sugar producers is based upon its loan programme for agricultural producers. Originally conceived as a way of evening out seasonal variations in commodity prices[2] the loan programme has become a price support mechanism because the loans are *non-recourse*. That is, if a producer decides not to pay the loan back, the government has no recourse but is left holding the commodity as its only security. Naturally, since the government did not wish to end up stocking all the US annual production, US farm bills have included the stipulation that the programme should run at no cost to the government, and various other (mainly border) measures have been added to ensure that the domestic price is always above the

---

2 Since the price of any commodity is lowest at harvest time, because of the large quantity coming into the market, it was thought that loaning a producer a reasonable price for his product at that time would enable him to store the product and sell at a better price later. He would then repay the loan plus interest.

loan rate. Thus the producers prefer to sell into the domestic market rather than take the loan from the government. Currently the loan rate for raw cane sugar is 18 cents/lb ($397/tonne) and for refined white sugar 23.43 cents/lb ($517/tonne) compared to world sugar prices around 12 cents/lb ($265/tonne) for raws and 15 cents/lb ($330/tonne) for whites.

The principal tool used to support the loan programme and ensure that domestic sugar prices do not fall below the loan rate is a variable import quota system (see Table 4.6). The total quota is set each year (although it can be adjusted during the year according to domestic price and production developments) as the difference between total estimated sugar consumption and total estimated domestic sugar consumption. Each participating country in the quota has been allocated a share, based on historical supply, which converts into a tonnage for that year. Since the USA lost a case brought by Australia in 1990 against its quota system in the GATT, the system has been referred to as a TRQ, administered on the basis of a low or zero tariff up to the variable quota quantity, and high or prohibitive quotas for quantities beyond the quota quantity. This interesting use of semantics has enabled the US sugar programme to escape unscathed from the Uruguay Round process!

Other measures used by the US to support the domestic sugar industry include marketing allotments, re-export programmes and section 22 quotas and fees.

Marketing allotments were introduced in the 1990 Farm Bill to protect a minimum import entitlement for foreign suppliers of 1.13 million tonnes, also introduced in that Farm Bill. The minimum import entitlement was a measure of the *Angst* induced by the precipitous fall in US imports after the introduction of import quotas (from 4 million tonnes in the early 1980s) and the harm this had caused foreign suppliers, particularly those from Latin America. In order to keep the domestic price above the loan rate, *without* cutting imports beyond 1.13 million tonnes, the domestic beet industry has to limit production or sales, holding sugar off the market, if the Secretary of Agriculture imposes marketing allotments when it is necessary to raise domestic market prices.

In order to support the domestic refining industry the import of quota exempt sugar is permitted provided it is for the purpose of re-export as refined sugar. Re-exports from the USA average around 450 000 tonnes annually.

When quotas were imposed some quantities of sugar escaped the restrictions by entering the USA in sugar-containing products. In 1983 action was taken by imposing a zero quota on products containing

Table 4.6 US sugar import quotas, 1994/95, tonnes, raw value

Countries holding US sugar import quotas	Share of base quota, %	Quota allocations, tonnes
Argentina	4.3	53 604
Australia	8.3	103 469
Barbados	0.7	8 726
Belize	1.1	13 713
Bolivia	0.8	9 973
Brazil	14.5	180 759
Colombia	2.4	29 919
Congo	*	8 468
Costa Rica	1.5	18 699
Côte d'Ivoire	*	8 468
Dominican Republic	17.6	219 404
Ecuador	1.1	13 713
El Salvador	2.6	32 412
Fiji	0.9	11 220
Gabon	*	8 468
Guatemala	4.8	59 837
Guyana	1.2	14 959
Haiti	*	8 468
Honduras	1.0	12 466
India	0.8	9 973
Jamaica	1.1	13 713
Madagascar	*	8 468
Malawi	0.7	12 466
Mauritius	1.2	14 959
Mexico	*	8 468
Mozambique	1.3	16 206
Nicaragua	2.1	26 179
Panama	2.9	36 152
Papua New Guinea	*	8 468
Paraguay	*	8 468
Peru	4.1	51 111
Philippines	13.5	168 293
St Christopher and Nevis	*	28 672
South Africa	2.3	8 468
Swaziland	1.6	19 946
Taiwan	1.2	14 960
Thailand	1.4	17 453
Trinidad and Tobago	0.7	8 726
Uruguay	*	8 468
Zimbabwe	1.2	14 960
Total	99.2	1 321 322

* Ten specified countries and areas have a total of 0.3% of the base quota, subject to minimum shipping quantities. *Source: USDA.*

more than 65% sugar. The USA has agreed to convert these quotas on sugar-containing products to tariffs under the 1994 Uruguay Round agreement on agriculture.

Like its EU counterpart, US domestic sugar policy has interacted strongly with the world sugar market. From the suspension of the US Sugar Act which governed imports up to 1974, a direct consequence of the world sugar price boom of that year, to 1982, when world prices fell sharply below the US domestic price and forced the introduction of country specific quotas, US sugar policy tried to balance supporting US producers with maintaining some contact, albeit sharply diminished, with the world market. The most far reaching consequence is that the maintenance of domestic sugar prices at a level attractive to domestic sugar producers has provided a protective umbrella under which the now massive HFCS industry has grown and thrived, always able to sell HFCS at a discount to sugar and taking over completely, as a consequence, the largest market for sugar – soft drinks. The effect of US sugar policy is illustrated by the figures for US production, imports and consumption from 1981 to 1994, shown in Table 4.7.

Under the protection of the loan rate/import quota system, US production, particularly of beet sugar, grew continuously up to 1993. Output from 1983 to 1993 increased by 1.8 million tonnes (35%) at an annual growth rate of 3%. As sugar was progressively substituted by HFCS, always available at a substantial discount to white refined sugar, sugar consumption fell from 8.96 million tonnes in 1981 to 7.08

Table 4.7 US sugar production, imports and consumption, 1981–94, million tonnes, raw value

	Production	Net imports	Consumption
1981	5.79	3.70	8.96
1982	5.42	2.34	8.31
1983	5.21	2.47	8.07
1984	5.34	2.47	7.74
1985	5.42	1.91	7.29
1986	5.68	1.38	7.08
1987	6.63	0.63	7.38
1988	6.43	1.01	7.42
1989	6.21	1.32	7.56
1990	5.74	2.04	7.85
1991	6.48	1.73	7.89
1992	6.80	1.55	8.10
1993	7.04	1.49	8.19
1994	6.92	1.13	8.45

Source: ISO.

million tonnes in 1986 – a fall of 21% in only five years. Consequently, squeezed between the rise in production and the fall in consumption, net imports fell dramatically: from 3.7 million tonnes in 1981 to only 0.63 million tonnes in 1987. Since 1992 US net imports have stabilized at around 1.3–1.5 million tonnes. The minimum quota level under the regulations is 1.13 million tonnes.

There is no doubt, too, that the sharp reduction in US sugar imports during the 1980s had a profound effect on the world sugar market and prices.

Japan

Japan has a highly complex support system. With production of between 0.9–1.0 million tonnes it is a substantial producer, encompassing beet sugar production in the north and cane sugar production in the south. Only a broad overview of the system will be given here. As can be seen from Tables 4.1 and 4.2, Japan has the world's highest level of producer support for sugar and the highest level of price subsidization by the consumer.

The body responsible for the administration of the system in Japan is the Raw Silk and Sugar Price Stabilization Association (SPSA) which sets minimum prices for beet and cane which processors must pay in order to receive their own price support. Processors, for example, receive rebates from the government to cover raw material costs. The SPSA buys the sugar from domestic processors at a price high enough to cover their costs, and then sells it back to the same firms at a price which enables them to compete with cheaper imported sugar. The money for this subsidy comes from direct government aid and a fund made up of revenue from import duties and a levy on HFCS production.

To support the domestic subsidization the SPSA employs border measures designed to raise the price of imported sugar. The SPSA buys all imported sugar at an average import price, based on a moving average of the London Daily Price. The imported sugar is then resold after adding a levy and a surcharge to bring the world price plus the tariff up to a domestic 'target price'. The target price is, of course, below the domestic cost of production. The import surcharge and levy have been replaced by a bound (high) tariff under the terms of the 1994 Uruguay Round agreement on agriculture. As in the USA, the existence of a high level of domestic support and the consequent high internal prices led to the development of a large HFCS industry, although unlike the USA some attempt has been made to regulate the industry and provide more equal competition between the sugar and HFCS industries. HFCS became incorporated into the sugar regime in 1982 when the surcharge on production was imposed to help fund the sugar stabilization fund.

Canada

Canada is not a major sugar producer, with production of around only 120 000 tonnes annually, but it is included here as an example of a different approach to support, which may, in turn have led to the rather small growth in production.

Canada uses the deficiency payment method to support sugar producers. That is, the deficiency between the cost of production of sugar and the domestic price obtained is made up to growers and processors. In the case of Canada the deficiency payment is shared equally by the federal government, the provincial government and the producers, and is calculated on the basis of 75% of current cash costs and 20% of the moving average of the price received for sugar beet during the previous 15 years. The Canadian sugar economy is thereby freed to operate at the world market price plus a minimal tariff, with obvious benefits for consumers (see Table 4.2) compared to the USA, EU and Japan. Because of the relatively low sugar price in Canada the sugar industry has not been troubled by the HFCS industry, which has found it more profitable to export to the USA.

Developing countries

India

India is the world's largest sugar economy and is also important because its immense swings from importer to exporter can and do have a strong effect on the world sugar market. Indian sugar policy is complex because it embodies two, apparently opposite goals. One is to have available sufficient production for consumption to be maintained or expanded, the other is to provide sugar for consumption at the cheapest possible price. The first goal of keeping production rising requires relatively high farm prices. Average prices to the consumer are kept low through a complex dual price system. Apart from periodically raising the minimum cane price the main instrument the government uses is the ratio between levy sugar (sugar purchased compulsorily from mills by the government at a low price and sold cheaply in special shops) and free market sugar. Currently the ratio is 60% of production to the free market and 40% of production to levy sugar. This has been the proportion since the late 1980s, changed after India was forced to import extensively in 1985–86. In 1967/68, when the policy was introduced, the ratio was the opposite: 60% of production becoming levy sugar and only 40% going to the free market. In order to give incentives for the increasing production necessitated by population growth the government has been forced to raise the allowance of free market sugar, which is obviously more profitable for mills. Currently even lower rates of levy sugar apply in early and late season as a measure to extend production, and new factories are free from levy sales for 8–10 years, depending on capacity, while expansions of existing factories are exempt for up to 5 years. Operating a dual price system while trying to prevent major production swings would be complicated enough, but the task is rendered even more difficult because Indian sugar growers have an alternative outlet for their cane. Half the cane grown in India is used for the production of open pan sugars (the so-called primitive or artisan sugars: gur, khandsari and jaggery). Open pan sugars, largely a rural-based, village industry, escape many of the taxes and levies applied to mill sugar, and, of course, can all be sold on their respective free markets. Consequently, open pan sugar manufacturers are often in a position to offer higher cane prices than millers, and when this happens mill sugar (vacuum pan sugar) production can fall sharply while open pan sugar production rises. Therefore if the government has got its cane prices, levy sugar proportions and other incentives wrong, as sometimes happens, it can be left having to import large quantities or having large stocks of sugar for export. This is when the Indian sugar economy can react strongly with the world market – for example, in 1985–86, when world prices were very low, India was in deficit and imported strongly. The result was that world prices bottomed out and rose, and although India purchased its sugar relatively cheaply, it could be said that India rescued the world market from its doldrums. The opposite happened in 1994 – the world market was already tight when India came into the market and prices were pushed up to four year highs – and high prices have always brought the danger of substitution.

However the government adjusted production incentives and in 1995/96 India will have a record crop, a massive 3 million tonnes up on the previous year, and a surplus of almost 2 million tonnes.

China

With the reduction of imports by the USA in the 1980s and the FSU in the 1990s, China has become potentially the world's largest importer. China's sugar policy is undergoing a period of transition, and it may be some years before a coherent picture emerges.

Change began in China in 1988 when a poor crop required the import of almost 4 million tonnes of sugar at an unacceptable cost in foreign exchange. The sugar area was expanded under a compulsory planting programme. Between 1987 and 1991 cane area was expanded by 35% and beet sowing by 57%. Sugar production rose from 4.7 million tonnes in 1987/88 to 8.6 million tonnes in 1991/92. China, for the first time, became a net exporter of sugar, mainly to the Asian FSU and production processing and consumption were freed from a wide range of controls, including the compulsory planting programme. The immediate result was that many farmers switched to more lucrative cash crops, and, with some bad weather also occurring, Chinese production fell back to the extent that imports of around 2 million tonnes were necessary in 1995/96. However, the government remains convinced that increased planting in new production areas, which still receive incentives, will more than offset the loss due to switching to other crops.

Thus with policy changes made in the late 1980s China briefly achieved the policy goal of self-sufficiency, albeit at a low per capita consumption level (6 kg compared to a world average of 20 kg). Whether self-sufficiency remains an objective is unclear; but avoiding large import bills will certainly be given a high priority. Therefore further adjustments in production and consumption policy can be expected to keep imports within manageable levels and the rate of production growth in line with the rate of consumption growth.

Thailand

Thailand is an example of an export orientated developing country where the principal objective is to ensure an adequate return to the grower. Given the volatility of the world sugar market and that direct subsidies were ruled out, the solution that evolved through the 1980s was to set a domestic price high enough so that domestic returns plus export returns were adequate to maintain the producer. Thailand operates with three quotas: A quota sugar for the domestic market, restricted to 1.3 million tonnes and sold at a high price; B quota sugar (about 300 000 tonnes) which represents sugar governed by long-term contracts, and C quota sugar (the balance) where the option exists to sell at the world market price or accept the daily B quota price. Domestic (A quota) sugar retails at more than double the export price. Therefore one quarter of the crop generates almost two-thirds of the revenue. By restricting growth in the domestic market and placing the burden on consumers (Thailand's per capita consumption in 1994 was 24.9 kg compared to the world average of 20.4 kg) 'Thailand's sugar policy regime seems to have done a relatively good job of achieving the objective of fostering a large and efficient sugar industry at a low cost to the treasury' (Early and Westfall).

Egypt

Egypt is an example of a developing importing country where the double objective of self-sufficiency and keeping the price as low as possible for consumers is being pursued. The goal of self-sufficiency is pursued not only to save on the import bill: Egypt is an example of a country where sugar, because of its agro-industrial aspect, is considered a tool of development, providing investment and employment in agricultural regions.

Three government ministries act as agents in the implementation of sugar policy. The Ministry of Agriculture supplies inputs to farmers and sets the cane price; the Ministry of Industry, through a government owned company, contracts with farmers for delivery of cane to the mills; the Ministry of Supply purchases half of the sugar companies' output and distributes it through a ration system or sells it at free market prices in ministry operated shops. The ration system was to be phased out by mid-1995 and all domestic cane production sold on the free market.

Sugar and the Uruguay Round agreement on agriculture

Although this chapter has been confined to domestic policy and its interaction with the world sugar economy, mention should be made of the Uruguay Round agreement on agriculture because, as has already been seen in the discussion of EU, US and Japanese policy, it has had and will continue to have an impact on domestic policies. The principal Uruguay Round reforms relating to agriculture are the market access commitment, tariffication and domestic support for agriculture and subsidized exports. Signatory countries are required to import a minimum share of 3% of their domestic market in 1995, rising to 5% by end-2000. Non-tariff barriers and variable import levies are to be replaced by a base rate tariff. Tariffs are then bound and reduced progressively by an average of 36% over all commodities over the five year transitional period (up to end-2000), with a minimum reduction for any individual commodity of 15%. Domestic support for agriculture is to be reduced by 20% from the 1986–88 base period for all commodities, and subsidized exports are to be reduced by 21% in volume and 36% by value by end-2000.

The sugar policies of developed countries have thus been left largely untouched by the Uruguay Round and, therefore, the Round will have only a minor impact on the world sugar market.

A modest reduction in subsidized EU exports, a lowering of the Japanese tariff on sugar and modest increases in access to some countries would slightly reduce surpluses of sweeteners, but not enough to have a measurable impact on prices. Tariff barriers in the USA, Europe and Japan will remain well above the likely sugar price in 2000. Perversely, many countries set base (initial) tariffs at a level higher than existing tariffs, so that when reduced progressively protection would remain at a high level. Consequently the level of protection actually rose as a result of the Uruguay Round (Prieto). Clearly the Uruguay Round has not delivered any significant reform of interventionist sugar policy.

At best, the Uruguay Round brings sugar into the mainstream of the GATT/WTO multilateral regulatory system. It delivers guarantees on access, provisions which prevent further increase in protection, and more transparent trade policy instruments (tariffs).

Tariffication has been a small step in the direction of the removal of quantitative restrictions on trade and opens the way for phased reductions in the future. In the long term this may lead to an actual reduction in protection.

5

Supply

World production

S ugar is one of the most autarkic[1] of soft commodities. Today, among countries with a significant capability of agricultural production, only New Zealand, Norway and the Republic of Korea are not producers of some quantity of sugar.

In 1994 sugar was produced in 120 countries or territories. Total production amounted to 110.289 million tonnes of which 34.089 million tonnes was produced from sugarbeet (31%) and 76.199 million tonnes from sugar cane (69%). Up until 1994 the world record for production had been 117.565 million tonnes, recorded in 1992. (In the period October 1995–September 1996, a new world record production of 120 million tonnes is expected to be established.)

Sugar production is spread over the whole world, with three major producing areas:

- Northern hemisphere beet producers – Eastern and Western Europe, Central Asia, North Africa and North America.
- Equatorial cane – Asia, Africa and North, Central and South America.
- Southern hemisphere cane – Oceania (Australia and Fiji), Southern Africa and South America (Brazil and Argentina).

In the USA, Australia, North Africa, Middle East, India, Brazil and Argentina cane production extends into sub-tropical regions. (Japan and Spain also have small areas of cane cultivation.) Except for Colombia, Hawaii and Peru, which uniquely have 12 month produc-

---

1 Autarky = desire for self-sufficiency.

tion cycles, sugar production is concentrated over 3–5 month campaigns timed to take advantage of maximum sugar content. This characteristic creates a strong seasonality in sugar output, availability and exports and can lead to world price volatility during a year. Northern hemisphere beets are harvested largely within the three month period from October to December; equatorial cane is processed mainly from November to April; and southern hemisphere cane from May to December. Consequently, from November to April world stocks of sugar build up rapidly and in a surplus year this can exert downward pressure on prices. Conversely, after April stocks begin to decline, reaching their lowest point in August or September, and this can cause seasonal price rises in a normal year and rapid increases in prices in a deficit year. The seasonal distribution of production for the world and some typical major producing countries is shown in Fig. 5.1. The highly seasonalized nature of production also has implications for the use of capital in sugar harvesting and processing. Capital intensive sugar mills and factories are idle for more than half of the year (except in Russia where beet factories are used to refine raw sugar during the off-season). Beet harvesters, cane mechanical harvesters where they are used (Australia and Cuba) and mechanical loaders are also idle for much of the year. The under-utilization of capital which cannot be used for other purposes has an important bearing on the cost of sugar production, which is high compared with other agricultural products.

The geographical distribution of world sugar production in 1994 is shown in Table 5.1. Asia (30% of world production in 1994, mainly cane) and Europe (25%, mainly beet) are by far the world's most productive continents. Central and South America (mainly cane) together accounted for another 26% in 1994. Although sugar production is widespread in Africa, the continent represented only 7% of world total production in 1994. Major producers are spread across the globe.

The concentration of production in large producers is illustrated by the fact that two-thirds of world production came from the 10 largest producers in 1994. The dynamism of world production can be deduced from the record production levels given for the 10 countries shown in Table 5.2. All the records were obtained in the 1990s and most date from the most recent completed calendar year.

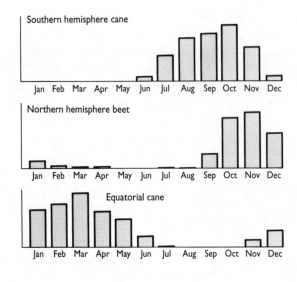

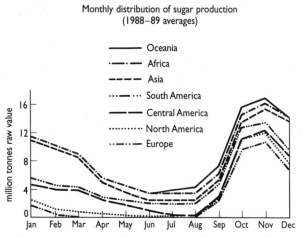

5.1 Seasonal distribution of sugar production (source: ISO).

Developments in world production: global production trends

Since 1950, when world sugar production was 33.427 million tonnes, output has increased by a factor of four, an annual growth rate of 2.75%. In most years world production has had a tendency to keep pace with, or outstrip, world consumption. In only 11 years – 1962, 1966, 1972, 1979, 1980, 1986–89 and 1993–94 – out of the 39 years

Table 5.1 Geographical distribution of world sugar production, 1994, million tonnes, raw value

	Beet	Cane	Total	Share of world total, %
Europe	27.249	0.268	27.518	25
North America	3.970	3.126	7.096	7
Central America	–	11.430	11.430	10
South America	0.505	17.412	17.917	16
Asia	1.886	31.434	33.320	30
Africa	0.478	6.733	7.212	7
Oceania	–	5.797	5.797	5
World	34.089	76.199	110.289	

Source: ISO.

Table 5.2 Ten largest sugar producers, 1994, million tonnes, raw value

1	EU	15.718	(17.384, 1993)
2	Brazil	12.270	(12.27, 1994)
3	India	11.900	(13.873, 1992)
4	USA	6.921	(7.045, 1993)
5	Australia	5.217	(5.215, 1994)
6	China	5.075	(8.864, 1992)
7	Thailand	4.168	(5.078, 1992)
8	Mexico	4.025	(4.360, 1993)
9	Cuba	4.017	(8.445, 1990)
10	Ukraine	3.632	(4.16, 1993)

Notes: Share of top ten producers in 1994 world production = 66%. Figures in brackets are record production and year of record. *Source: ISO.*

from 1955 to 1994 has world production been less than world consumption. Figure 5.2 shows that while the overall trend in global production is positive, there is also a cycle of approximately four to nine years when production dips below trend and world consumption. It can also be seen from Fig. 5.2 that this is due largely to variations in cane sugar production. Several factors explain this phenomenon. Sugar cane is a perennial crop, remaining in the ground for five to seven years. Once planted, it tends to be harvested irrespective of price, as long as the price is above the marginal cost of harvesting. Following a short period of high prices, world sugar production can increase beyond world consumption. Prices decline but the tendency to keep producing from planted cane means that it takes two to five years before production reacts to the lower prices. However, sugar cane is grown in tropical or sub-tropical regions where severe weather disruptions – hurricanes or droughts – can

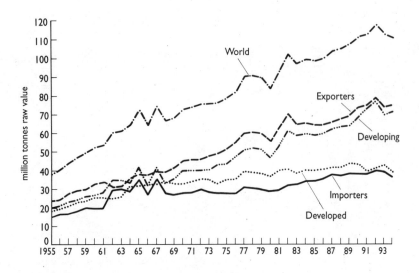

5.2   Global production trends (source: ISO).

occur. Sugar cane is a heavy user of water and yields fall considerably if there is dry weather or drought. Every four to nine years, a coincidence of bad weather in several cane producing regions has caused a sharp drop in cane sugar production. In 1962, 1972, 1979 and, to a lesser extent, 1990, the fall in world production precipitated sharp rises in world sugar prices. As a result, cane area was increased and subsequently production rose sharply (see Fig. 5.2). Sugarbeet, in contrast, is an annual crop grown, from sowing to harvesting, in only six months. Unless affected by drought (e.g. the EU in 1994) beet sugar production tends to be much more stable.

Another tendency, since the 1950s, is for factory capacity to outstrip consumption growth, meaning that in years of excellent weather for growth of both beet and cane, world sugar production far exceeds world consumption. Such years tend to follow periods of high world prices, exacerbated by increased planting of beet and cane. Two recent examples are 1982 (following the 1979–81 high world price period) when world production reached 102 million tonnes compared to world consumption for that year of 93.967 million tonnes and 1992, when world production of 117.565 million tonnes was recorded, compared to world consumption of 112.8 million tonnes. The build-up of world stocks resulting from these sudden surges in production tends to depress world prices in subsequent years until production readjusts and the stocks are cleared. It is sometimes argued that high world prices are necessary to trigger investment in new productive capacity. Not only is there no

Table 5.3 Beet and cane sugar production, 1955–94, million tonnes, raw value

	1955	1960	1965	1970	1975	1980	1985	1990	1994
Beet sugar	15.621	22.838	27.328	29.321	31.273	33.011	36.835	40.699	34.089
% share	40	44	42	40	40	39	37	37	31
Cane sugar	23.304	29.461	37.550	43.575	47.574	51.478	61.530	70.195	76.199
% share	60	56	58	60	60	61	63	63	69
World total	38.925	52.299	64.878	72.896	78.847	84.489	98.365	110.89	110.28

Source: ISO.

evidence for this, but conversations with factory managers suggest that every year, when maintenance is carried out during the off-season, improvements leading to an increase in capacity of at least 2% (the average growth rate in world consumption) are made. In addition, as part of national or regional programmes, new mills are being constructed worldwide, irrespective of the world price. The capital intensity of sugar production means that investment decisions are taken with a long-term perspective rather than being influenced by short-term variations in the world price.

Contrary to many perceptions, the share of beet sugar in world production has declined since it peaked in 1960, in spite of the rapid increases in EU production after 1975. Beet and cane sugar production for 1955–94 is shown in Table 5.3.

After World War II, reconstruction in Eastern and Western Europe led to rapidly rising beet production, whereas developing countries, many still colonies, where cane sugar production was concentrated, grew only slowly. Following the world price booms of 1962 and 1974, and particularly after the first oil price shock of 1973, cane production surged and outgrew beet sugar production, which had also accelerated due to a sharp increase of production quotas and internal prices in the EU in the aftermath of the 1974 world price boom.

Yields, however, have followed a different path. Figure 5.3 shows a comparison between world beet and cane yields between 1964 and 1993. It can be seen that between 1973 and 1988 beet sugar yields were consistently below cane sugar yields, but from 1989 beet sugar yields have overtaken those of cane sugar. The explanation lies in the EU, where subsidized production of beet sugar has been profitable enough for money to be spent on research and development. New beet varieties and improved general agronomy have led to a sharp increase in yields, and new varieties and techniques can be expected to spread to other, lower yielding, beet areas such as Eastern Europe.

A comparison of beet and cane yields for selected, representative countries is shown in Table 5.4.

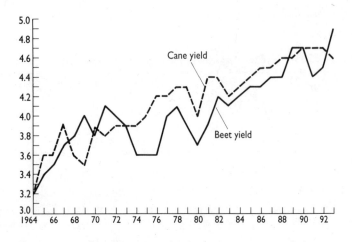

5.3 A comparison between world beet and cane yields, 1964-93 (source: FAO Production Yearbooks).

Table 5.4 Beet and cane yields, 1991-94, tonnes sugar, raw value/hectare

	1991	**1992**	**1993**
World beet	4.4	4.5	4.9
EC–12	8.0	8.5	8.8
Russia	—	1.7	1.9
Ukraine	—	2.5	2.5
USA	5.3	5.3	5.8
World cane	4.7	4.7	4.6
Australia	10.1	12.2	12.2
Cuba	5.4	4.6	3.8
Swaziland	12.9	12.5	11.6
Thailand	4.4	5.7	4.0

Sources: FAO, ISO.

Table 5.4 underlines the influence of the EU on world beet yields. With EU yield rising to 8.8 tonnes raw sugar per hectare in 1993, world beet yield rose to 4.9 tonnes raw sugar per hectare and exceeded the average yield of world cane (4.6 tonnes raw sugar per hectare). The world average of almost 5 tonnes/hectare is achieved in spite of very low yields registered in Russia and Ukraine. Cane yields also show strong variation between countries, and a wider difference between high and low yields. Australia and Swaziland (irrigated) attain yields exceeding 12 tonnes/hectare, while Cuba and Thailand struggle to achieve 5 tonnes/hectare. (For more detail of EU yields see Table 5.6.)

Due to more expensive inputs, especially energy (cane sugar mills

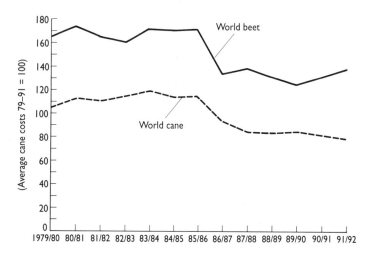

5.4 World beet and cane sugar overall production costs 1979/80–1991/92 crop years (source: Landell Mills Commodities).

are supplied with energy by burning bagasse, the residual after crushing cane, whereas beet sugar factories must buy in energy), the cost of production of beet sugar remains significantly higher than that of cane sugar. According to Landell Mills Commodities, the world average cost of production of beet sugar in 1991 was 70% higher than the comparable figure for cane sugar (see Fig. 5.4). Since 1989, beet and cane costs have diverged further (Fig. 5.4).

Production trends by country

Table 5.5 shows the evolution of the ten largest sugar producers from 1955 to 1994. In 1955 Cuba was the largest producer followed by the USA, USSR, Brazil and India. Before the formation of the EC, France, FR Germany and Italy all figured in the top ten. West Indies, then a colonial entity, had a total production exceeding one million tonnes and supplied the UK. Cuba supplied the USA. The USSR was an exporter. Features since 1955 have been the substantial increases in Brazil and India throughout the period; the rise of Australia since entering the top ten in 1960 and, more recently – since 1985 – of Thailand; the increases in the USSR up until 1990, when the break-up of the Soviet Union left only Ukraine of the FSU republics at number ten in 1994; and the precipitous decline in Cuban production

Table 5.5 Evolution of ten largest producers, 1955–94, million tonnes, raw value

	1955	1960	1965	1970	1975	1980	1985	1990	1994
1	Cuba 4.528	Cuba 5.862	USSR 9.7	EC 9.087	EC 11.128	EC 13.545	EC 13.860	EC 16.939	EU 15.718
2	USA 4.265	USSR 5.702	EC 6.772	USSR 8.847	USSR 8.200	USSR 7.174	Brazil 8.455	India 12.068	Brazil 12.270
3	USSR 3.716	USA 4.576	Cuba 6.082	Cuba 7.559	Cuba 6.427	Brazil 8.270	USSR 8.261	USSR 9.159	India 11.900
4	Brazil 2.073	Brazil 3.319	USA 5.691	USA 5.399	Brazil 6.299	Cuba 6.805	Cuba 7.889	Cuba 8.445	USA 6.921
5	India 1.616	India 2.814	Brazil 4.614	Brazil 5.019	USA 5.955	USA 5.313	India 7.016	Brazil 8.007	Australia 5.217
6	France 1.595	France 2.267	India 3.493	India 3.959	India 5.048	India 4.528	USA 5.415	China 6.250	China 5.075
7	FR Germany 1.298	FR Germany 1.877	China 2.200	China 3.050	China 4.000	Australia 3.489	China 4.300	USA 5.740	Thailand 4.168
8	Philippines 1.244	Philippines 1.398	Mexico 2.121	Australia 2.507	Australia 2.958	China 2.800	Australia 3.439	Australia 3.612	Mexico 4.025
9	West Indies 1.112	Poland 1.392	Australia 2.073	Mexico 2.402	Philippines 2.672	Mexico 2.719	Mexico 3.308	Thailand 3.542	Cuba 4.017
10	Italy 1.077	Australia 1.367	Philippines 1.658	Philippines 2.171	Mexico 2.636	Philippines 2.332	Thailand 2.393	Mexico 3.384	Ukraine 3.632

Source: ISO.

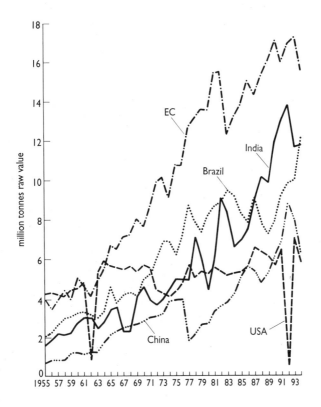

5.5   Evolution of five largest producers, 1955–94 (source: ISO).

following the loss of its major, subsidized, USSR market. The progress of the five largest producers from 1955 to 1994 is shown in Fig. 5.5.

EU

Sugar is produced in all 15 countries which make up the EU (see Table 5.6). Except for small quantities (around 20 000 tonnes) of cane sugar produced in Southern Spain, and around 400 000 tonnes of cane sugar produced in French Départements Outre Mer (DOMs), mainland sugar is all produced from beets. France and Germany are the principal producers.

The EU sugar regime and its effect on sugar production has been discussed in detail in Chapter 4 and will only be summarized here. Before 1970 the EC was a net importer of sugar. But the accession of the UK and the 1974 world sugar price boom brought some policy changes which resulted in the EC eventually (by 1980) becoming a major sugar exporter. A and B production quotas were raised

Table 5.6 EU-15: production and yields, 1994/95

	Production, million tonnes, raw value	Yield, tonnes white sugar/ hectare
Austria	0.425	7.74
Belgium/Luxembourg	0.943	8.59
Denmark	0.487	6.71
Finland	0.174	4.69
France	4.591	9.90
Germany	3.985	7.21
Greece	0.272	6.19
Holland	1.051	8.44
Ireland	0.237	5.86
Italy	1.621	5.23
Portugal	0.007	—
Spain	1.213	6.23
Sweden	0.368	6.37
UK	1.371	8.01
EU–15	16.739	7.53

Source: Zuckerwirtschaft.

significantly in 1974 and EC production increased rapidly in the period 1975–80. In 1980 there was another world sugar price boom, and intervention prices were again raised. EC production continued to expand in the early 1980s in spite of rapidly declining world sugar prices. Since the mid-1980s, EC sugar production has tended to level off (except for new accessions – Spain and Portugal – and the former German Democratic Republic (GDR)). Area has declined, but yields have continued to rise as some of the profits from sugar production have been diverted into improved beet varieties, better agronomic practices, etc. Yields in France exceed 9 tonnes of white sugar/ hectare, and the EU average exceeds 7 tonnes of white sugar/hectare. Under the EU sugar regime, large-scale production of sugar is highly profitable, and sugarbeet production gives the best returns of any large-scale crop. Production, consumption and trade statistics from 1970 to 1995 are shown in Table 5.7.

From 1973 to 1993 EC production grew by 7.2 million tonnes. Of this, only around 2.5 million tonnes was due to accessions, and the adjusted annual growth rate is 2.05%. This growth in production, including gains in yields, can be ascribed to the good conditions for producing sugar under the protection of the sugar regime of the CAP.

Table 5.7 EC/EU: production, consumption and trade, 1970–95, million tonnes, raw value

	Production	Consumption	Net imports	Net exports
1970	9.087	10.692	1.042	—
1971	10.287	10.461	1.009	—
1972	9.935	10.474	0.374	—
1973	10.177	11.116	0.312	—
1974	9.237	11.698	1.037	—
1975	10.818	9.541	1.452	—
1976	10.778	10.751	0.209	—
1977	12.458	9.871	—	0.966
1978	12.816	10.550	—	1.910
1979	13.613	10.813	—	2.146
1980	14.529	12.401	—	2.583
1981	16.572	12.093	—	3.760
1982	16.653	12.187	—	3.734
1983	13.693	11.944	—	3.063
1984	14.534	12.072	—	2.544
1985	14.965	12.022	—	2.338
1986	15.111	12.211	—	2.546
1987	14.401	11.922	—	3.737
1988	15.377	12.240	—	3.241
1989	16.124	12.686	—	3.257
1990	17.175	13.067	—	3.633
1991	15.995	13.001	—	3.152
1992	17.101	13.682	—	3.197
1993	17.383	13.116	—	4.119
1994	15.718	13.441	—	3.263
1995	15.500*	13.600*	—	2.900*

*Estimate. Source: ISO.

Brazil

In the mid-1990s Brazil has leapt into second place amongst sugar producers, overtaking India, which had a poor crop, in 1994. From production of 8 million tonnes in 1990, Brazil produced 12.27 million tonnes in 1994, an increase of 4.27 million tonnes (56%) at an annual growth rate of 11.2%. This rapid rise in production was closely connected with the Brazilian alcohol (ethanol) programme (for a detailed discussion of the Brazilian alcohol programme, see Appendix III), and the diversion of additional cane from a good cane crop into the production of sugar, rather than ethanol. World sugar prices in the 1990s have been attractive for Brazilian producers in the Centre/South region who are amongst the most efficient producers in the world.

Sugar production is confined to the Centre/South region (principally São Paulo state) and the North/North-east (principally Penambuco state). The Centre/South currently produces around three-quarters of Brazil's sugar, up to about 9 million tonnes, and the North/North-east around 3 million tonnes. Up to 1990 the Centre/South production, in the form of white sugar, was mainly for domestic consumption, while the North/North-east produced mainly raw sugar for export. However, with the recent increase in production occurring entirely in the Centre/South, exports from that region have increased significantly and now represent more than half of Brazil's total exports.

Brazil's pro-alcohol programme began in the late 1970s as a reaction to the first oil price shock of 1973. The objective was to produce enough alcohol, from sugar cane, to fuel all the cars in Brazil. Large areas of land, mainly in São Paulo state, previously used for cattle raising were planted in sugar cane and a large number of dedicated distilleries were constructed. Cane crushing capacity was quadrupled. Legislation required all new cars to be alcohol powered (the first stage required that all cars use 20% alcohol in a mix with gasoline). By the mid-1980s alcohol production had reached around 11 million litres and only one-third of the sugar cane produced was being used for sugar production. All new cars were powered by alcohol. In the 1970s Brazil had been in the top three of sugar exporters, along with Cuba and Australia, and had regularly produced 8.5–9 million tonnes of sugar. Rising alcohol demand in the mid- to late 1980s led to cane being diverted to alcohol production. Brazilian sugar production fell from 9.266 million tonnes in 1987 to 7.326 million tonnes in 1989. Exports in 1989 were only 0.965 million tonnes compared to 2.424 million tonnes in 1987. The alcohol crisis of 1989 brought some policy changes. Regulations governing new cars were relaxed to allow more gasoline driven cars to be purchased and imports of alcohol to top up domestic production were allowed. Alcohol demand has consequently levelled off at around 13 million litres and a succession of good cane crops in 1993, 1994 and 1995 has led to the rapid increase in sugar production discussed above.

Table 5.8 shows production, consumption and net exports for Brazil for 1970–95.

India

India pursues a policy of self-sufficiency, sometimes successfully as in 1995 and 1996, sometimes unsuccessfully as in 1994 and 1986 when it imported large quantities.

Table 5.8 Brazil: production, consumption and net exports, 1970–95, million tonnes, raw value

	Production	Consumption	Net exports
1970	5.019	3.495	1.130
1971	5.298	3.797	1.230
1972	6.151	4.125	2.638
1973	6.937	4.266	2.975
1974	6.931	4.576	2.303
1975	6.299	4.989	1.730
1976	7.236	5.091	1.252
1977	8.758	5.060	2.487
1978	7.913	5.289	1.924
1979	7.362	6.009	1.942
1980	8.270	6.264	2.662
1981	8.726	5.872	2.670
1982	8.941	6.097	2.788
1983	9.555	5.209	2.801
1984	9.258	6.201	3.040
1985	8.455	6.080	2.609
1986	7.999	6.589	2.554
1987	9.266	6.573	2.424
1988	7.874	6.241	1.686
1989	7.326	7.401	0.965
1990	8.007	6.614	1.639
1991	9.453	7.276	1.613
1992	9.925	7.349	2.273
1993	10.097	7.575	3.008
1994	12.270	7.874	3.616
1995	14.100*	8.250*	5.000*

*Estimate. Source: ISO.

The pursuit of self-sufficiency in India is complicated by having two apparently opposing goals: one is to ensure that production is sufficient, which implies the highest possible prices to growers; the other is to provide sugar as cheaply as possible to the population, which is achieved through a complex two-tier pricing system – the so-called levy sugar, sold at a low price through special shops, and 'free market' sugar, sold at the higher, free market price. The main instrument used to regulate this complex marketing system is the proportion of levy to free sales and this is controlled by the government. Free market sales are clearly more profitable for millers and growers. When instituted in 1968 the proportion was 60% levy sugar and 40% free sales. These proportions have been steadily changed to encourage higher production (growers and millers receive better returns from free sale sugar) and now stand at 60% free sale and 40% levy sugar, a complete reversal. The sugar situation in India is

Table 5.9 India: production, consumption and net trade, 1985–96, million tonnes, raw value

	Production	Consumption	Net trade
1985	7.016	8.974	−0.085
1986	7.594	8.693	−1.740
1987	9.215	9.732	−0.918
1988	10.207	10.175	—
1989	9.912	10.575	—
1990	12.068	11.075	—
1991	13.112	11.721	+0.335
1992	13.873	12.387	+0.549
1993	11.750	12.989	+0.352
1994	11.900	13.700	−2.635
1995	15.850*	13.650*	+2.200**
1996	16.500*	14.300*	+2.200**

*Estimates. **Surplus of production over consumption. Source: ISO.

complicated by the fact that only around half the cane goes into centrifugal sugar. The other half is used for open pan sugars. These sugars are outside the levy system and escape other taxes. Therefore manufacturers can often offer better cane prices to growers. At these times open pan sugar production rises and centrifugal sugar production falls, causing regulatory problems for the government and bringing about the need to import – sometimes heavily (1986 and 1994). The success, or otherwise, of the Indian government's self-sufficiency policy is shown in Table 5.9.

India achieved remarkable growth in production from 1985 to 1992 of 6.86 million tonnes, an annual growth rate of 10.2%. Consumption has grown at much the same rate.

Adequate supplies of cane and adequate mill capacity are available in India for production and consumption to continue expanding without recourse to imports if the problem of cane diversion to open pan sugars does not arise. This depends on the price millers can offer to growers, which in turn depends on the minimum cane price set by the Indian government or states, and the proportion of free sale sugar (which is more profitable to mills and they can therefore pay a higher cane price), again set by the government. Table 5.9 shows that from 1988 to 1992 this was managed successfully, but in 1993 and 1994 cane was diverted to open pan sugars and heavy imports were required in 1994. The Indian government will continue to attempt to manage its sugar cycle to achieve self-sufficiency. India will never be a permanent net importer from the world market, and will import only when its complex system gets out of balance. Intense efforts are being made to improve the yield of cane to meet consumption needs, and as with Pakistan, the possibility of replacing some of the open pan industry with white, mill centrifugal sugar exists.

China

China has long been considered by many to be the potential saviour of the world sugar market. With a per capita consumption of only 6 kg (compared to a world average of 20 kg) there is clearly considerable scope for improvement in spite of traditional dietary habits which do not include sugar as an important source of energy. (Rice has been and will remain the main provider of calories.) Yet there is no statistical evidence that sugar consumption is given a high priority. On the contrary, consumption has always been allowed to rise in line with rises in production and imports, except in years of crop problems and low production, have been kept at an average of 1.545 million tonnes from 1980 to 1990. Table 5.10 shows production, consumption and net trade figures for 1985-94.

From Table 5.10 it can be seen that production increased from 4.8 million tonnes in 1985 to 8.863 million tonnes in 1992, an increase of 4 million tonnes at a remarkable annual growth rate of 9.1%. Over the same period consumption increased by only 1.265 million tonnes, an annual growth rate of 2.6%.

A good example of how production and consumption are managed is provided by the period 1988-94. In 1988 a poor crop meant China had to import 3.7 million tonnes at a high cost in foreign exchange. The government instituted compulsory planting schemes for both beet and cane. By 1992 a remarkable 80% increase in total

Table 5.10   China: production, consumption and net trade, 1985-94, million tonnes, raw value

	Production	Consumption	Net trade
1985	4.800	6.350	−1.964
1986	5.700	6.700	−0.808
1987	5.450	7.000	−1.710
1988	4.875	7.200	−3.682
1989	5.350	7.150	−1.139
1990	6.250	7.125	−0.527
1991	6.943	7.350	−0.645
1992	8.863	7.615	+0.705
1993	8.092	7.720	+1.555
1994	6.325	7.900	−1.238

Source: ISO.

production had been achieved, and in 1992 and 1993 China became a major world net exporter, exporting respectively 700 000 tonnes and 1.555 million tonnes in those two years. The additional production did not go into consumption, but to exports.

In 1994 the compulsory planting order was dropped and a combination of poor weather and farmers switching to more lucrative cash crops led to a sharp decline in production and China became a net importer, once more, of 1.238 million tonnes. The government believes that this deficit will be made up by production from 'new cane areas' which still receive some government support.

Thus, having achieved self-sufficiency at the low per capita level of 6 kg in 1992 and 1993, China still seems intent on maintaining self-sufficiency, or limiting the level of imports, in the future. China's future as an importer is very closely linked to government policy. Some hope has been expressed that the newly urbanized middle class in China will push up sugar consumption and imports. However, the majority of China's population remains rural, where sugar is almost unknown. In the past the government has stepped up the production and import of saccharin, to sweeten soft drinks, when demand has risen and there has also been discussion about setting up a major HFCS industry in China based on locally produced corn. Therefore China's imports cannot be expected to average much more in the 1990s than they did in the 1980s (1.5 million tonnes).

USA

Sugar is produced from both beet and cane in the USA. Cane sugar is produced in the states of Louisiana, Florida, Texas and Hawaii, and in Puerto Rico, and beet sugar in the Midwest (Michigan, Ohio, Minnesota, North Dakota, Colorado, Nebraska, Wyoming, Montana, Idaho and Oregon) and California. In 1994 total production was 6.92 million tonnes, of which 3.795 million tonnes was beet sugar (55%) and 3.125 million tonnes (45%) cane sugar.

US sugar policy and its effect on production were discussed in detail in Chapter 4 and will only be summarized here. From the introduction of country specific quotas in 1982 and the setting of the support price (the loan rate) at a level significantly above the world price (currently the loan rate is 18 cents/lb for raw cane sugar and 23.43 cents/lb for refined cane sugar), US production of sugar has expanded. Production in 1982 was 5.42 million tonnes and has grown to reach 6.92 million tonnes in 1994, growth of 1.5 million tonnes at an annual growth rate of 2.06%. Most of the growth has come from

Table 5.11 USA: production, consumption and net imports, 1970–95, million tonnes, raw value

	Production	Consumption	Net imports
1970	5.734	10.547	4.803
1971	5.570	10.530	5.068
1972	5.724	10.619	4.951
1973	5.729	10.630	4.831
1974	5.399	10.325	5.188
1975	5.955	9.141	3.311
1976	6.438	10.000	4.159
1977	5.764	10.361	5.271
1978	5.133	9.954	4.237
1979	5.435	9.876	4.422
1980	5.313	9.330	3.215
1981	5.788	8.958	3.697
1982	5.418	8.310	2.343
1983	5.215	8.074	2.466
1984	5.342	7.738	2.473
1985	5.415	7.290	1.910
1986	5.676	7.085	1.384
1987	6.631	7.385	0.632
1988	6.429	7.420	1.011
1989	6.206	7.561	1.321
1990	5.704	7.848	2.045
1991	6.477	7.887	1.732
1992	6.805	8.098	1.545
1993	7.045	8.192	1.489
1994	6.921	8.454	1.132
1995	7.100*	8.400*	1.055*

*Estimate. *Source: ISO.*

beet sugar, especially after the introduction of a process to de-sugar molasses in the late 1980s. With consumption declining sharply up to 1986 (consumption fell from 8.3 million tonnes in 1982 to 7.085 million tonnes in 1986), due to the substitution of HFCS for sugar, and only regaining its 1982 level in 1994, US imports, strictly controlled by the quota, have declined sharply. Production, consumption and net imports for 1970–95 are shown in Table 5.11.

Australia

Australia has consistently been one of the world's largest producers and is almost unique in that it is largely export orientated – more than 80% of its production is exported, and overwhelmingly to the free market. Australia began its recent, major expansion with a general

Table 5.12 Australia: production, consumption and exports, 1970–95 million tonnes, raw value

	Production	Consumption	Exports
1970	2.507	0.721	1.642
1971	2.732	0.717	1.779
1972	2.869	0.717	2.315
1973	2.583	0.756	2.124
1974	2.938	0.764	1.828
1975	2.930	0.778	1.976
1976	3.395	0.781	2.620
1977	3.452	0.785	2.965
1978	2.978	0.786	2.002
1979	2.960	0.787	2.003
1980	3.415	0.783	2.411
1981	3.509	0.793	2.982
1982	3.652	0.783	2.504
1983	3.256	0.759	2.425
1984	3.627	0.749	2.591
1985	3.439	0.764	2.651
1986	3.439	0.818	2.710
1987	3.571	0.817	2.826
1988	3.759	0.844	2.980
1989	3.887	0.881	3.149
1990	3.612	0.864	3.069
1991	3.195	0.834	2.456
1992	4.362	0.829	2.907
1993	4.448	0.909	3.444
1994	5.217	0.927	4.524
1995	5.025*	0.950*	4.000*

*Estimate. *Source: ISO.*

deregulation of the industry, inspired by the Uruguay Round, in 1989. The ban on imports was lifted and replaced with a tariff, and, although land assignment for growing cane continued, it would no longer be a constraint on the growth of production. This led to a rapid rise in cane area and, as weather permitted, a sharp increase in production. From 1990, when sugar production was 3.612 million tonnes, output rose by 1.6 million tonnes (44%, at an annual growth rate of 9.6%) by 1994 to a record 5.217 million tonnes. Production is mainly located along the coast of Queensland, with a small production for domestic consumption in northern New South Wales, and a new production area recently opened up in Western Australia. Production, consumption and exports for 1970–95 are shown in Table 5.12.

Cuba

Up until 1960 Cuba was the world's largest sugar producer, from 1965 to 1975 the third largest, and from 1975 until the break-up of the USSR in 1991 the fourth largest. The sugar industry of Cuba, like those of Australia and Thailand, is export orientated, but Cuba sells largely under special, bilateral trade arrangements; up to 1960 to the USA, under the US Sugar Act, and since 1960 to the USSR, its satellites and China. In 1985 85% of Cuban production was exported. Production, consumption and exports for 1970–95 are shown in Table 5.13.

With an apparently insatiable market in the USSR, its satellites and China, post-revolutionary Cuba tried to increase production through the 1960s and managed a record output of 7.559 million tonnes in 1970. However, the effort drained the industry and production fell away in 1971 and 1972, falling to 4.688 million tonnes in 1972. The

Table 5.13 Cuba: production, consumption and exports, 1970–95, million tonnes, raw value

	Production	Consumption	Exports
1970	7.559	0.619	6.906
1971	5.950	0.616	5.511
1972	4.688	0.471	4.140
1973	5.383	0.464	4.797
1974	5.926	0.522	5.491
1975	6.427	0.499	5.744
1976	6.152	0.532	5.764
1977	6.953	0.519	6.238
1978	7.662	0.552	7.231
1979	7.800	0.519	7.269
1980	6.805	0.530	6.191
1981	7.926	0.552	7.071
1982	8.039	0.649	7.734
1983	7.460	0.678	6.792
1984	7.783	0.728	7.016
1985	7.889	0.887	7.209
1986	7.467	0.762	6.703
1987	7.232	0.772	6.482
1988	8.119	0.745	6.978
1989	7.579	0.882	7.123
1990	8.444	0.937	7.172
1991	7.233	0.956	6.767
1992	7.219	0.962	6.085
1993	4.246	0.796	3.662
1994	4.017	0.664	3.188
1995	3.400*	0.650*	2.750*

*Estimate. *Source: ISO.*

1974 world sugar price boom created the conditions for another attempt at expansion, and production grew rapidly through the 1970s to reach 8.039 million tonnes by 1982, an expansion of 3.35 million tonnes (71%) from 1972 at an annual growth rate of 5.5%. Between 1983 and 1990, when a record production of 8.444 million tonnes was achieved, production stabilized, depending on weather conditions, in the range 7.2–8.4 million tonnes. The economic shock waves from the break-up of the USSR were felt soon after 1991. Application of fertilizer virtually ceased and spare parts for field machinery, especially harvesters, and mills were in short supply. Production fell from 7.219 million tonnes in 1992 to 4.246 million tonnes in 1993, 4.017 million tonnes in 1994, and an all-time low of 3.4 million tonnes in 1995. In 1995 contracts were signed with foreign investors to supply essential inputs, especially fertilizer, in return for a share of the resulting increase in sugar production. These measures, and other measures to deregulate the industry (state farms were converted into co-operatives) and produce a more market orientated sugar economy, should lead to a recovery in Cuban production, possibly to around 5-6 million tonnes depending on world market conditions. But levels of production of 7-8 million tonnes may never be attained again.

Thailand

As with Australia and Cuba, production in Thailand is export orientated. In 1994 65% of its production was exported. Like Australia, Thailand's exports are overwhelmingly to the free market. Thailand is significant because it successfully achieved a contra-cyclical expansion in production when world prices were at their lowest ever level in real terms. (Normally countries begin expansions at times of high world prices, only to find that when the additional production comes on stream prices are at a low level.) Production, consumption and exports for 1970–95 are shown in Table 5.14.

Thailand has only become a major producer and exporter since 1980. In 1970 it had a relatively small industry, producing less than half a million tonnes and exporting 52 000 tonnes. Encouraged by the world sugar price boom of 1974, production was expanded to reach 2.36 million tonnes by 1977. From 1978 to 1981 production was restrained by the 1977 ISA, but in 1982, with good weather conditions, production reached 3.017 million tonnes. From 1983 to 1988, during which time world prices were low (although Thailand was planning and executing a major expansion), output remained in the range between 2.1 and 2.7 million tonnes. However, in 1988,

Table 5.14 Thailand: production, consumption and exports, 1970–95, million tonnes, raw value

	Production	Consumption	Exports
1970	0.495	0.371	0.052
1971	0.640	0.404	0.145
1972	0.702	0.413	0.439
1973	0.839	0.433	0.258
1974	0.985	0.499	0.564
1975	1.216	0.548	0.668
1976	1.757	0.569	1.145
1977	2.361	0.594	1.675
1978	1.664	0.607	1.029
1979	1.981	0.620	1.210
1980	0.778	0.632	0.460
1981	1.702	0.642	1.155
1982	3.017	0.604	2.045
1983	2.113	0.660	1.411
1984	2.550	0.701	1.444
1985	2.393	0.721	1.781
1986	2.718	0.744	2.049
1987	2.532	0.883	2.072
1988	2.639	0.886	1.961
1989	4.338	0.981	3.105
1990	3.542	1.105	2.496
1991	4.248	1.189	2.863
1992	5.078	1.264	3.719
1993	3.825	1.368	2.401
1994	4.168	1.480	2.720
1995	5.500*	1.600*	3.800

*Estimate. *Source: ISO.*

when world prices began to rise (the average raw sugar price for 1988 was 10.2 cents/lb, compared to 6.75 cents/lb in 1987 and 4.06 cents/lb in 1985), production jumped by 1.7 million tonnes (64%) to reach a then record of 4.338 million tonnes in 1989. From 1990 Thai production has been periodically affected by drought but reached 4.248 million tonnes in 1991 and a new record 5.078 million tonnes is expected to be posted in 1995. Sugar is produced in two main regions in Thailand: the Central belt and the North-east where most of the post-1980 expansion took place.

6

Demand

An important source of energy

S ugar is a valuable, basic part of most diets. In developed
countries it supplies 10–15% of energy intake (see Table 6.1). In
some developing countries the proportion of energy supplied
by sugar can reach 20%. However, in low income developing
countries per capita consumption can be very low, less than 10 kg
annually. As might be expected, sugar has a low income elasticity in
high income (developed, industrial) countries but a much higher
income elasticity in developing countries. Dietary habits also play a
part in determining demand. In some parts of Asia (e.g. China, as we
have seen) sugar is not part of the traditional diet – energy comes
from rice – and this restrains consumption growth. Sugar is, however,
consumed in every country of the world.

Current consumption patterns

Table 6.2 shows the ten largest world consumers and continental and
world consumption totals for 1994. Ten countries alone account for
61% of total world consumption. Asia, in spite of areas of low per
capita consumption, makes up 37% of world consumption, including
as it does the giants India and China. On the other hand, North
America, with only two countries, consumes more sugar than the
whole of the African continent.

Table 6.1 Share of sucrose in total energy intake in developed and developing countries, 1988–90

	%	Per capita consumption, kg/year
Developed countries		
USA	15	50.5*
	10	31.6
Australia	17	50.9
UK (1985)	14	43.4
FR Germany (1985)	12	33.0
Japan	9	22.9
Developed countries total	12	37.9
Developing countries		
Mexico	18	50.4
Cuba	21	81.2
Guatemala	19	38.9
Brazil	18	45.8
Colombia	16	35.9
Argentina	10	29.3
Average South America	16	39.6
Algeria	11	30.1
Egypt	11	33.4
Nigeria	2	3.8
Zaire	2	3.1
South Africa	12	38.1
Average Africa	6	13.8
Pakistan	9	19.4
India	6	13.1
China	3	6.4
Indonesia	6	14.6
Philippines	11	23.8
Thailand	9	17.9
Average Asia	5	11.8
Developing countries total	7	15.2
World	8	20.8

*Sucrose and HFCS. *Sources: WSRO, USDA, ISO, FAO.*

Table 6.2 Ten largest consumers, continental and world consumption, 1994, million tonnes, raw value

			Share of world consumption, %
1	India	13.70	12
2	EU	13.44	12
3	USA	8.45	7
4	China	7.90	7
5	Brazil	7.87	7
6	Russia	5.25	5
7	Mexico	4.35	4
8	Pakistan	2.90	3
9	Japan	2.66	2
10	Ukraine	2.49	2
	Total		61
	Europe	31.08	27
	North America	9.63	8
	Central America	6.87	6
	South America	13.27	12
	Asia	41.83	37
	Africa	9.52	8
	Oceania	1.20	1
	World	113.80	

Source: ISO.

Per capita consumption patterns

World per capita sugar consumption in 1994 was 20.4 kg (see Table 6.3). It had been steady at around 20 kg from 1970. This apparent stability, however, masks the true picture: developed country per capita consumption has been falling as that of developing countries has risen. In developed countries, sugar consumption has come under pressure from three sides: health, diet and substitutes. Wide publicity has been given to various attempts since the early 1970s to associate sugar with diseases such as diabetes, hyperphycemia and obesity, etc (see Chapter 8 and Appendix II). Although all were eventually disproved, public awareness was raised and there is no doubt this has continued to have a negative effect on sugar consumption in developed, industrial countries. Perhaps more significantly, post World War II diets in developed industrial countries have had to

Table 6.3   Per capita consumption, 1994, kg/annum

Europe		**36.9**
of which:	EU	38.5
	Poland	44.2
	Russia	34.4
	Turkey	29.3
North America		**33.2**
of which:	Canada	40.2
	USA	32.4
Central America		**44.0**
of which:	Cuba	60.6
	Dominican Rep.	37.9
	Guatemala	40.3
	Mexico	46.8
South America		**43.0**
of which:	Argentina	37.9
	Brazil	51.2
	Colombia	32.1
	Venezuela	35.4
Asia		**12.8**
of which:	China	6.5
	India	15.2
	Indonesia	15.1
	Iran	26.8
	Japan	21.5
	Korea, Rep.	19.4
	Malaysia	39.8
	Pakistan	22.9
	Philippines	28.7
	Thailand	24.9
Africa		**13.6**
of which:	Algeria	29.6
	Cameroon	6.4
	Egypt	29.4
	Kenya	21.2
	Ghana	7.2
	Morocco	32.1
	Nigeria	5.5
	Senegal	17.3
	South Africa	36.7
	Togo	6.9
	Zaire	2.5
Oceania		**44.2**
of which:	Australia	52.1
	New Zealand	52.3
Developed countries		37.9
Developing countries		15.2
World		20.4

Source: ISO.

adjust to more sedentary, less manual employment. Consequently, average daily requirements for energy have fallen, and sugar, since part of its role in food is to supply calories, has suffered along with other dietary components from this decline in calorific intake. Coupled with this, low population growth rates have led to an increase in the average age of the population, and older people require and consume fewer calories.

In contrast, in developing countries, where population growth rates are higher, the average age of the population is falling and per capita sugar consumption levels are rising, in some cases rapidly, if the population can afford to buy sugar. In developing countries sugar is valued as an energy provider as well as a taste enhancer.

The substitution of HFCS for sugar in (principally) the USA and Japan is discussed in more detail in Chapter 8. However, it is important to note here that in the USA, HFCS, under the protection of sugar support legislation, substituted for approximately 3 million tonnes of sugar and, in addition, took over the most important and fastest growing use for sugar: soft drinks. Subsequent growth in sweetener use by soft drinks accrued to HFCS. In Japan the substitution was less severe, but nevertheless amounted to approximately 1 million tonnes. The substitution of HFCS for sugar was a major factor in the decline in consumption in developed countries from the mid-1970s.

Table 6.3 illustrates the distinct regional patterns of per capita sugar consumption. Developed countries typically have a consumption of between 30 and 40 kg/year. Europe, with 36.9 kg, and North America, with 33.2 kg, follow this pattern. In the early 1970s the USA had a per capita consumption exceeding 50 kg/year but the introduction of HFCS after the world sugar price boom of 1974 resulted in the loss of the entire soft drinks sector to HFCS by the mid-1980s. Per capita consumption rates in Central and South America are the highest in the world. Although they are developing countries, many of them low income, most are surplus (exporting) producers, and sugar is available and cheap to purchase. In addition, sugar is important for cultural reasons, particularly when it is associated with high levels of coffee drinking. There is a strong contrast between Central/South America and Asia/Africa. As we have seen, sugar is not a traditional part of the food culture in Asia. Therefore even higher income countries such as Japan and Korea have relatively low rates of intake of 21.5 and 19.4 kg, respectively. (Both countries also have HFCS industries.) Even surplus producers such as Thailand and the Philippines (24.9 and 28.7 kg, respectively) have lower levels than comparable Central/South American exporters. Of the populous Asian countries, only Malaysia (39.8 kg) has per capita consumption equivalent to the level found in developed countries. Clearly, many Asian countries are low income and this as well as dietary habits has a bearing on per capita consumption. It should be noted, however, that if account is taken of open pan sugars India has a per capita consumption of all sugars exceeding 20 kg/year.

Africa, with a per capita consumption in 1994 of 13.6 kg, is also well below the world average. In spite of higher levels in North Africa (Algeria, 29.6 kg; Egypt, 29.4 kg and Morocco, 32.1 kg) and South Africa (36.7 kg), the other countries represented in Table 6.3 are more typical of the continent – Cameroon, 6.4 kg; Ghana, 7.2 kg; Nigeria, 5.5 kg; Togo, 6.9 kg; Zaire, 2.5 kg. There the problem is, quite simply, low income. Sugar production is spread thinly across the continent and only Côte d'Ivoire, Ethiopia, Malawi, Mauritius, South Africa, Sudan, Swaziland, Zambia and Zimbabwe are surplus countries (nine countries out of a total of fifty in Africa). Most countries south of the Sahara cannot afford to import the quantities that would meet potential demand.

Global consumption trends

From 1950 to 1994 world sugar consumption grew at an annual rate of 3.1% almost quadrupling from 29.791 million tonnes to 113.798 million tonnes. However, the growth rate slowed over this period, as Table 6.4 shows.

As noted in the section on per capita consumption patterns, the world trend masks the dynamics of world consumption development. Figure 6.1 shows that while the growth rate of world consumption has slowed down, it has been the sum of two divergent trends by developed and developing countries. Both grew at approximately the same rate in the years of reconstruction after World War II but in the

Table 6.4 World consumption growth rates, 1950–94, %

1950–60	5.1
1960–70	3.9
1970–80	2.1
1980–90	2.0
1990–94	1.2

Source: ISO.

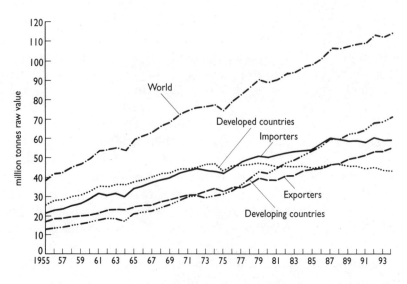

6.1 Global consumption trends (source: ISO).

mid-1970s both changed course. In developed countries three events coincided. As we have seen, sugar came under attack for health reasons, the slow process of dietary adjustment to smaller energy needs began to bite, and, after the world sugar price boom of 1974, HFCS was substituted for sugar in the USA and Japan. Consequently, sugar consumption in developed countries today has fallen to around 35 kg per capita. Consumption in developing countries, however, began to accelerate from the same period. This was triggered by the first oil price shock in 1973, which shifted income in the direction of developing countries, and was reinforced by the second oil price shock of 1980. The process began with a surge in sugar consumption by oil-exporting developing countries. In other developing countries increased sugar production also enabled consumption to grow. Consequently, in 1981 total developing country consumption exceeded that of developed countries for the first time and in 1994 was 24.85 million tonnes higher at 69.323 million tonnes. The dynamism and dominance of developing country consumption has had a profound effect on the world sugar economy, a point that will be discussed in Chapter 9 in the context of the world sugar market. Table 6.5 shows the evolution of developed and developing country consumption from 1955 to 1994. The share of developing countries in world consumption almost doubled from 32% to 61% over the period.

Table 6.5 Developed and developing country consumption, 1955–94, million tonnes, raw value

	Developed	Developing	Developing share, %	Growth rates Developed	Developing
1955	26.198	12.463	32	–	–
1960	33.153	16.064	33	+4.8	+5.2
1965	38.541	20.585	35	+3.1	+5.1
1970	44.947	27.173	38	+2.9	+5.7
1975	44.259	30.176	41	–0.4	+2.1
1980	47.845	40.771	46	+1.6	+6.2
1985	45.755	52.015	53	–1.0	+5.0
1990	47.192	60.631	56	+0.6	+3.1
1994	44.475	69.323	61	–1.2	+3.4

Source: ISO.

Consumption trends by country

Table 6.6 shows how the top ten world consumers have evolved and illustrates the remarkable rise in sugar consumption in most countries from 1955 to 1994. The exceptions are the USA and, to a lesser extent, Japan.

USA

US consumption peaked in 1973 at 10.46 million tonnes when annual per capita consumption was 55 kg. Then, as a consequence of the world sugar price boom of 1974, consumption declined as HFCS was progressively substituted for sugar in the soft drinks industry. US sugar consumption reached its post-1974 low point in 1986 when it fell to 7.085 million tonnes (representing a per capita consumption of only 29.3 kg), lower than it had been in 1955 (7.74 million tonnes).

US total and per capita consumption, shown in Table 6.7, have both grown since the low point of 1986, to reach in 1994 8.454 million tonnes and 32.4 kg respectively. In spite of the decline, the USA retains third place amongst world consumers, having been the largest from 1955 to 1965, before being overtaken by the USSR and the EC.

Table 6.6 Evolution of ten largest consumers, 1955–94, million tonnes, raw value

	1955	1960	1965	1970	1975	1980	1985	1990	1994
1	USA 7.74	USA 8.41	USA 10.17	EC 10.69	USSR 11.30	USSR 12.30	USSR 12.61	USSR 13.40	India 13.70
2	USSR 3.95	USSR 6.70	USSR 9.10	USA 10.40	EC 9.54	EC 10.97	EC 10.64	EC 13.07	EU 13.44
3	UK 2.73	UK 2.90	EC 6.30	USSR 10.25	USA 9.14	USA 9.34	USA 8.34	India 11.08	USA 8.45
4	Brazil 1.95	Brazil 2.48	Brazil 2.95	India 4.94	Brazil 4.99	Brazil 6.26	India 8.24	USA 8.90	China 7.90
5	India 1.74	India 2.23	UK 2.94	Brazil 3.50	China 4.20	India 5.04	China 6.35	China 7.35	Brazil 7.87
6	FR Germany 1.52	FR Germany 1.78	India 2.78	China 3.34	India 3.86	China 3.60	Brazil 6.20	Brazil 7.28	Russia 5.25
7	France 1.24	China 1.70	China 2.30	Japan 3.10	Japan 3.18	Mexico 3.15	Mexico 3.34	Mexico 4.42	Mexico 4.35
8	Japan 1.15	France 1.47	Japan 2.03	Mexico 1.90	Mexico 2.53	Japan 2.98	Japan 2.75	Japan 2.83	Pakistan 2.90
9	Mexico 0.80	Japan 1.41	Mexico 1.48	Poland 1.42	Poland 1.59	Indonesia 1.55	Indonesia 1.73	Pakistan 2.66	Japan 2.66
10	South Africa 0.61	Mexico 1.12	Poland 1.20	Spain 0.93	Spain 1.10	Poland 1.53	Poland 1.69	Indonesia 2.63	Ukraine 2.49

Source: ISO.

Table 6.7   USA: total and per capita consumption, 1970-94

	Total, million tonnes, raw value	Per capita, kg/annum
1970	10.401	50.8
1975	9.141	42.0
1980	9.330	41.0
1985	7.290	30.5
1990	7.848	30.9
1994	8.454	32.4

Source: ISO.

Japan

Japan followed a similar pattern, for the same reasons, to the USA. Consumption peaked in 1974 at 3.34 million tonnes, representing an annual per capita consumption of 30.4 kg, and reached its low point in 1987: 2.69 million tonnes (22.1 kg per capita consumption). Again the substitution of HFCS was responsible for the decline. Consumption in Japan rose to 2.8 million tonnes in the late 1980s–early 1990s. Both total consumption and per capita consumption have fallen again in the mid-1990s due to further inroads by HFCS. In 1994 total consumption was 2.657 million tonnes and per capita consumption was 21.5 kg. Total and per capita consumption for Japan is shown in Table 6.8.

Table 6.8   Japan: total and per capita consumption, 1970-94

	Total, million tonnes, raw value	Per capita, kg/annum
1970	3.029	29.0
1975	2.796	25.2
1980	2.982	25.5
1985	2.891	23.9
1990	2.833	22.9
1994	2.657	21.5

Source: ISO.

USSR/FSU

The USSR/FSU is another case of decline in a developed country, but for different reasons. The break-up of the USSR in 1991 ended the era of heavily subsidized sugar prices, and per capita consumption in

Table 6.9   USSR/FSU: total and per capita consumption, 1970–94

	Total, million tonnes, raw value	Per capita, kg/annum
1970	10.247	42.2
1975	11.304	44.4
1980	12.300	46.3
1985	12.610	45.3
1990	13.400	46.2
1994	10.075	34.4

Source: ISO.

Russia fell from almost 50 kg in the Soviet period to only 30 kg by 1994. Consumption in the Ukraine held up better because Ukraine is a surplus, exporting country with no problems with availability of sugar. Total and per capita consumption for the USSR/FSU is shown in Table 6.9.

USSR consumption peaked in 1988 at 14.35 million tonnes, representing a per capita high of 50.3 kg. As the Gorbachev era progressed there was a decline, but in 1990 consumption was still 13.4 million tonnes (46.2 kg per capita). However, the decline after the break-up of the USSR was rapid, and by 1994 FSU consumption had fallen 4.275 million tonnes (30%) from the Soviet peak in 1988 to only 10.075 million tonnes (34.4 kg per capita). Nevertheless, the FSU remains the third largest consuming region and Russia, with a consumption of 5.25 million tonnes, was the world's sixth largest consumer in 1994.

The expansion in USSR consumption took place after the Cuban Revolution in 1959, when not only did the USSR take large quantities of Cuban sugar (from 2 rising to 4 million tonnes) but a programme of raising domestic production also began. In 1960 Soviet consumption was 6.365 million tonnes, with a per capita level of only 29.7 kg, and domestic production had risen to 10.078 million tonnes. Imports from Cuba were 1.332 million tonnes and consumption had risen in only 9 years by 55% (an annual growth rate of 5%) to 9.889 million tonnes (41.1 kg per capita). From 1970 onwards the rise was slower, but still spectacular, up to the 1988 peak of 14.35 million tonnes. The increase from 1970 to 1988 was 4.46 million tonnes (45%) at an annual growth rate of 2.1%.

EU

In 1994 the EU was the world's second largest consumer of sugar, after India, with a total of 13.44 million tonnes at a per capita level of

Table 6.10 EC/EU: total and per capita consumption, 1970–94

	Total, million tonnes, raw value	Per capita, kg/annum
1970	7.593	42.1
1975	9.541	36.7
1980	10.972	40.3
1985	10.732	39.1
1990	13.067	38.1
1994	13.441	38.5

Source: ISO.

38.5 kg. Although total consumption has increased through enlargement, per capita growth has been small in recent years, constrained not by HFCS growth, as in the USA and Japan, but by concerns about health and diet. Total and per capita consumption is shown in Table 6.10.

Per capita consumption fell in 1975 in reaction to the 1974 world sugar price boom, regained 40 kg by 1980, but subsequently fell again due to the accession of Spain and Portugal, which had lower per capita consumption levels than their northern neighbours.

India

In 1994 India was the world's largest consumer of sugar, with an offtake of 13.7 million tonnes representing a per capita level 15.2 kg (compared to the world average of 20.4 kg). If consumption of open pan sugar is taken into account, per capita consumption of all sugars in India exceeds 20 kg. India is a good example of a dynamic developing country where both total and per capita consumption of sugar are growing rapidly (see Table 6.11).

Table 6.11 India: total and per capita consumption, 1970–94

	Total, million tonnes, raw value	Per capita, kg/annum
1970	3.767	6.9
1975	3.859	6.5
1980	5.042	7.5
1985	8.974	12.0
1990	11.075	13.3
1994	13.700	15.2

Source: ISO.

Per capita consumption in India has doubled since 1980. The overall annual growth rate from 1970 to 1994 was a remarkable (for consumption) 5.8%, compared to the world consumption growth rate over the same period of 2% per annum. India maintains a high consumption growth rate: from 1990 to 1994 growth was 5.48% per annum. India's consumption increased by 2.625 million tonnes from 1990 to 1994, 49% of the increase in world consumption of 5.38 million tonnes over the same period. India is the dynamo of and the principal contributor to world consumption growth. In India sugar consumption is strongly associated with tea drinking and the preparation of confectionery for religious festivals.

China

China has a very low per capita consumption of sugar, only 6.5 kg in 1994, which has not grown appreciably since 1984. In China, as we have already seen, sugar is not an important or traditional part of the diet – rice being the principal source of energy. However, through population growth, total consumption also grows, and in 1994 China was the fourth largest world consumer at 7.9 million tonnes. Total and per capita consumption for China is shown in Table 6.12.

Table 6.12 China: total and per capita consumption, 1970–94

	Total, million tonnes, raw value	Per capita, kg/annum
1970	3.150	4.2
1975	4.300	5.1
1980	3.600	3.8
1985	6.350	6.0
1990	7.125	6.2
1994	7.900	6.5

Source: ISO.

Up to 1980 the Chinese total consumption growth rate did exceed the population growth rate: from 1970 to 1985 the annual growth rate of sugar consumption was comparable with that of India at 5.1%. After 1985 growth slowed appreciably, to 2.46% from 1986 to 1994, only slightly exceeding the population growth rate. With rapid urbanization and the movement towards a freer market economy, many observers believe that the creation of a soft-drink quaffing middle class will lead to an increase in the consumption growth rate above the rate of growth of population. Whether this eventuates will depend on government policy decisions, not only on consumption but also concerning the role of domestic production and imports. (For more detailed discussion of the interaction between consumption, production, imports and exports, see Chapter 5.)

Brazil

Brazil is a good example of a sugar surplus developing country where the availability and relative cheapness of sugar has led to a high level of per capita sugar consumption. In 1994 Brazil's per capita consumption was 51.2 kg, one of the highest – for a large country – in the world, having peaked at 52.1 kg in 1989. In Brazil sugar has a very important place in the diet, providing 18% of energy intake. Brazil was the fifth largest consumer of sugar in the world in 1994, with an offtake of 7.87 million tonnes. Sugar consumption is strongly associated with coffee drinking, and Brazil has also a high level of coffee intake. Total and per capita consumption for Brazil is shown in Table 6.13.

Apart from the period between 1980 and 1985 Brazil, like India, has shown rapid consumption growth, well exceeding the population growth rate. Overall, from 1970 to 1994, the annual growth rate was 3.6%, compared with the world rate of 2% and the Indian growth rate over the same period of 5.8%. Since 1990 the consumption growth rate has accelerated as production has risen sharply. From 1990 to 1994 the annual growth rate in consumption was 4.45%, representing an increase of 1.259 million tonnes or 23% of the world increase in consumption over the same period. (Together India and Brazil accounted for 72% of the increase in world consumption from 1990 to 1994.)

Table 6.13   Brazil: total and per capita consumption, 1970-94

	Total, million tonnes, raw value	Per capita, kg/annum
1970	3.495	37.4
1975	4.990	45.3
1980	6.264	50.9
1985	6.080	44.8
1990	6.615	45.8
1994	7.874	51.2

Source: ISO.

Table 6.14 Mexico: total and per capita consumption, 1970–94

	Total, million tonnes, raw value	Per capita, kg/annum
1970	1.992	41.2
1975	2.525	42.0
1980	3.152	44.7
1985	3.548	45.3
1990	4.424	54.5
1994	4.350	46.8

Source: ISO.

Mexico

Mexico has the highest level of per capita soft drink consumption in the developing world, and consequently has a high per capita sugar consumption level: 46.8 kg in 1994, having peaked at 54.5 kg in 1990. Like Brazil, Mexico is a major producer of sugar with good availability, and government controlled sugar prices up to 1995 have helped to maintain the high level of consumption. In 1994 Mexico's total sugar consumption was 4.35 million tonnes, the seventh highest in the world. Total and per capita consumption for Mexico is shown in Table 6.14.

Apart from a post-1990 decline, Mexico's sugar consumption has grown strongly. From 1970 to 1994, the annual growth rate was 3.45%, above that of the population growth rate. Up to 1990 the rate was 4.3% per annum.

Pakistan

Pakistan has a remarkable record of strong consumption growth, with a growth rate exceeding even that of India. Between 1980 and 1985 total consumption almost doubled, and between 1986 and 1994 it more than doubled. The per capita consumption level rose from a very low level of 4.8 kg in 1970 to 22.9 kg in 1994, exceeding the world average by 2.7 kg. The annual growth rate from 1970 to 1994 was a stupendous 6.9%, and the growth rate actually accelerated after 1985: from 1986 to 1994 it was 9.5% per annum. The extremely rapid increase in Pakistan's consumption over the period was based on an equally rapid increase in production rather than imports. After 1990 seven new mills were built and white, mill, centrifugal sugar almost completely replaced open pan sugar. In 1994 Pakistan produced 3.043

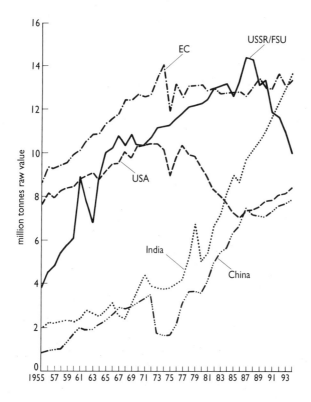

6.2 Evolution of five largest consumers, 1955–94 (source: ISO).

Table 6.15 Pakistan: total and per capita consumption, 1970–94

	Total, million tonnes, raw value	Per capita, kg/annum
1970	0.625	4.8
1975	0.520	7.4
1980	0.781	9.6
1985	1.400	14.6
1990	2.290	20.4
1994	2.900	22.9

Source: ISO.

million tonnes of sugar, more than 1 million tonnes more than the quantity produced in 1990 (1.989 million tonnes). In 1994 Pakistan's consumption was 2.9 million tonnes, making it the eighth largest producer in the world in that year. Total and per capita consumption for Pakistan is shown in Table 6.15.

Table 6.6 shows the rise through the ranks of developing countries, particularly India, Pakistan, China and Brazil, emphasizing the stagnation or decline in developed countries in stark contrast to the dynamic growth of developing countries. Figure 6.2 shows the evolution of the top five consuming countries in 1994, from 1955 to 1994.

7

Exporters and importers

Exports

World net exports in 1994 amounted to 22.839 million tonnes. Of this total 8.236 million tonnes (36%) came from developed countries (largely EU and Australia) and 14.603 million (64%) from developing exporters. The geographical distribution of world exports in 1994 is shown in Table 7.1.

Apart from Africa, exports are reasonably evenly distributed around the continents. However, in 1994 this was due partly to the sharp decline in Cuban exports after the break-up of the USSR in 1991. In 1990, for example, Central America accounted for 35% of world net exports.

Table 7.1 Geographical distribution of world exports, 1994, million tonnes, raw value

		Share of world total, %
Europe	3.834	17
Central America	4.910	21
South America	4.606	20
Asia	3.040	13
Africa	1.448	6
Oceania	5.005	23
World	22.839	

Source: ISO.

Table 7.2 Ten largest net exporters, 1994, million tonnes, raw value

1	Australia	4.523
2	Brazil	3.602
3	EU	3.263
4	Cuba	3.188
5	Thailand	2.720
6	Guatemala	0.752
7	Colombia	0.724
8	Mauritius	0.552
9	Fiji	0.473
10	Turkey	0.385
	Total of ten largest	20.200

Note: Share of ten largest in world total = 88%.

In volume terms world net exports are concentrated. The five largest net exporters alone account for 75% of world net exports; the ten largest for 88%. However, in contrast to most other soft commodities, sugar has many countries of origin. In 1994, a total of 29 countries were net exporters and if countries which either export less they import or re-export (i.e. importing raw sugar and re-exporting white sugar, e.g. USA, Canada and the Republic of Korea) are taken into account, the total number of countries of origin in 1994 rises to 71. The ten largest net exporters for 1994 are shown in Table 7.2.

In 1994, 50% of gross world exports were white sugar. The share of white sugar in total sugar trade has risen sharply in recent years, and was particularly high in 1994 because India – as happens periodically when the Indian sugar production cycle is in deficit (the previous occurrence was 1985) – imported large quantities of white sugar (2.635 million tonnes). The main origins of white sugar are the EU, Brazil and Thailand. Other exporting (beet) white sugar producers are Austria, Turkey and Poland. The major re-exporters of white sugar (toll refined from raw sugar) are the Republic of Korea, China, Singapore, Malaysia, USA and Canada. Re-exports of white sugar for 1994 are shown in Table 7.3.

The world export market today

The world export market is currently dominated by five large exporters: Australia, Brazil, the EU, Cuba and Thailand. In 1994 the five accounted for net exports totalling 17.3 million tonnes, 76% of the world total.

Table 7.3 Re-exports of white sugar, 1994, million tonnes, raw value

Canada	0.064
China	1.026
Hong Kong	0.040
Korea, Rep.	0.284
Malaysia	0.159
Singapore	0.023
USA	0.471
Total	2.067

Source: ISO.

Table 7.7 later in this chapter shows that **Australia** expanded its industry and exports significantly after 1985. A process of deregulation was undertaken, including a freeing of the regulations for assigning land to cane cultivation, and this led to an expansion of production from 3.9 million tonnes in 1988 to 5.22 million tonnes in 1994 (an increase of 34% in four years). Exports rose from 3.15 million tonnes in 1989 to 4.52 million tonnes in 1994 (plus 43%). Australia exports overwhelmingly raw sugar, mainly to its closest markets in the Far East – Japan, China, Korea, Malaysia, Singapore – and Canada.

Brazil was a major world exporter through both the 1960s and 1970s and up to the early 1980s (see Table 7.7). However, from the mid-1980s until 1990, priority in the use of cane was given to the production of alcohol, and by 1990 Brazilian exports had fallen to 1.64 million tonnes (compared to 2.59 million tonnes in 1985). In the 1990s alcohol production has levelled off and imports of alcohol have been permitted. The increased cane supply coming from good crops in 1994 and 1995 has been diverted to sugar production, with the result that output rose more than 2 million tonnes to 12.27 million tonnes in 1994 and is expected to exceed 14 million tonnes in 1995. Consequently, Brazil's exports leapt to 3.6 million tonnes in 1994, putting Brazil into second place after Australia. A feature of the resurgence of Brazilian exports in the mid-1990s has been the quantities of direct (plantation) white sugar exports coming from the Centre/South region. Brazil has since the late 1970s been a major white sugar exporter, but mainly on the basis of refined raws from the North/North-east region. Since the post-1990 increase in production has occurred in the Centre/South, a significant part of the sugar exported has been direct mill white sugar from that region. In 1994 Brazil exported around half of its sugar as raws and half as whites. (For a more detailed discussion of the interaction between the alcohol programme and sugar production, see Chapter 5 and Appendix III.)

The principal markets for Brazil are South America, the USA, the Middle East, West Africa and, in 1994, India.

It is significant that the **EC** appears in Table 7.8 in 1970 and 1975 (and before that the UK) as a major importer. The sharp increase in EC production and imports after the 1974 world sugar price boom has already been documented in Chapters 4 and 5. Suffice to say that the EC was consistently in second place to Cuba in the world hierarchy after 1980, until overtaken by Australia and Brazil in 1994. The EU exports white sugar. Its principal markets are the Middle East and Africa.

The situation in **Cuba** has been discussed in detail in Chapter 5 and will be referred to again later in this chapter. Until the dissolution of the Soviet Union, Cuba was consistently the world's largest exporter by a wide margin (see Table 7.7). In pre-revolutionary times it exported around 5 million tonnes, mainly to the USA, and after the revolution increased exports to 6 rising to 7 million tonnes, mainly to the USSR and its satellites, and China under special bilateral arrangements. In 1994, when it slipped to fourth place, Cuba's main market remained Russia and the other republics of the FSU, while it exported also to Japan, Canada, Latin America, North Africa and the Middle East. Cuba was in the 1970s and 1980s an exporter of up to 1 million tonnes of white sugar, but currently exports only raws.

The rapid rise of **Thailand,** from 1970, to be a major exporter, has been discussed in Chapter 5. Thailand first appeared in the league table in 1975, in eighth place (Table 7.7), and exports rose strongly in the late 1980s. Thailand exports up to 1 million tonnes of white sugar, the balance as raws. Thailand's main markets are in the Far East, especially China.

Mention needs to be made of the rise of **Guatemala** and **Colombia** to become established medium sized exporters in the 1990s. Both countries expanded production and exports significantly in the late 1980s and the 1990s. Guatemala increased production from 0.72 million tonnes in 1988 to 1.23 million tonnes in 1993 (an annual growth rate of a remarkable 11.3%) and exports from 0.39 million tonnes to 0.72 million tonnes (an annual growth rate of 13%) over the same period. Colombia increased production from 1.36 million tonnes in 1988 to 1.96 million tonnes in 1994 (an annual growth rate of 6.3%) and exports from 0.24 million tonnes to 0.72 million tonnes (an annual growth rate of a stupendous 20%) over the same period. Around 40% of Guatemala's exports and 60% of Colombia's exports are white sugar. Both countries export mainly to Central and South America.

Mauritius and **Fiji** export the bulk of their sugar, as raws, to the EU under the sugar protocol of the Lomé Convention (see Chapter 4).

Imports

In spite of the fact that sugar is produced in most countries in the world, the number of self-sufficient or surplus producers is relatively small (29 in 1994, as discussed in the previous section of this chapter). Consequently the number of importers is large, and world imports are much more diffuse. In 1994 a total of 117 countries or territories were *net* importers. The total of all countries making some import (gross importers) was 150.

World net imports in 1994 were 22.869 million tonnes, 20% of world consumption. Of that total 7.521 million tonnes (32%) were imported by developed countries and 15.348 million tonnes (68%) were purchased by developing countries. The world import market is therefore dominated by developing countries. The geographical distribution of net imports for 1994 is shown in Table 7.4.

Table 7.4 Geographical distribution of net imports, 1994, million tonnes, raw value

		Share of world total, %
Europe	3.065	13
North America	2.217	10
Central America	0.244	1
South America	1.086	5
Asia	11.964	52
Africa	3.678	16
Oceania	0.214	1
World	22.869	

Source: ISO.

Asia accounted for more than half of world net imports in 1994. Africa (16%), Europe (13%) and North America (10%) were the only other continents with significant imports whereas Central/South America and Oceania are largely surplus, exporting regions.

Table 7.5 shows the ten largest net importers for 1994. It can be seen from Table 7.5 that imports are much more diffuse than exports: the ten largest importers account for 57% of world net imports compared to the 88% of world exports accounted for by the ten largest exporters. It should also be noted that 1994 was an exceptional year for India. In a cycle with a periodicity of approximately ten years, production dipped substantially below consumption and India was forced to import heavily to meet demand. The previous time this had occurred was in 1985.

Table 7.5   Ten largest net importers, 1994, million tonnes, raw value

1	India	2.635
2	Russia	1.963
3	Japan	1.699
4	China	1.238
5	USA	1.132
6	Canada	1.085
7	Korea, Rep.	0.991
8	Malaysia	0.823
9	Algeria	0.810
10	Iran	0.645
	Total of ten largest	13.021

Note: Share of ten largest in world total = 57%.

The world import market today

As stated earlier, the world import market is much more diffuse than the world export market. In 1994, the five largest importers purchased 8.7 million tonnes, 38% of the world market, compared with the 76% accounted for by the five largest exporters. The other important feature of the world import market is its domination by developing countries which take more than 60% of all imports. As noted elsewhere (see Chapter 4 and Chapter 5) **India** appears only periodically on the import market, when its sugar production cycle is at a low point. This occurred in 1994, and 1985–6 and 1955 (Table 7.8). India purchases white sugar, and its main suppliers are the EU and, in 1994, Brazil.

Russia is the major sugar importing remnant of the USSR, which was consistently the largest world importer from 1980 to 1990 after US imports began their decline in the aftermath of the 1974 world sugar price boom. Russia imports mainly raw sugar and its principal supplier remains Cuba. The other republics of the FSU are significant importers of sugar, importing together 1.37 million tonnes of sugar in 1994. The most significant of the republics in 1994 were Belarus (0.38 million tonnes), Uzbekistan (0.31 million tonnes) and Kazakhstan (0.19 million tonnes). China and Cuba are the main suppliers to the FSU republics.

In spite of the sharp fall in imports to **Japan** after the 1974 world sugar price boom, it retains its third place amongst importers. The main sources of supply for Japan are Australia, Thailand, Cuba and South Africa. Japan imports only raw sugar.

The interaction between production, consumption and trade in

China was discussed in some detail in Chapter 4. China has been a major importer since the 1970s, but shows extreme variation in the quantity according to the level of domestic production. For example, in 1988 China had net *imports* of 3.68 million tonnes, in 1993 net *exports* of 1.55 million tonnes; in 1994 it imported 1.24 million tonnes and held fourth position. China imports raw sugar and its main suppliers are Thailand, Cuba and Australia.

US sugar policy, and its effects on production and imports (including the substitution of HFCS for sugar under the shelter of the protective umbrella raised for sugar) were discussed in some detail in Chapter 4. Up to 1975 the USA was, by a wide margin, the largest world importer. From 1975 to 1980 it maintained second position to the USSR. By 1994 it had slipped to fifth position with imports of only 1.13 million tonnes. Except in poor production years, net imports remain close to the minimum quota level of 1.15 million tonnes. The principal sources of sugar for the USA are Latin America (except, of course, Cuba) and the Philippines. The USA imports raw sugar.

Since its imports stopped growing in 1970, **Canada** has been the most consistent of all importing countries, regularly importing close to 1 million tonnes. Canada's main suppliers are Cuba, Australia and Swaziland. Canada imports raw sugar.

Korea and **Malaysia** are similar in that both import raw sugar for refining and both make re-exports of refined sugar, mainly in the Far East. In 1994 Korea imported a total of 1.27 million tonnes of sugar and re-exported 0.28 million tonnes of refined sugar. The principal sources of sugar for Korea are Australia, Thailand and South Africa. Malaysia, in 1994, imported a total of 0.98 million tonnes of raw sugar and re-exported 0.16 million tonnes of white sugar. Malaysia's main suppliers of raw sugar are Australia, Thailand and Fiji.

Imports by **Algeria** have grown consistently over the period since 1955 and in 1994 it imported 0.81 million tonnes. Algeria imports up to 200 000 tonnes of raw sugar for refining, and the balance is imported in the form of white sugar. Principal suppliers are the EU (whites), Cuba (raws) and Brazil (whites).

In the mid-1970s, when oil prices were rising, **Iran**'s imports grew rapidly, peaking at 0.88 million tonnes in 1978. Since the end of the Iran–Iraq war considerable effort has gone into increasing production, with the goal being self-sufficiency in sugar. From 0.6 million tonnes in 1988, production rose to 0.95 million tonnes in 1994 when Iran imported 0.64 million tonnes, mainly from the EU, Brazil and Turkey.

Table 7.6 Regional balances, 1994, million tonnes, raw value

	Production	Consumption	Imports	Exports	Net trade
Europe	27.52	31.08	7.21	7.98	+0.77
% share			25	27	
North America	7.06	9.63	2.75	0.53	−2.22
% share			9	2	
Central America	11.43	6.87	0.35	5.00	+4.65
% share			1	17	
South America	17.41	13.27	1.24	4.76	+3.52
% share			4	15	
Asia	31.43	41.83	13.42	4.99	−8.93
% share			47	16	
Africa	7.21	9.52	3.97	1.74	−2.23
% share			13	6	
Oceania	5.80	1.20	0.23	5.02	+4.79
% share			1	17	
World	110.29	113.8	30.07	30.04	

Source: ISO.

Regional movements

Table 7.6 shows regional balances for sugar in 1994. Asia was by far the largest deficit area, with net imports of 8.93 million tonnes. Asia accounted for 47% of world gross imports, containing as it does major 1994 importers in India and China. Nevertheless, with exporters like Thailand and Philippines in the region, Asia made up 16% of gross exports. The other deficit continents were North America and Africa, with net imports of 2.22 million tonnes and 2.23 million tonnes respectively in 1994. Europe, accounting for 25% of world gross imports and 27% of world gross exports, showed a small surplus of 0.77 million tonnes in 1994, partly because of the sharp fall in FSU imports. The three main surplus producing regions were Central America (4.65 million tonnes), South America (3.52 million tonnes) and – the largest – Oceania (4.79 million tonnes).

Developments in the trade since 1955

The evolution of the ten largest exporters from 1955 to 1994 is shown in Table 7.7 and Table 7.8 shows the evolution of the ten largest importers over the same period.

Table 7.7 Evolution of ten largest exporters, 1955–94, million tonnes, raw value

	1955	1960	1965	1970	1975	1980	1985	1990	1994
1	Cuba 4.65	Cuba 5.63	Cuba 5.32	Cuba 6.91	Cuba 5.74	Cuba 6.19	Cuba 7.21	Cuba 7.17	Australia 4.52
2	West Indies 0.93	Dominican Rep 1.1	Australia 1.21	Australia 1.64	Australia 1.83	EC 2.89	EC 2.98	EC 3.63	Brazil 3.60
3	Philippines 0.91	Philippines 1.1	Philippines 1.1	Philippines 1.18	Brazil 1.73	Brazil 2.66	Australia 2.65	Australia 3.06	EU 3.26
4	Australia 0.63	Taiwan 0.91	Brazil 0.82	Brazil 1.13	India 1.05	Australia 2.44	Brazil 2.59	Thailand 2.50	Cuba 3.19
5	Taiwan 0.59	Brazil 0.85	Taiwan 0.81	Dominican Rep 0.79	Philippines 1.0	Philippines 1.79	Thailand 1.78	Brazil 1.64	Thailand 2.72
6	Dominican Rep 0.58	Australia 0.79	Mauritius 0.6	South Africa 0.69	Dominican Rep 0.97	Dominican Rep 0.79	South Africa 1.0	South Africa 0.83	Guatemala 0.75
7	Brazil 0.58	West Indies 0.71	Dominican Rep 0.52	Mauritius 0.62	South Africa 0.74	South Africa 0.75	Dominican Rep 0.72	Mauritius 0.61	Colombia 0.72
8	Mauritius 0.49	Peru 0.51	Poland 0.52	Mexico 0.61	Thailand 0.67	Mauritius 0.65	Philippines 0.59	Guatemala 0.55	Mauritius 0.55
9	Peru 0.48	Mauritius 0.32	Mexico 0.51	Taiwan 0.43	Mauritius 0.47	Fiji 0.45	Mauritius 0.57	Swaziland 0.44	Fiji 0.47
10	France 0.42	South Africa 0.28	Jamaica 0.41	India 0.34	Peru 0.42	Taiwan 0.41	Fiji 0.42	Colombia 0.42	Turkey 0.38

Source: ISO.

Table 7.8 Evolution of ten largest importers, 1955–94, million tonnes, raw value

	1955	1960	1965	1970	1975	1980	1985	1990	1994
1	USA 3.66	USA 4.63	USA 3.65	USA 4.80	USA 3.31	USSR 4.82	USSR 4.30	USSR 3.94	India 2.63
2	UK 1.55	UK 1.87	UK 1.92	Japan 2.48	USSR 3.18	USA 3.21	Japan 1.98	USA 2.04	Russia 1.96
3	Japan 0.99	USSR 1.45	USSR 1.56	USSR 1.49	Japan 2.44	Japan 2.31	China 1.96	Japan 1.75	Japan 1.70
4	USSR 0.77	Japan 1.25	Japan 1.47	EC 1.04	EC 1.45	Canada 0.89	USA 1.91	Mexico 1.55	China 1.24
5	Canada 0.65	Canada 0.61	Canada 0.86	Canada 0.98	Canada 0.95	Iran 0.78	India 1.74	Canada 0.92	USA 1.13
6	India 0.47	China 0.46	Iran 0.43	China 0.44	Iran 0.68	Mexico 0.76	Canada 1.09	Algeria 0.81	Canada 1.08
7	Morocco 0.33	Morocco 0.35	Morocco 0.34	Bulgaria 0.38	Korea, Rep. 0.36	Iraq 0.74	Egypt 0.71	Egypt 0.80	Korea, Rep. 0.99
8	Chile 0.25	Iran 0.30	Iraq 0.31	Malaysia 0.37	Spain 0.34	China 0.71	Iran 0.63	Korea, Rep. 0.74	Malaysia 0.82
9	Iran 0.21	Algeria 0.26	Switzerland 0.26	Vietnam (S) 0.36	Iraq 0.33	Nigeria 0.71	Iraq 0.58	Turkey 0.63	Algeria 0.81
10	Algeria 0.17	Iraq 0.21	Algeria 0.25	GDR 0.30	Malaysia 0.33	Algeria 0.58	Korea, Rep. 0.57	Malaysia 0.54	Iran 0.64

Source: ISO.

94

1955–60

In 1955 the USA (3.66 million tonnes) and the UK (1.55 million tonnes) were the major importing countries. Both were preferential markets and not part of the so-called free world market. In the USA, the US Sugar Act applied: countries had quotas to supply sugar at agreed preferential prices. The principal supplier was Cuba, which in 1955 exported 2.55 million tonnes to the USA. The other major supplier in 1955 was the Philippines, with 0.89 million tonnes. Imports into the UK were at that time governed by the Commonwealth Sugar Agreement (CSA) also with quotas and a preferential price. Major suppliers in 1955 were the West Indies (0.5 million tonnes), Australia (0.46 million tonnes), Mauritius (0.33 million tonnes) and South Africa (0.18 million tonnes). Major non-Commonwealth suppliers were Cuba (0.38 million tonnes) and the Dominican Republic (0.29 million tonnes).

Because of the size of these special preferential arrangements, the free market in 1955 was, proportionately, rather small. Out of a world total of net imports of 11.415 million tonnes, free market requirements were 4.65 million tonnes – 41%. The other major importers in 1955 were Japan (free market) with 1 million tonnes and Canada (under the Commonwealth arrangement) with 0.65 million tonnes. The principal origins of Japanese imports in 1955 were Taiwan (0.32 million tonnes), Cuba (0.29 million tonnes), Australia (0.11 million tonnes), Brazil (0.11 million tonnes) and Indonesia (0.11 million tonnes). Major suppliers to Canada were Guyana (0.11 million tonnes), Australia (0.10 million tonnes), Mauritius (0.9 million tonnes) and Jamaica (0.08 million tonnes).

A feature of the import market in 1955 was the presence of India (0.47 million tonnes). India has a well documented sugar cycle. Almost half of its consumption comes from open pan sugars and they compete with white mill (centrifugal) sugar for supplies of cane. Because open pan sugars are not part of the highly controlled sugar policy system (as we have seen, they are largely a village-based industry) they can often offer higher prices for cane. In years when total cane supply is lower (usually due to monsoon failure) cane is diverted to open pan sugars and production of white mill sugar is insufficient to meet demand and India must import. The Indian sugar cycle has a periodicity of approximately ten years, and at this frequency India appears in the world import market – 1955 was such a year. In other years India is a sugar exporter.

On the export side in 1955, Cuba (4.65 million tonnes) was by far dominant. As already mentioned, Cuba's main markets were the USA,

UK and Japan. West Indies (to UK) and the Philippines (to USA) exported about 0.9 million tonnes, and a group of countries – Australia, Taiwan, Dominican Republic, Brazil, Mauritius, Peru and France – exported between 0.4 and 0.6 million tonnes.

By 1960 an event had occurred which fundamentally and profoundly affected the world sugar economy. This was the Cuban Revolution of 1959. The USA reacted by placing an embargo on the import of all goods from Cuba. As has been noted, Cuba was the major supplier to the USA under a preferential agreement (the US Sugar Act) and also the main free market origin. The USSR agreed to import most of the diverted Cuban sugar. Other quantities went to the USSR's Eastern European satellites (Poland, Hungary, Bulgaria, Romania and Czechoslovakia), other European socialist countries (Albania and Yugoslavia), and China, North Korea and North Vietnam in Asia. At that time the USSR did not require all the sugar it agreed to purchase from Cuba (note that in 1955 imports by the USSR were 0.77 million tonnes) and its own industry was about to undergo expansion. The USSR, therefore, became a major re-exporter of white sugar (refined Cuban raw sugar) to developing countries. The protocols governing exports by Cuba to COMECON and other socialist countries represented a new and large special (preferential) arrangement in the world sugar market. Exports of sugar by the USSR for 1960–72 are shown in Table 7.9.

The disruption caused to established world sugar flows by the US embargo on Cuban sugar was exacerbated by the encouragement given by the USA to Latin American and Philippines producers to increase production and replace Cuba in the US Sugar Act quota imports. World sugar prices, which initially rose sharply because of US attempts to secure non-Cuban supplies (and a fall in world production in 1960), fell to extremely low levels for the mid-1960s as a consequence. The 1958 ISA, which together with its 1953 predecessor

Table 7.9 Exports of sugar by the USSR, 1960–72, million tonnes, raw value

Year	Value	Year	Value
1960	0.26	1967	1.20
1961	0.95	1968	1.46
1962	0.90	1969	1.39
1963	0.92	1970	1.52
1964	0.43	1971	1.40
1965	0.73	1972	0.06
1966	1.16		

Source: ISO.

had regulated the free market through the 1950s, was unable to operate in the changed situation, and a UN conference to negotiate a successor agreement in 1961 failed.

The first repercussions of the Cuban Revolution can be seen in Table 7.8, where the USSR moved from fourth place in 1955 (0.77 million tonnes) to third place in 1960 (1.45 million tonnes).

1960–65

The USA remained the largest importer in the period 1960–65 but after a sharp rise in production from 1963 to 1965 imported less (3.65 million tonnes). By 1965 the Philippines (1.07 million tonnes), Mexico (0.46 million tonnes), Dominican Republic (0.45 million tonnes), Brazil (0.29 million tonnes), Peru (0.28 million tonnes) and Australia (0.19 million tonnes) had replaced Cuba as principal suppliers. Cuba had diversified its exports to the USSR (2.46 million tonnes), China (0.4 million tonnes), Czechoslovakia (0.24 million tonnes), German Democratic Republic (GDR) (0.17 million tonnes) and Bulgaria (0.16 million tonnes), and increased its exports to Japan (0.42 million tonnes).

1965–70

Through the 1960s consumption in both the USA and Japan grew rapidly and imports by the USA reached 4.8 million tonnes in 1970 and those by Japan 2.48 million tonnes. The USA continued to draw its imports principally from the Philippines (1.18 million tonnes) and Latin America – the Dominican Republic (0.66 million tonnes), Brazil (0.62 million tonnes), Mexico (0.59 million tonnes) and Peru (0.41 million tonnes). The only other supplier of note was Australia (0.19 million tonnes). The major sources of Japan's imports were Cuba (1.13 million tonnes), Australia (0.53 million tonnes), South Africa (0.39 million tonnes), Brazil (0.15 million tonnes) and Taiwan (0.11 million tonnes). On the export side, Cuba continued to develop its market in socialist countries. Of total exports in 1970 of 6.91 million tonnes, 3.1 million tonnes were consigned to the USSR, 0.53 million tonnes to China, 0.35 million tonnes to GDR, 0.23 million tonnes to Bulgaria and Czechoslovakia, 0.15 million tonnes to North Korea and 0.1 million tonnes to Romania. Japan remained the principal free market destination with 1.22 million tonnes, but Cuba was expanding markets in developing countries, e.g. Malaysia, 0.21 million tonnes and

Syria, 0.1 million tonnes. The exporters' hierarchy remained largely the same, but India (0.34 million tonnes) made an appearance.

1970–75

1974 witnessed an event that was to have significant repercussions for the world sugar market. In that year there was a spectacular sugar price boom and the world (free market) price reached 64 cents/lb in October 1974, having been less than 2 cents/lb in the late 1960s. The ground was laid for the 1974 boom in 1972 when Cuba had a poor crop – production fell to 4.69 million tonnes from 5.95 million tonnes in 1971 and 7.56 million tonnes in 1970. The USSR, which itself had a poor crop in 1971, began buying increased quantities from the free market to meet its requirements for both its domestic consumption and export commitments. World stocks of sugar were reduced, and in 1974 world production failed to grow and there was a deficit of more than 1 million tonnes of world production compared to world consumption. The steeply rising sugar prices brought chaos to the market, especially the special (preferential) arrangements. The US Sugar Act was suspended, never to be re-introduced, and the CSA was in disarray. The problem was that world free market prices had risen above the preferential prices of these two special arrangements and sugar was diverted to the free market. Although welcome to exporters at the time, the exceptionally high prices damaged the world sugar market in the long term. Three negative long-term consequences of the 1974 price boom can be cited:

- The encouragement given to the nascent HFCS industries in the USA and Japan, already mentioned, led to a precipitous decline in US consumption and imports and a serious decline in consumption in Japan by the mid-1980s.
- The price boom coincided with the setting of new production quotas and support prices in the EC sugar regime of the CAP. Production quotas were raised by 24% in 1974 and a further 23% in 1975 to 13.4 million tonnes compared with EC consumption of 11.5 million tonnes. Support prices were raised by 12% in 1974, 15% in 1975 and a further 9% in 1976, encouraged by the belief, prevalent at the time, that the world sugar economy was entering a phase of permanent deficit. These moves were to lead to a significant expansion in production and would convert the EC from a net importer into a major exporter by 1980. Also, in 1975, the UK formally acceded to the EC and the CSA was converted into

the sugar protocol of the Lomé Convention, under which UK import quotas were reserved for developing Commonwealth countries; Australia lost its quota.

- Many importing countries, unable to afford and frightened by the level of world prices, embarked on expansion programmes. The increasing share of world consumption met by domestic production led to stagnation and decline in world net import requirements in the 1980s.

On the import side, 1975 saw the USSR move into second place (3.18 million tonnes up from 1.56 million tonnes in 1965) and the EC in fourth place at 1.45 million tonnes because of the accession of the UK, a deficit country (see previous years: the UK had consistently been the second or third largest world importer from 1955 to 1965). In 1975 developed countries continued to hold the first five positions and six of the top ten.

On the export side some significant changes occurred. The Indian sugar cycle was in surplus in 1975 and India entered the export list in fourth position with exports of 1.05 million tonnes. And, foreshadowing future developments, Thailand appeared for first time at number eight, exporting 0.67 million tonnes. Taiwan, caught in the vice of rising consumption and falling production, did not figure in the 1975 top ten and would reappear only once – in 1980. (By 1994 Taiwan would be a net importer.) Peru, about to suffer a long drought from which production would never recover, made its last appearance in 1975.

1975–80

Nineteen eighty was another boom year for world sugar prices. Although prices did not hit the heights of 1974 – prices peaked at 47 cents/lb in October 1980 compared to a peak of 64 cents/lb in 1974 – the annual averages were remarkably similar, 29.7 cents/lb for 1974 and 28.7 cents/lb for 1980. Again the immediate precursor for the boom was a coincidence of poor crops in the USSR and Cuba. Production in the USSR fell from 9.35 million tonnes in 1978 to 7.93 million tonnes in 1979, and continued to fall in the two years following to a nadir of 6.41 million tonnes in 1981. Production in Cuba fell by 1 million tonnes in 1980 to 6.8 million tonnes from 7.8 million tonnes in 1979. As a result, the USSR entered the free market for large quantities of sugar, with net imports of 4.82 million tonnes in 1980 of which 2.33 million tonnes came from the free market.

Although world production and exports had grown rapidly in the aftermath of the 1974 sugar price boom, so had imports. The sudden appearance on the free market of the USSR, armed with hard currency, for more than 2 million tonnes, depleted world stocks below the level needed to sustain normal trade and prices rose rapidly. Between 1975 and 1980 world net imports rose by 4.7 million tonnes (25%) to reach 23.1 million tonnes. Another important factor, which also underlay the price booms of 1974 and 1980, contributed to this rapid growth. The immediate antecedent of the 1974 boom was the first oil price shock of 1973. This placed additional income in the hands of developing countries, particularly oil-exporting developing countries. Virtually all the growth in world net imports from 1975 to 1980 came from developing countries, particularly those exporting oil. The second oil price shock funded the 1980 boom in the sense that imports by developing countries did not fall in spite of sharply rising prices. World net imports continued to rise throughout the early 1980s, peaking at 26.4 million tonnes in 1982, still a record level today (e.g. world net imports in 1994 were 22.87 million tonnes, 3.5 million tonnes (13%) below the 1982 peak). This is a major difference compared with the 1974 boom – world net imports in 1975 fell by 0.9 million tonnes (5%) from 1974.

In 1980, on the export side, another dramatic repercussion of the 1974 price boom is evident – the EC jumped to second place amongst net exporters with exports of 2.89 million tonnes, having been a net importer of 1.45 million tonnes only five years earlier. The reasons for this transformation have been discussed earlier: it represented a massive shift in the structure of trade, especially as EC exports were in the form of white sugar, immediately available for consumption and produced from a crop (beets) with an annual growing cycle more readily able to respond to market conditions than cane. On the import side the emergence of the USSR as the largest net importer has already been noted. US net imports had declined from their peak of 5.19 million tonnes in 1974 to reach 3.21 million tonnes by 1980, as the consumption of HFCS rose steadily and was given further impetus by the 1980 price boom. Similarly net imports by Japan had peaked at 2.83 million tonnes, also in 1974, and by 1980 had declined to 2.31 million tonnes, as HFCS gained a foothold. Although the first four places in Table 7.8 are still held by developed countries, places five to ten are now occupied by developing countries (Iran, Mexico, Iraq, China, Nigeria and Algeria), four of them oil exporters importing between 0.6 and 0.8 million tonnes.

Table 7.10 World production and consumption, 1980–85, million tonnes, raw value

	Production	Consumption	Surplus/Deficit
1980	84.49	88.65	−4.16
1981	92.76	89.91	+2.85
1982	102.00	93.97	+8.03
1983	96.97	93.76	+3.21
1984	99.22	96.68	+2.54
1985	98.36	97.86	+0.50
Cumulative surplus, 1980–85			12.97

Source: ISO.

1980–85

The reaction to the 1980 price boom was swift and fierce. In 1980, it will be recalled, world free market raw sugar prices averaged 28.7 cents/lb. In 1985 they averaged 4.06 cents/lb, a fall of 86% in five years. The low point, probably the lowest price for raw sugar ever in real terms, was reached on 20 June 1985 when an ISA daily price of 2.61 cents/lb was posted. In reaction to the 1980 boom, world production had increased rapidly and world stocks built up to unprecedented levels. World production and consumption of sugar for 1980–85 is shown in Table 7.10.

At the same time as world production was increasing rapidly, world consumption maintained its normal 2% growth rate, and, because of the high prices, grew only 1.4% between 1980 and 1981. The stocks built up in the early 1980s were not cleared and world prices remained depressed until 1989.

In the aftermath of the 1980 price boom, two important policy changes occurred. In the EC in 1980, the support (intervention) prices for sugar were raised by 15%. This underpinned the rapid increase in EC production in the early 1980s (EC sugar production rose sharply from 13.545 million tonnes in 1980 to 15.515 million tonnes in 1982). In the USA, in 1982, country specific import quotas were introduced. The total of the quotas was set each year at the anticipated difference between consumption and domestic production. Individual country quotas were allocated pro rata, according to the average share of US imports of each country over the five years up to 1982. Imports within the quota would receive the US domestic price for raw sugar, then (and now) higher than the world price. The reasons for this somewhat brutal move, which was to have a profound effect on US net imports

Table 7.11 USA: production, consumption, imports, re-exports and net imports, 1977–87, million tonnes, raw value

	Production	Consumption	Imports	Re-exports	Net imports
1977	5.76	10.36	5.29	0.02	5.27
1978	5.13	9.95	4.26	0.02	4.24
1979	5.43	9.88	4.44	0.01	4.42
1980	5.31	9.33	3.80	0.59	3.21
1981	5.79	8.96	4.65	0.95	3.70
1982	5.42	8.31	2.39	0.05	2.34
1983	5.21	8.07	2.67	0.20	2.47
1984	5.34	7.74	3.02	0.30	2.47
1985	5.42	7.29	2.27	0.36	1.91
1986	5.68	7.08	1.80	0.41	1.38
1987	6.60	7.41	1.22	0.59	0.63

Source: ISO.

and the world sugar market, was falling US consumption due to the inroads made by HFCS. US refiners, however, continued to import around 4 million tonnes of sugar, necessitating large re-exports of refined sugar and driving down the price received by domestic sugar producers. US production, consumption, imports, re-exports and net imports for 1977–87 are shown in Table 7.11.

Table 7.11 illustrates the connection between the decline in US consumption since 1977 and the steep reduction in US net imports since quotas were introduced in 1982. The imposition of a quota system by the USA meant that the effects of declining sugar consumption due to the growth of HFCS were borne entirely by the world sugar market. A domestic problem was solved by transforming it into an international problem and increasing steeply the level of protection for both the domestic sugar industry and the world sugar economy which cost the world market 3 million tonnes of prime imports.

On the export side, in 1985 the EC maintained its second position with almost 3 million tonnes and Cuba had record (still standing) net exports of 7.21 million tonnes. Thailand, which had suffered from drought in 1980, maintained its progress, exporting 1.78 million tonnes. Thailand was about to begin a massive, contra-cyclical, expansion programme which would increase production and exports to the extent that it would become the fourth largest exporter by 1990. In contrast, the Philippines, where production was falling and consumption rising rapidly, exported only 0.59 million tonnes and made its last appearance in the top ten in eighth position.

The USSR maintained its position as largest net importer in 1985

Table 7.12   Net imports by China, 1980-90, million tonnes, raw value

	Net imports	World price, cents/lb
1980	0.71	28.70
1981	1.04	16.80
1982	2.41	8.30
1983	1.65	8.50
1984	1.22	5.20
1985	1.96	4.10
1986	0.79	6.00
1987	1.67	6.75
1988	3.68	10.20
1989	1.14	12.80
1990	0.53	12.55

Source: ISO.

with 4.3 million tonnes. US imports had fallen sharply since 1980 to 1.91 million tonnes, due to the accelerated pace of HFCS penetration after the 1980 world price boom. US net imports would reach their lowest ever level of 0.63 million tonnes in 1987 when HFCS took over 100% of sweetener input into soft drinks. Japanese net imports were also lower in 1985, falling to 1.98 million tonnes, and would fall further. Developing country imports were high in 1985 – higher than their rapid rate of growth would suggest. India had reached another deficit point in its sugar cycle and imported 1.74 million tonnes, making it the fifth largest importer that year (India had been the fourth largest exporter ten years earlier). China, which had also been a cyclical importer in terms of quantity, imported 1.96 million tonnes net in 1985, putting it in third position, higher than the US. Throughout this period, China had been sensitive to world prices, tending to import more when world prices were low. Net imports by China for 1980–90 are shown in Table 7.12.

China's net imports peaked in 1988, after which the country began a production expansion programme which made it a net exporter by 1992.

1985–90

By 1990, a new order of exporters was becoming established. Gone from the top ten were the Dominican Republic (net exports in 1990 0.37 million tonnes) and the Philippines (net exports in 1990 0.26 million tonnes), both caught in a squeeze between rising consumption and falling production. Into the top ten net exporters came Guatemala (0.55 million tonnes) and Colombia (0.42 million tonnes). Net exports by Brazil were (temporarily) lower, at 1.64 million tonnes. In Brazil consumption had risen in the second half of the 1980s and production of fuel alcohol from sugar cane had fallen. In the late 1980s supply of cane-based fuel alcohol, used for powering most of the cars in Brazil, had fallen to crisis levels and ethanol had to be imported. By 1990, to ensure the future of the fuel alcohol programme, cane had been diverted to ethanol production and sugar production and exports had fallen.

In 1990, on the import side, a new order was beginning to impose itself. Developing countries like Algeria (0.81 million tonnes), Egypt (0.8 million tonnes), the Republic of Korea (0.74 million tonnes) and Malaysia (0.54 million tonnes) had firmly established themselves as medium sized constant importers. Mexico (1.55 million tonnes, fourth largest importer in 1990) is another special case. From the 1950s to 1980 Mexico had been a net exporter, twice (1965 and 1970) appearing in the top ten. In 1980 Mexico suffered a severe drought and was forced to import 0.76 million tonnes to meet consumption needs. As an oil exporter Mexico was not affected by the high world prices. From 1985 Mexico returned to being a net exporter, peaking in 1988 with net exports of 1.01 million tonnes. However, in the late 1980s the painful process of privatizing the state owned sugar industry began and production fell rapidly. In 1990 Mexico appeared on the world market buying 1.55 million tonnes of sugar. Turkey, normally a net exporter, suffered a severe drought in 1989/90 and imported 0.63 million tonnes in 1990. The USA also had a poor crop in 1990 (production fell to 5.7 million tonnes from 6.2 million tonnes in 1989), and imports rose to 2.04 million tonnes from the nadir of 0.61 million tonnes in 1987. Imports by Japan fell further to 1.75 million tonnes.

1990 saw another cyclical peak in the world raw sugar price, which averaged 12.55 cents/lb for the year, compared to an average of 4.06 cents/lb in 1985. The massive stocks that had been built up in the early 1980s had by 1990 been cleared, partly through normal imports and a decline in the rate of increase of world production in the second half of the 1980s, and partly through unusually high imports by India (1985 and 1986) and China (1988). Poor crops in 1990 in the USA, Mexico and Turkey exacerbated the situation, and the years 1986 to 1989 had been deficit years in the world sugar economy. World sugar production and consumption for 1986–90 is shown in Table 7.13.

World stocks fell proportionately lower in relation to world consumption than they had been in 1980: the stock/consumption

Table 7.13 World production and consumption, 1986–90, million tonnes, raw value

	Production	Consumption	Deficit/Surplus
1986	100.02	101.25	−1.23
1987	103.53	105.66	−2.13
1988	104.59	105.86	−1.27
1989	107.18	107.30	−0.12
1990	110.89	108.42	+2.47
Cumulative stocks change, 1986–90			−2.28

Source: ISO.

ratio (stocks measured at 31 December) in 1990 was 41% compared to 44% in 1980. Yet the world price average for 1990 was only 44% of that in 1980. This fundamental change in the world price formation process was due to far-reaching changes in the structure of the world import market. In 1975, two-thirds of the world import market was accounted for by high income–low price elasticity developed countries (mainly the USA, Japan and Canada). As documented in this chapter, from 1975 developed country imports declined and developing country imports rose, so that by 1990 the situation had been reversed and two-thirds of the world import market was made up of developing countries with lower incomes and a much higher price sensibility (see Fig. 7.1). Their higher price elasticity meant that when prices began to rise in 1988, and continued rising through 1989 and 1990, developing countries reacted by buying less and the momentum provided by high income countries determined to secure

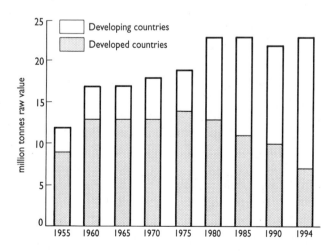

7.1 Evolution of world trade (net imports), 1955–94 (source: ISO).

normal supplies irrespective of the price which had been present in 1974 and 1980 was lacking; raw sugar prices, consequently, peaked at 16 cents/lb, compared to 47 cents/lb in 1980 and 64 cents/lb in 1974. (Structural change and its consequences will be discussed in more detail in Chapter 9.)

1990-94

In 1991 a third momentous event fundamentally changed the structure of the market – the dissolution of the USSR (the other two events with similar far-reaching effects were the 1959 Cuban Revolution and the 1974 world sugar price boom). As we have seen, since 1960 the USSR had become the world's largest net importer. When the other socialist countries are added, the protocol for Cuban exports to socialist countries at its peak governed total exports of 5–6 million tonnes. This special arrangement largely took the form of barter trade for oil, industrial products and grains, and equivalent prices are therefore difficult to estimate; it is generally accepted, however, that the exchange prices were equivalent to between two (at world price peaks) and eight times the world price (some estimates have put the equivalent prices under the protocol in excess of 40 cents/lb). Clearly this level of return underpinned the Cuban economy. In the USSR, however, sugar prices were heavily subsidized (sugar prices remained at 1917 levels for more than 70 years!) and, fuelled by increases in domestic production as well as the ready availability of Cuban sugar, per capita consumption had by 1988 reached 50 kg. Similar levels of consumption were normal in other COMECON countries for the same reasons. Internal sugar prices had first been raised under *perestroika* in 1990, but after 1992 world prices prevailed and sugar consumption fell rapidly in Russia to around 30 kg. Since production also fell, imports did not fall by as much as consumption, but by 1994 Russia was importing only 1.96 million tonnes, and the whole of the FSU only 1.72 million tonnes (taking into account exports by the Ukraine, a large surplus republic), compared to net imports of 5.44 million tonnes in 1989 and 3.94 million tonnes in 1990 for the USSR. Total consumption in the FSU in 1994 was only 10.07 million tonnes, compared to Soviet consumption of 13.4 million tonnes in 1990 and a peak of 14.35 million tonnes in 1988. (Students of the fall of the USSR may recall that 1988 was the year that Gorbachev sharply raised vodka prices and rationed its sale; millions of Russians and Ukrainians stepped up, or turned to, the manufacture of 'moonshine' vodka, consuming vast additional

Table 7.14 Cuba: production and exports, 1990–94, million tonnes, raw value

	Production	Exports
1990	8.44	7.17
1991	7.23	6.77
1992	7.22	6.08
1993	4.25	3.66
1994	4.02	3.19

Source: ISO.

quantities of sugar.) This massive, once and for all decline in consumption and imports was a significant shock to the world sugar economy, and the repercussions in changing and diverting established trade flows continue to be assimilated by the world sugar market, a process which is likely to continue throughout the 1990s. The ramifications of the collapse of the USSR were not confined to the FSU. As previously stated, the subsidized prices under the Cuban sugar protocol were fundamental to the Cuban economy (at the time of the collapse 80% of Cuba's export earnings and 50% of its GDP came from sugar). Lacking hitherto cheap oil, spare parts and, most importantly, fertilizers, and in the context of an economic crisis, Cuban sugar production went into a precipitous decline. Sugar production and exports for Cuba for 1990–94 are shown in Table 7.14.

So, a major trade flow, which, along with the Lomé – ACP – exports to the EU, could be said to have survived the post-colonial era intact as a preferential arrangement, was dissolved for ever. Even if Cuba's production recovers, as it probably will (but not to the level attained in 1990), it will sell much smaller quantities to the FSU, and all its exports will be made at free market prices, not preferential terms.

Imports in 1994 reflected the new order. The USA, after a steady rise in production since 1990, imported only 1.13 million tonnes. Imports by Japan fell again, to 1.7 million tonnes, almost 1 million tonnes below the 1970s' peak. India found itself, again, in considerable deficit (the previous occurrence had been 1985–86) and was the largest importer with 2.63 million tonnes. Russian imports have already been discussed. Developing countries dominated the top ten. China, having been a net exporter in 1992 and 1993, returned as a net importer with 1.24 million tonnes.

Similarly, on the export side, the new order was confirmed. Australia, having posted a substantial increase in production to a record 5.2 million tonnes in 1994 (in 1989 Australia produced 3.89 million tonnes, then a record, increasing to 4.36 million tonnes in

1992 and 5.22 million tonnes in 1994), was the world's largest net exporter with a record 4.52 million tonnes. Brazilian production, having recovered from the alcohol crisis affected levels of 7.33 million tonnes in 1989 and 8 million tonnes in 1990, reached a record of 12.27 million tonnes in 1994, and exports rose to 3.6 million tonnes making Brazil the second largest exporter in 1994. Thailand maintained fifth position with net exports of 2.72 million tonnes. Guatemala and Colombia continued their rise through the exporter ranks, exporting 0.75 million tonnes and 0.72 million tonnes respectively.

Conclusions

Table 7.15 and Fig. 7.1 show the evolution of world trade (net imports) from 1955 to 1994. It can be seen that world trade grew quite rapidly up until 1980 but has since stagnated. From 1955 until 1980 world trade almost doubled, growing at a rate of 2.9% per annum, which is comparable with the growth rate of world

Table 7.15 Evolution of world trade (net imports), 1955–94, million tonnes, raw value

	Total	Developed countries	Developing countries
1955	11.701	8.899	2.802
% share		76	24
1960	16.749	12.962	3.788
% share		77	23
1965	17.151	12.878	4.273
% share		75	25
1970	17.658	12.944	4.713
% share		73	27
1975	18.401	13.534	4.868
% share		74	26
1980	23.056	12.788	10.268
% share		56	44
1985	23.013	11.285	11.639
% share		49	51
1990	23.138	10.326	12.217
% share		47	53
1994	22.869	7.179	15.691
% share		31	69

Source: ISO.

consumption over the same period. Two contrasting periods can be identified. Up to 1975 absolute growth was mainly in developed countries recovering after World War II and building sugar production policies designed to achieve self-sufficiency. The annual growth rate in developed country imports up to 1975 was 2.2%, compared to that of developing countries, starting from a much lower base, of 2.9%. Following the first oil price shock of 1973 imports by developing countries, particularly oil exporters, began to grow very rapidly while developed country imports, in the aftermath of the 1974 world sugar price boom, began a decline which was to be continuous up to 1994. Between 1975 and 1980 developing countries' imports grew by 5.4 million tonnes (111%) at an annual rate of 17%. Their share of world imports jumped to 44%, from 26% in 1975.

Since 1980 the rate of growth of developing country imports has slowed (to 3.3% per annum from 1980 to 1994) and has been balanced almost exactly by the decline in developed country imports, which accelerated upon the break-up of the USSR. Consequently, since 1980, total world net trade has shown no growth whatsoever.

Table 7.15 and Fig. 7.1 clearly illustrate what has been a continuing theme throughout this volume: the immense structural change that the world market has undergone since 1955. In Part III the impact of this structural change on the price formation process and general market behaviour will be discussed. With startling symmetry, the percentage shares of developed and developing countries in world imports were exactly reversed from 1955 to 1994 (see Table 7.15). As already noted, the share of developing countries began to grow quickly after 1975 while the share of developed countries has been in continuous decline from the same date, slipping to only 31% in 1994 when the developing countries' share rose to 69%.

8

Substitute products

Alternative sweeteners

D espite considerable opposition from vested interests the anti-sugar lobby succeeded to a certain extent in convincing certain sectors of the population that they just might live a little longer if they ate less sugar. This led to the proliferous use of artificial sweeteners. Initially some of these were considered to be a source of cancer but eventually they got the all clear from the health authorities.

As discussed in Chapter 6, imports of sugar into the USA and Japan fell dramatically following the price booms of 1974 and 1980, due to the rapid increase in HFCS use in the market. In addition, saccharin use in low calorie soft drinks became very popular with consumers The efficaciousness of artificial sweeteners is still subject to debate but, nevertheless, their use in diet soft drinks continues to grow and has also been extended to non-diet drinks.

Consumers in general, in their search for anything that could prolong their life, are becoming increasingly diet conscious and take particular care of their calorie intake. This has led manufacturers of colas and soft drinks to increase the use of saccharin to such an extent that in the UK warnings will soon be printed on labels. The intake of high levels of saccharin continues to worry the UK government's Food Advisory Committee because it has been linked to cancer in laboratory animals. Manufacturers are reluctant to put such information on labels, including those for concentrated drinks, leaving parents confused as to what they can safely give young children. Foods advertised as being low in sugar could be high in saccharin and this applies to iced lollies, tinned soups and toothpaste as well as fizzy drinks.

Alternative sweeteners fall into two categories – natural and manufactured. Natural non-sugar sweeteners are dominated by high fructose syrup (HFS) usually, but not always, made from maize (corn) and known as HFCS. Manufactured (or intense) sweeteners are led by saccharin and aspartame.

Natural sweeteners

HFS, or isoglucose as it is known in Europe, can be produced from any feedstock that contains a sufficient amount of starch. The most prominent source is maize (corn) but smaller producers include potatoes, wheat, maple and yams (sweet potatoes). HFS is only available in liquid form, so its applications are limited and substitutions are not complete. It also creates problems of storage and transport, both of which have to be kept to a minimum. Trade is confined to cross-border transactions and production is geared largely to domestic use.

HFS comes in two strengths, HFS–42 and HFS–55. The figures indicate the strength of fructose (%) of each and the former is used in the production of jams, ice cream, pastries and tinned fruit while the latter is used mainly by the soft drink bottling industry. The average bushel of maize wet-milled in the USA contains 31.5 lb of recoverable starch (dry weight) which in turn produces about 33.33 lb of corn sweetener. This apparent anomaly is due to the chemical gain in converting starch to sweetener.

The process of making sweeteners from starch was known in the nineteenth century but it was not until the surge in sugar prices in the early 1970s that HFS production made an economic impact. The high price of sugar at that time enabled the production of HFS to benefit from advances in technology and to reach industrial quantities. Production trebled and it continued to be economically viable when sugar prices fell again in 1975/76.

Production costs are sensitive to many variables and it is therefore difficult to predict with any accuracy the future rate of growth. Most estimates are made by private consultancies and are not readily available. The main variable is the cost of the starch. Availability can fluctuate according to export demand in the case of US maize, and domestic demand in the case of Japanese yams. For HFCS, the raw material is a traded commodity with a variable price. To reach a net starch cost it is necessary to deduct the proceeds from the sale of the by-products from the cost of the maize. Set-up costs for the production of HFS are very high. F O Licht, a leading sugar and sweetener research company, estimates that each bushel (25.4 kg) of newly built daily grinding capacity can require investment of up to $3000, while expansion of existing plant costs around $1600 per bushel.

During the surge in sugar prices in 1980, HFS production flourished. The equally dramatic decline in prices, however, incurred some losses from 1982/83. Availability and price of sugar, while important, are not the only determinants in the production of HFS; sufficient supplies of starch, government support and a well-developed food production and consumption infrastructure are also important prerequisites. The first plants were built in the USA and Japan, which together currently account for nearly 85% of world output. The USA is the world's biggest maize producer and Japan gets its supplies from maize imports (from the USA) and its domestic potato crop.

There is little doubt that the specious health scares associated with sugar have greatly aided the expansion of HFS production. In both the USA and Japan favourable pricing policies and attractive tax structures have been very helpful and output continues to expand in both countries.

In the USA, which accounts for 75% of world production, HFCS output for the year ending 30 September 1995 was expected to reach 7.75 million short tons dry basis, a 4% increase on the previous year. In addition, glucose syrup and dextrose production are together forecast to total 3.8 million tons. Japanese production, on the other hand, remained static in the four years from 1990 before resuming its expansion in 1994/95 when output was forecast to reach around 900 000 tonnes.

Elsewhere, the greatest potential for growth is in the Far East. Taiwan and South Korea both benefit from considerable government intervention in favour of HFS and in China both Coca-Cola and PepsiCo are investing heavily in new plant. In 1995, however, both these companies were still using sugar in their soft drinks manufactured in the country as the plant had not yet come on stream. In Hungary and Egypt production is increasing but it remains static within the EU where the current quota structure restricts its growth.

Owing to its poor storage qualities, production of HFS is closely allied to consumption growth and the figures given above reflect that growth. However, the potential for further expansion is considerable. In the USA alone, during 1995, additional capacity totalling about 2 million short tons is expected to be completed. Production of HFS is shown in Table 8.1.

Table 8.1   HFS production, 000 tonnes, dry basis

	1994/95	1993/94	1990/91
Belgium/Luxembourg	72	72	72
Spain	83	83	83
Total EU	303	310	292
Hungary	50	40	40
FSU	40	20	8
Total Europe	448	385	358
Egypt	77	71	40
Argentina	145	158	154
Canada	240	260	250
USA	7 031	6 759	5 872
All America	7 441	7 197	6 294
China	50	35	30
Japan	870	754	783
Korea, Rep.	330	285	276
Taiwan	200	160	110
All Asia	1 541	1 308	1 260
World	9 510	8 965	7 956

Source: F O Licht.

Trade in HFS is small and largely confined to cross-border transactions. Exports from the USA to Canada and Mexico increased in 1994/95 but the former market is highly price sensitive and the latter has a flourishing sugar industry to protect and is strongly resisting further inroads. Adverse weather conditions in the US Corn Belt during planting and harvesting in 1995 pushed maize prices to their highest levels for some years. This may affect HFCS production in 1995/96.

The net corn sweetener cost to Midwest maize refiners averaged 3.44 cents/lb, dry basis, for the year ending September 1994 compared with 2.39 cents for the previous year. For the October–December 1994 quarter, the costs averaged 2.30 cents.

Manufactured sweeteners

Manufactured, or high-intensity, sweeteners are increasingly being used in a wide range of so-called diet foods and soft drinks. Also known as low-calorie sweeteners, the most widely used ones are 200–300 times sweeter than sugar. The three most common types are aspartame, saccharin and acesulfame-K (ace-K) which have all been approved for use in the USA. Others are pending approval.

The consumption prospects of these sweeteners seem likely to expand as the range of foods and beverages sweetened by them increases. Soft drinks and ice cream toppings are the chief uses of high-intensity sweeteners, while others include powdered gelatine desserts, tinned fruit, ice creams, confectionery and chewing gum. Their use as a table-top powdered sweetener (direct sugar substitute) is confined to aspartame and, although widely used by diabetics, is not yet great enough to be an important end-use.

Aspartame

Aspartame is about 200 times as sweet as sugar and is now the leading intense sweetener. Discovered in 1965, it is composed of two amino acids, phenylalanine and aspartic acid. Like all other proteins, it provides four calories/g but because it is so sweet only very small amounts are needed to reach the equivalent of sugar. Aspartame gradually loses its sweetness over time and needs to be protected from high heat in baking. In its encapsulated form it remains protected until the final stages of baking when the sweetener is released. It is ten times more expensive than saccharin. The US patent for aspartame ran out in December 1992, since when it has been a completely free market, expanding rapidly, particularly in the EU.

Saccharin

Saccharin is 300 times as sweet as sugar and was discovered over 100 years ago. It is a coal tar product and is not metabolized, so it has no calories. It does, however, have a very bitter aftertaste which can only be removed by blending with other sweeteners. When blended with aspartame, the aftertastes cancel each other out. In 1977, it was banned in the USA as research indicated it might be carcinogenic but Congress imposed a moratorium on the ban. Notwithstanding the medical implications, saccharin is the second most widely used intense sweetener.

Acesulfame–K

Ace-K is 200 times sweeter than sugar and, like saccharin, is calorie free. It also has a bitter aftertaste that can only be removed by mixing with other sweeteners. So far, its use is confined to smaller markets such as certain flavours of chewing gum and approval is awaited for use in the US soft drink market.

Cyclamate

Cyclamate is 30 times as sweet as sugar and before it was banned was frequently blended 50/50 with saccharin in soft drinks. However, it was banned in 1970 following claims that it was carcinogenic. In June 1985 that was found to be untrue. It is a high quality sweetener with very little aftertaste. It is also soluble which makes it a useful additive in foods and beverages.

Others

Other high-intensity sweeteners include sucralose, derived from and 600 times as sweet as sugar and produced by Tate & Lyle. Another is alitame, 2000 times the sweetness of sugar, which is also composed of two amino acids (alanine and aspartic acid). However, due to the strength of its sweetness, alitame contributes very few calories.

Consumption growth of intense sweeteners is patchy. Following the decision of the UK government in 1993 to abolish minimum sugar levels in non-diet beverages, consumption increased significantly. Manufacturers were able to make substantial cost savings by replacing sugar with intense sweeteners and, by marketing the drinks as lite or sugar-free, sales boomed.

It is a different story, however, in the USA, where there are distinct signs of a topping out of sales of high-intensity sweeteners. Although still, by a long way, the world's leading consumer, sales fell in both 1992 and 1993 before picking up slightly in 1994 and 1995. This was due to changing drinking habits towards pure fruit juices and ready-to-drink teas and coffees, none of which contain any artificial sweeteners. This could have a significant effect on future prospects since it is estimated that some 80% of aspartame sales in the USA are to the beverage industry.

Elsewhere, the Far East has an expanding industry. Although accurate statistics are virtually non-existent, Chinese production and consumption make China the most important market in the region.

Artificial sweeteners will continue to be used as a sugar substitute for diabetics and slimmers.

Consumption trends

Prospects for continued growth in HFS consumption are very bright since 75% of HFS distribution involves the soft drinks industry where average world annual consumption is 32 eight-ounce servings per capita. In the emerging countries of Asia and Eastern Europe the current average is only around six such servings, so it can be seen that the possibilities are very encouraging.

World consumption rose from 700 000 tonnes in 1975 to 10.1 million tonnes in 1995 and is forecast to reach 13.5 million by the end of the century. Boosted by above average growth in Mexico, North America's share of this total is expected to reach 9.5 million tonnes, an increase of more than two million over 1995. Mexico's consumption was 90 000 tonnes in 1995 and is expected to exceed 540 000 tonnes by the year 2000.

In the EU, consumption is around 3% of the world's total and is expected to remain so for the next few years. Asia is expected to increase (at North America's expense) to 20% by 2000, from around 19% in 1995.

Annual growth of HFS consumption is forecast to grow at 5% for HFS–55 and 3% for HFS–42. Around 25% of growth in world nutritive sweetener consumption is expected to be satisfied by HFS. Asia continues to be a major area of growth and as production grows there so will consumption. If sugar prices rise significantly (i.e. in excess of 13 cents/lb) then massive substitution is likely to take place and growth prospects for all alternative sweeteners will be almost limitless.

Sugar and health

Sugar plays many roles in our daily diet: as a taste enhancer, a bulking agent, a preservative and as a provider of texture. It is also an antioxidant. Its chief value, however, is in providing energy, through calories, and in making a variety of foods more palatable. It is, therefore, a very versatile and pleasant food that performs a valuable function towards our well being.

That has not, however, prevented so-called nutritional experts telling us that sugar is bad for us. There is, as a result, a public perception that sugar, is, in some way, a harmful constituent of the diet. Hence, it has been possible to advertise sugar-free as a positive selling point. The only consolation is that sugar is not the only food to be so treated. At one time bread and potatoes were thought to be bad for health but now such roughage is strongly recommended. Fat was considered fatal until someone wrote a book entitled *Eat Fat and*

Grow Thin. There was a time when more than two glasses of wine a day was a sign of advanced alcoholism; now, in moderation, wine is recommended as highly beneficial.

So, it can be seen that diet and nutrition is an inexact science that is susceptible to fashion. Sugar, unfortunately, has long been a target of faddists and a powerful anti-sugar lobby has appeared.

For over 40 years the adverse effects of sugar on our health have been in the news but perhaps the most damaging report was one published in 1991 by the World Health Organization (WHO), which has been at the forefront of the anti-sugar lobby for years. This report did little harm to the overall consumption of sugar but may have prevented its growth. The areas of attack were fourfold. Firstly, the report stated that if more than 10% of energy needs are gleaned from sugar this will lead to obesity. Secondly, sugar contributes to colon and breast cancers. Thirdly, sugar can cause diabetes, heart disease and hypertension and, fourthly, sugar causes dental caries, especially in children.

All these claims have been discounted as unproven and scientifically unsound by the pro-sugar lobby in subsequent reports, but disinformation by opposing parties, together with distorted statistics and manipulation of the media have instilled into the minds of people in developed countries a feeling that sugar is bad. Although sugar has been blamed for many diseases, including those mentioned above, extensive and expensive research has failed to come up with any substantive argument in support of any of these claims. It is only when the consumption of sugar is grossly excessive, leading to obesity, that the claims bear fruit but the same can be said about excessive consumption of anything.

Perhaps the chief reason for the anti-sugar lobby's crusade is the now somewhat flawed perception that sugar supplies only calories and no other nutrients, vitamins, minerals or proteins. But sugar stands as an energy source in its own right and brings to food consumption many desirable properties, making food more palatable and more varied. The charge that additional sugar intake is at the expense of other carbohydrates such as starch is not supported by any evidence. It is interesting to note that there is clear evidence that sugar consumption seems to discourage the consumption of fat.

Another accusation levelled at the industry is that excess sugar intake leads to obesity. Of course it does, just as the excessive intake of almost anything will lead to obesity. Changes in body fat are governed by the balance between energy intake and energy expenditure. Taking in more than is used up will cause weight gain since excess energy from any food is converted into body fat. Nutrition experts have found that people who remove sugar from their diet simply eat more fat. Recent research in Canada and the USA has shown that sugar suppresses appetite better than fat and that low-fat foods are unlikely to shrink waistlines since people will compensate by eating other foods.

Fat has long been considered the dieter's biggest enemy but there is a school of thought that reckons that sugar could be a key to successful weight control. All energy-giving food gets turned into sugar in the blood. If the blood-sugar level is too high it gets turned into fat but if it is too low it can lead to lethargy.

Several authors have tried to prove that the correlation with heart disease rates is stronger with the consumption of sugar than with that of fats, and that sugar, because it can be addictive, contributes to colon and breast cancers. These accusations have been refuted by many individual pieces of research and several expert committees have published reports casting apodictic doubt on such claims. This book is not the proper forum for a scientific debate on such matters. Suffice it to say that many eminent bodies, led by the Royal College of Physicians, have concluded that there is no evidence linking sugar intake and coronary heart disease or cancer. Similarly, a separate report states that there is no evidence to support a direct causal role for sugar in the development of diabetes other than as a non-specific source of calories.

Under experimental conditions, large doses of sugar taken in solution can cause aggressiveness in adults. In children, however, the result is far more likely to be listlessness and apathy, although irritability and naughtiness do sometimes manifest themselves. On the other hand, evidence also shows that this does not happen when children simply eat sugar-containing foods.

The WHO report's arbitrary upper limit of 10% of energy needs from sugar was prompted chiefly by the desire to protect children from the ravages of dental caries. This is a problem, as there is no denying the fact that excessive sugar consumption can lead to dental caries, particularly in children. It is sensible, therefore, to try and limit the consumption and the frequency of use of foods that are high in sugar, particularly amongst the very young. To counteract this problem, great strides have been made in preventing dental caries with the use of fluoride, especially in toothpaste. Improved oral hygiene practices have also played their part. The incidence of tooth decay has fallen dramatically in developed countries in recent years.

Another culprit is soft fizzy drinks. It is now thought that these can cause erosion of teeth in children, particularly teenagers, who tend to subject their teeth to attack for long periods by, for instance, allowing one can of drink to last a long time. Backed up by two recent government surveys, many scientists, researchers and dentists believe that the soaring consumption of fizzy drinks is leading to an epidemic of tooth erosion amongst youngsters. The enamel coating on the inside of the front teeth gets etched away by the effects of the acid in the drinks (see Appendix II for further discussion).

At the time of the WHO report, the USA was getting around 15% of its energy from sugar but overall per capita consumption remained constant at around 31 kg per year. Efforts to prevent chronic diseases through dietary intervention are not appreciated in developed countries as they are seen as an infringement of the individual's freedom of choice. There is a natural resentment and underlying resistance to being told what to eat. The fact remains that there are no properly conclusive scientific reasons for stating that sugar is harmful to health if, like all things, it is taken in moderation. Sugar calories are no more implicated than calories from other foods.

Another report, however, published by two US academics towards the end of 1995 in the *Journal of the American Medical Association* debunks the theory, prevalent for over 70 years, that temper tantrums, poor performance at school and other childish misdemeanours are caused by refined sugar. In 1922 and 1947, two separate reports suggested that behavioural problems in childhood could be caused by sugar and arose largely from unsubstantiated parental preconceptions reflecting their own expectations. The new report analysed the case histories of 1800 children in 23 separate studies which showed that, despite marked differences in social background and age, children's reactions to sugar were equally reassuring. It found that sugar did not affect either the behaviour or the learning ability of the children.

Damaging propaganda and unfavourable perceptions make it necessary to continue scientific research on all nutritional aspects of sugar to prove conclusively that it is not harmful. Perhaps then the anti-lobby will turn its attentions elsewhere. An encouraging sign of a change in people's perception of sugar is the result of a recent survey that the number of those with a positive attitude towards sugar doubled to over 50% in the five years to 1994.

It is quite clear that sugar plays a valuable role in the diet of developed and developing countries both as an important energy source and as a taste enhancer. A recent study carried out by a team led by a leading nutritionist at King's College, London, found that sugar does not make sugar fat nor does it displace other important items in the diet. In fact, it could actually improve the diet because the evidence is that children who eat more sugar eat less fat. The results of the study were published in 1995 in the *Journal of Human Nutrition & Dietetics*, and showed that those children who ate the most sugar were the least likely to be overweight. The denigration of sugar as empty calories by critics is naive, the report states, since most sugar is eaten with a great variety of nutrients to which it contributes taste and texture as well as energy.

The trade

9

Trends in the world trade

Factors contributing to volatility

In 1993, sugar was the second most important soft commodity in world trade (after cereals) in value terms, with a total value of US$10.68 billion.[1] Many countries are highly dependent on sugar for export revenue.[2] In price terms sugar has been the most volatile of all commodities (see Table 9.1 and Fig. 9.1). A number of factors contribute to this volatility.

Residuality

Only 21% of world production currently enters trade. This produces a gearing effect – a relatively small change in world production can, if cleared through the price-forming (free) market, be magnified almost five times in proportionate terms. For example, a 1 million tonnes increase in world production (0.8%) would, if it appeared on the world market, increase export availability by 4.4%. This effect is exaggerated because the existence of special (preferential) arrangements reduces

---

1 Compared to an import value of US$38.42 billion for grains and US$7.45 billion for coffee in 1993.

2 In 1986, sugar accounted for 76% of all export earnings in Cuba, 37% of export earnings in Mauritius and 50% of export earnings in Fiji.

Table 9.1 Instability indices and trends in monthly market prices for selected primary commodities

Commodity	Weight[1] 1983-85 %	Instability index[2] (Percentage variation) 1962-89[5]	1962-80	1980-89[5]	Trend[3] — Annual average rate of change, % — In current dollars 1962-89[5]	1962-80	1980-89[5]	In constant dollars[4] 1962-89[5]	1962-80	1980-89[5]
Food and tropical beverages of which:	64.57	24.8	18.3	11.0	5.9	9.0	-4.8	-0.3	2.0	-6.3
Food	**50.05**	**27.9**	**24.4**	**22.9**	**4.6**	**8.0**	**-8.7**	**-1.6**	**1.0**	**-10.3**
Sugar	7.79	69.9	67.4	72.7	4.5	11.5	-20.6	-1.7	4.3	-22.1
Rice	1.83	29.6	23.2	24.1	3.1	6.5	-11.3	-3.1	-0.4	-12.8
Palm kernels	0.03	30.5	23.7	34.8	3.2	6.1	-9.5	-3.0	-0.8	-11.0
Palm oil	2.40	28.2	22.0	25.4	4.1	7.1	-8.5	-2.1	0.2	-10.1
Groundnuts	1.18	29.6	17.6	12.2	4.2	8.4	-8.6	-2.0	1.4	-10.1
Maize	1.50	20.8	17.2	16.6	4.2	6.8	-8.2	-2.0	-0.1	-9.7
Palm kernel oil	0.35	32.2	24.3	33.0	3.6	7.1	-7.7	-2.6	0.2	-9.3
Sunflower oil	0.42	30.4	23.6	20.4	4.3	8.2	-7.1	-1.9	1.2	-8.7
Wheat	1.54	23.0	21.8	12.8	4.6	6.6	-6.8	-1.6	-0.2	-8.3
Coconut oil	1.78	29.1	22.0	34.5	3.2	5.9	-6.2	-3.0	-0.9	-7.7
Copra	0.13	30.8	25.9	33.2	3.7	6.4	-6.1	-2.5	-0.5	-7.6
Soybean oil	0.92	28.2	22.6	22.0	4.2	7.4	-6.0	-2.0	0.5	-7.5
Groundnut oil	0.17	28.4	18.9	24.8	5.0	8.7	-5.7	-1.2	1.7	-7.3
Fishmeal	1.62	25.5	22.4	22.7	4.7	7.6	-5.5	-1.5	0.6	-7.1
Soybean meal	2.02	20.7	17.2	19.3	4.4	6.9	-5.1	-1.9	0.0	-6.6
Soybeans	1.24	20.7	16.9	16.4	4.4	7.2	-4.7	-1.8	0.2	-6.3
Beef	1.01	14.8	11.7	8.1	5.0	7.1	-2.7	-1.2	0.2	-4.2
Bananas	1.41	16.2	15.7	15.4	5.0	4.7	-0.6	-1.2	-2.0	-2.1
Pepper	0.31	25.5	14.5	34.6	6.6	7.1	17.7	0.4	0.2	16.1

Tropical beverages	14.52	26.2	25.5	12.7	7.1	10.0	-1.2	0.8	2.9	-2.8
Tea	1.89	22.2	20.9	17.0	3.4	3.3	-2.1	-2.2	-3.3	-3.7
Cocoa	2.48	34.6	27.7	12.8	8.2	13.0	-1.2	2.0	5.7	-2.7
Coffee	10.15	27.3	28.4	12.2	7.3	10.0	-0.1	1.1	2.9	-1.6
Agricultural raw materials	14.24	17.2	16.6	13.3	5.6	7.4	-2.5	-0.7	0.5	-4.0
Linseed oil	1.09	34.1	33.2	24.7	4.8	7.8	-8.3	-1.4	0.8	-9.9
Rubber	3.23	24.7	25.9	20.7	4.4	5.3	-5.3	-1.8	-1.5	-6.9
Cotton	2.81	20.8	15.3	13.0	5.1	7.5	-5.3	-1.1	0.6	-6.6
Sisal	0.08	36.4	41.3	7.9	5.2	7.1	-5.1	-1.0	0.1	-3.6
Wool	0.35	23.3	26.3	15.3	4.5	5.3	-2.0	-1.7	-1.5	-2.2
Hides and skins	0.37	22.2	25.2	16.4	5.2	7.8	-0.7	-1.0	0.9	-1.7
Tropical timber	5.69	19.1	16.9	12.7	7.2	8.7	-0.2	0.9	1.3	-1.2
Jute	0.15	16.1	10.4	26.2	1.1	1.5	0.4	-5.1	-5.0	-1.2
Minerals, ores and metals	21.19	15.8	12.3	16.7	4.0	6.3	-4.3	-2.2	-0.5	-5.8
Tungsten	0.06	47.6	30.0	17.7	5.9	14.7	-17.1	-0.3	7.4	-18.6
Tin	1.77	29.0	21.5	16.2	7.0	10.6	-11.8	0.8	3.5	-13.4
Lead	0.24	29.9	20.9	30.6	4.4	9.1	-8.0	-1.9	2.1	-9.5
Phosphate rock	1.00	37.3	34.4	12.6	7.0	10.4	-5.6	0.8	3.3	-7.2
Manganese ore	0.20	21.4	21.1	14.7	4.4	5.2	-3.9	-1.8	-1.5	-5.4
Copper	4.80	22.9	23.1	26.9	2.0	4.3	-3.6	-4.2	-2.4	-5.1
Iron ore	2.88	13.1	11.6	5.0	4.5	5.4	-2.4	-1.7	-1.4	-3.9
Aluminium	3.33	17.6	14.7	31.1	5.0	6.7	-1.7	-1.2	-0.2	-3.2
Zinc	0.21	26.3	26.5	22.3	5.7	8.4	-0.4	-0.5	1.4	-2.0
All commodities										
In current dollars	100.00	19.5	15.2	11.2	5.5	8.1	-4.1	-0.9	1.1	-5.6
In terms of Special Drawing Rights	—	15.5	12.6	7.9	4.7	6.3	-3.6	-1.7	-0.6	-5.3

Notes: [1]Derived from values of world exports. [2]The measure of instability is $\frac{1}{n}\sum_{(t=1,N)}|(Y-Y(t))Y(t)|$. where $Y(t)$ is the observed magnitude of the variable; $Y(t)$ is the magnitude estimated by fitting an exponential trend to the observed value and N is the number of observations. The vertical bar indicated the absolute value (i.e. disregarding signs). Accordingly, instability is measured as the percentage deviation of the variables concerned from their exponential trend levels for a given period. [3]The growth rate of each period has been calculated using the formula: $Log(p)=a+b(t)$ where p is the price index and t is time. [4]Constant 1980 dollars (current dollars divided by the United Nations index of export unit value of manufactured goods exported by developed market-economy countries). [5]Prices for 1989 are for the first seven months. *Source: UNCTAD Commodity Yearbook, 1989.*

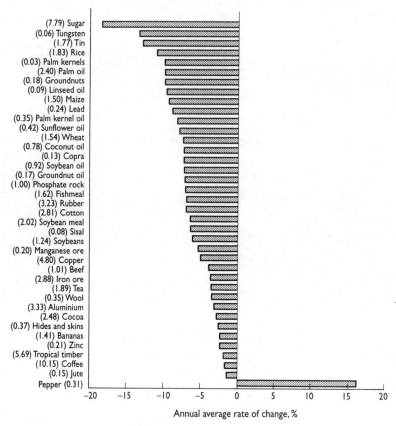

Note: Figures in parentheses refer to the weights

9.1 Instability indices and trends in monthly market prices for selected primary commodities (source: UNCTAD Commodity Yearbook 1989).

even further the size of the price-setting free market. Currently, special arrangements reduce total net imports by around 3 million tonnes (13%) but special arrangements in the 1950s made up almost 60% of the total net market.

Asset fixity

Sugar is both an agricultural and an industrial product. Taking into account cultivation equipment, harvesting equipment and mills/factories/refineries, the capital input is high – higher than any other comparable soft commodity. Since the equipment and mills are specialized and cannot be used for other purposes, there is a tendency both to maximize throughput and to continue producing so long as the marginal cost (of cane or beet harvesting, and the price paid for the raw material) is less than the marginal revenue, irrespective of the world price for sugar. Consequently, production can be raised even though prices are falling, driving prices down ever further (the early 1980s are a good example of this phenomenon).

Sugar cane growth period

Another example of asset fixity is the sugar cane growth period. Sugar cane is a perennial crop which stays in the ground for four to seven years. Therefore only one-quarter to one-seventh of the land is replanted each year. This contributes to rising prices because cane is relatively slow to respond. Falling prices are also accelerated because once cane is planted it is often cheaper to harvest it than to remove it.

Low price elasticity of developed importers

Developed importers tend not to respond to rising prices because of their high income and low price elasticity. Their priority in a rising market is to secure their normal or necessary supplies. This keeps up the momentum of a rising market, or accelerates it, until the desired quantity of sugar has been secured. Clearly, as Chapter 7 demonstrated, this factor is currently less important – developed countries represent less than one-third of the import market compared to two-thirds as recently as 1975.

Divergent growth trends in world production and consumption

As Chapter 6 showed, world consumption since 1955 has grown at a steady 2 million tonnes a year (currently 2% per annum), except in rare years of major shock (e.g. 1974 and 1980). World production, on the other hand, has a tendency toward lumpy growth – asset fixity and the sugar cane growth period referred to above mean growth in response to high prices is delayed, but may continue long after prices have begun to fall. In addition, sugar, especially that grown in the tropical belt, is vulnerable to weather shocks – hurricanes or droughts – causing sudden and unexpected falls in production. As a result of these two factors, the world sugar economy is usually either in surplus or deficit (sometimes massive – refer to the early 1980s), seldom in neat balance.

Protectionism

Currently, around one-quarter of world production is subsidized and most importing producers protect their domestic industries with tariffs or other trade barriers (most will be converted to tariffs under the GATT Uruguay Round agreement). Protection means that a large number of sugar producers are not exposed to the world price – they increase or decrease production purely in relation to domestic factors. They can exacerbate a rising world market price by producing less, or over-supply a falling world market by producing (and in some cases exporting) more. Two recent examples of the harm that can be done to the world market by protectionism are the rapid increase in EC production and exports in the early 1980s which contributed significantly to the sharp fall in world sugar prices, which in 1985 fell to an all-time low in real terms of 2.61 cents/lb; and the imposition of quotas by the USA in 1982 to protect its domestic industry from HFCS. US net imports fell from 3.7 million tonnes in 1981 to 0.63 million tonnes in 1987, significantly contributing to the build-up of world stocks during the early to mid-1980s.

The above list of factors contributing to volatility is not exhaustive, nor do they all have equal weight at any time or over time, but together they explain the volatility for which sugar has become, justly, famous. One more idea should be added: as Chapter 3 attempted to demonstrate, sugar is a highly political and social commodity and has been so since colonial times. It is affected by and intertwined with big events (the Cuban Revolution, the dissolution of the USSR) and it is not surprising, therefore, that it has been the subject of many attempts at international political regulation dating from the first ISA of 1864.

Structure of the world market – evolution

The proportion of consumption met by trade

Figure 9.2 shows the evolution of world net imports as a percentage of world consumption from 1955 to 1994. The proportion of consumption

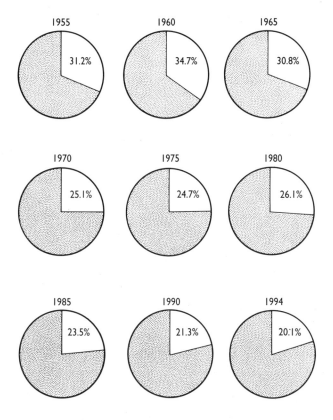

9.2 World net imports as % of world consumption (source: ISO).

met from trade peaked at almost 35% in 1960, but has been declining since, and this decline has accelerated since 1980. This is because, since 1960, the level of self-sufficiency in the world has risen. Importers have increasingly met rising demand by increasing domestic production. In many cases this is the consequence of the volatility of world prices – importers would rather increase production, at whatever cost, than become more dependent on a volatile world market subject to periodic high prices (1974 and 1980). At times of rising prices, developing importing countries would be forced to reduce imports and therefore reduce politically sensitive consumption. Therefore increasing domestic production has a certain attraction, which may be reinforced by national or regional socio-economic factors – supporting domestic sugar production may well be cheaper than directly supporting income in a region as well as reducing the import bill.

Table 9.2 illustrates increases in production, consumption and imports from 1980 to 1994. The figures are dramatic. Most of the

Table 9.2 Increases in production, consumption and imports, 1980–94, million tonnes, raw value

	1980	1994	Change	%
World consumption	88.65	113.80	+25.15	+28
World net imports	23.09	22.87	−0.22	−1
Production in importing countries	28.62	35.71	+7.09	+25

Source: ISO.

increase in world consumption of 25.15 million tonnes was met from trade. In fact, trade declined slightly over the period. On the other hand, production in importing countries rose by 7.1 million tonnes (25%). It should be noted that 1980 was a boom year (world raw sugar prices averaged 28.7 cents/lb) but prices swiftly declined to real all-time lows by 1985. These low prices persisted until 1987, yet imports did not increase over the whole decade. It is difficult to escape the conclusion that high prices damage the market by encouraging self-sufficiency and, once the investment in productive capacity is made, low prices do not encourage a reversal from increasing self-sufficiency to achieving consumption growth from imports. The decline in the proportion of imports should have increased volatility and up to 1980 this was the case but this effect has been nullified by the rapid growth in the share of price-sensitive developing countries in world imports.

The share of developing countries in imports

The evolution of the share of developing countries in net imports from 1955 to 1994 is shown in Fig. 9.3. In 1955 developing countries accounted for 31% of net imports. Rapid post-war growth in developed country imports reduced the share of developing countries to 23% by 1960. Their share increased gradually to 26% in 1975, and then, boosted by the transfer in income from the first oil price shock of 1973 and the rapidly increasing imports of oil-exporting developing countries, increased rapidly, reaching 45% by 1980. A further rise to 53% was registered in 1985, and then stagnation till 1980. The break-up of the USSR in 1991 and the concomitant fall in imports, coupled with imports by India and China in 1994, increased the share to two-thirds of the import market. The rising share of price-sensitive developing countries since 1975 has had a dampening effect on price volatility – prices did not rise as high in 1980 as they did in 1974, and since 1988 raw sugar prices have been confined within a range from 8 to 16 cents/lb while annual averages have varied between 8.97 and

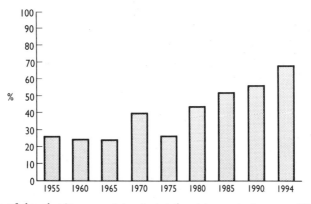

9.3 Share of developing countries in total net imports (source: ISO).

12.82 cents/lb. The seven year average (1988–94) was 10.81 cents/lb. It must be noted that the share of developing countries in the free market (excluding preferential imports and where the world sugar price is actually set) is higher than their share of total net imports. In 1955, when special (preferential) arrangements covered 60% of the total net market, developing countries accounted for 54% of free market net import requirements (or 31% of total net imports). By 1960 their share of the free market had risen to 56%, and by 1980 had settled at 50%. However, by 1990 the share of developing countries in the free market had risen to 65% (compared to their share of the total net market of 52%). The share of developing countries in the net free market of 1994 remained at 65% (see Fig. 9.4).

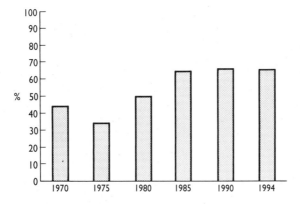

9.4 Share of developing countries in free market net imports (source: ISO).

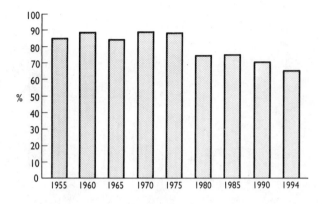

9.5   Share of developing countries in total net exports (source: ISO).

The share of developing countries in exports

The developing countries' share in exports has always been the antithesis of the import market. As Fig. 9.5 shows, up to 1975, their share had been between 85% and 90%. Cane production, which provided most of the sugar exports up to that time, was concentrated in developing countries. Australia was the only notable developed country exporter. From 1975, however, one of the significant structural changes to affect the post-war world sugar market occurred. This was the rise in EC production and exports. The effect that this had on the share is clearly evident from Fig. 9.4. By 1994 the share of developing countries had fallen to almost 65%.

The structural change engendered by the rise of EC exports was not merely arithmetic. EC exports were of white sugar, made from a plant – beet – with an annual crop cycle. In addition, the EC had a stocking policy which caused larger than normal stocks to be held. For these two reasons, the EC was able to respond more rapidly to changes in conditions and prices on the world sugar market. This enhanced responsiveness on the supply side has been a small but important factor in the growing stability, since the mid-1980s, of the world sugar market. The growing share of white sugar in total world exports is shown in Table 9.3.

Special (bilateral) arrangements

A characteristic of the world sugar market has been the proportion of total trade accounted for by special trade arrangements, with

132

Table 9.3   Share of white sugar in total world exports, 1978–94, %

1978	28	1987	37
1979	27	1988	34
1980	32	1989	34
1981	35	1990	37
1982	34	1991	39
1983	34	1992	49
1984	35	1993	53
1985	36	1994	51
1986	37		

Source: ISO.

quantitative and prices fixed at government level. Generally, although not always (the exceptions being world price peak periods up to 1980), special arrangement prices have been above the free market price. This characteristic has had the effect of marginalizing the free, price-setting, market even more, especially in the early post-war years. Table 9.4 shows the share of total net imports accounted for by the principal examples of special arrangements.

Table 9.4   Summary of special arrangements and their market share, 1955–94. million tonnes, raw average

	Average special arrangement	Average total net imports	Share of special arrangement, %
1955–59			
CSA	1.5		
US Sugar Act	4.0		
	5.5	12.5	44
1960–74			
CSA	1.5		
US Sugar Act	4.4		
Cuba–socialist countries	3.1		
	9.0	17.4	51
1975–91			
Lomé Convention (EC)	1.4		
Cuba–socialist countries	5.1		
	6.5	22.8	29
1992–94			
Lomé Convention (EC)	1.4		
Cuba–Russia/China	2.4		
	3.8	23.4	16

Source: ISO.

Up until 1959, when the Cuban Revolution caused the supply of Cuban sugar under the US Sugar Act to be terminated (Cuba's quota under the Act was approximately 2.7–3.0 million tonnes), special arrangement imports accounted for an average of 44% of the world sugar market (i.e. the free market was only 56% of the total market). The establishment of the protocol governing Cuban exports to socialist countries in 1960 raised the share of special arrangements even further. From 1966 to the price peak year of 1974, when both the CSA governing UK imports and the US Sugar Act were suspended, special arrangement imports rose to average 9 million tonnes, representing an average share of total net imports of 51%. In 1975 the CSA was replaced by the sugar protocol of the Lomé Convention when the UK formally acceded to the EC, with a slightly reduced quantity. The US Sugar Act was never re-enacted. However, the quantities imported under the Cuba–socialist countries protocol rose significantly to average 5.1 million tonnes in the years 1975–91. However, the loss of the US Sugar Act resulted in a reduced average total of special arrangement imports of 6.5 million tonnes (1975–91) and the average share of special arrangements in total net imports fell to 29% over the period.

The demise of the USSR (following the independence of its buffer states in 1989–90) has further reduced the importance of special arrangements compared to the years before 1975. The average quantity for 1992–94 has fallen to under 3 million tonnes and the average share to 16%.

It has been argued that the imposition of country specific quotas by the USA in 1981/82, which continue to operate, represent a special arrangement. Raw sugar imports within the quota ceiling receive the US internal price, currently 18 cents/lb, and, since 1982, higher than the world sugar price. However, the USA imposed the quota system unilaterally so that neither quotas nor prices were fixed at an intergovernmental level. Consequently, the US quota system has been excluded from this analysis and US imports are considered to be free market imports. US imports under quota have ranged between 0.63 million tonnes and 2.72 million tonnes between 1982 and 1994, with an average for the five most recent available years (1990–94) of 1.59 million tonnes. Variations from year to year are due to variations in domestic production (as import quotas are set annually to make up the difference between consumption and domestic production) and, up to 1987, falling consumption due to the inroads made by HFCS.

One of the defining characteristics of special bilateral arrangements is that the price is fixed and is normally significantly higher than the world sugar price (except in world sugar price boom years such as 1974 and 1980).

Under the sugar protocol of the Lomé Convention, participating countries (see Chapter 4) receive the raw equivalent of the intervention (support) price. The intervention price is currently 67–68 ECU/100 kg (37.9–38.5 cents/lb) and the raw equivalent is 52.37 ECU/10 kg (29.6 cents/lb). The world raw sugar price is currently 13 cents/lb.

The US loan rate effectively sets the US domestic price for both raw and refined. Importers under the quota system in force receive the US domestic price for all quantities within the quota. The US loan rate (support price) is currently set at 18 cents/lb for raw sugar and 23.43 cents/lb for refined beet sugar.

Up to 1992, when free market prices were introduced for both oil and sugar exchanged under bilateral barter, it was exceptionally difficult to quantify the Cuba–USSR–COMECON sugar protocols. Sugar was exchanged for oil, machinery, spare parts, cereals and many other goods. Even if the goods had an international value that could be quantified there was still the question of quality. Nevertheless, several attempts were made to place a value on the sugar Cuba supplied to USSR–COMECON. One of the most comprehensive was by Perez-Lopez (see Table 9.5).

Table 9.5 Estimated Soviet subsidy prices for Cuban sugar, 1970–85, US cents/lb, raw sugar

	Soviet contract price	World market price	Preferential USA	Preferential EC
1970	6.11	3.75	8.07	5.09
1971	6.11	4.53	8.52	5.16
1972	6.11	7.43	9.09	6.79
1973	12.02	9.63	10.24	6.66
1974	19.64	29.96	29.50	10.66
1975	30.40	20.50	22.43	25.79
1976	30.95	11.57	13.31	14.82
1977	35.73	8.09	11.00	12.46
1978	40.78	7.84	13.93	15.11
1979	44.00	9.66	15.56	19.29
1980	47.45	28.67	30.11	22.09
1981	35.10	16.89	19.73	18.93
1982	39.00	8.41	19.92	18.12
1983	46.00	8.47	23.04	17.57
1984	44.00	5.20	21.74	16.04
1985	45.00	4.06	20.34	15.89

Source: Early and Westfall, after Perez-Lopez.

Perez-Lopez estimated that from 1978 onwards the Soviet subsidized prices exceeded 40 cents/lb when converted to their market equivalent. In 1985 this was more than 10 times the free market raw sugar price.

It is clear that the scale of special arrangements has contributed significantly to the volatility of sugar prices. Between 1960 and 1975, when the world sugar market was adjusting to the diversion of Cuban sugar to the USSR and other socialist countries, the free market, on average, was less than half of the total of world net imports. This marginalization made the free market particularly vulnerable to relatively small changes in the quantities demanded or cleared through it. It is no coincidence that the highest ever price peaks for sugar, in 1974, occurred during this period.

Conversely, the reduction in the share of special arrangements from 1975, to their current share of 16%, has contributed to the increased price stability of the world sugar market since 1988.

ISAs

The extreme volatility of world sugar prices, up to 1980, noted throughout this chapter, has resulted in many multilateral, inter-governmental attempts at stabilization. ISAs with economic clauses were negotiated in 1953, 1958, 1968 and 1977. Thus, of the 45 years from 1950 to 1994, 19 were covered by intergovernmental treaties designed to keep the world free market sugar price within stated ranges. The principal instrument used was adjustable export quotas, increased or suspended when prices rose toward the ceiling price and reduced, within limits, when prices fell. In the 1977 ISA, which ran from 1978 to 1984, the defence of the upper limit was strengthened by limited stocking provisions, of 2.2 million tonnes (not, therefore, buffer stocks). These stocks were scheduled for phased release as prices approached the upper end of the range.

Figure 9.6 summarizes the price ranges of the four post-war ISAs and compares them to the actual world raw sugar price. Except for the 1953 ISA, it cannot be said that ISAs succeeded in their price objectives. None were able to deal with exceptional circumstances. The 1958 ISA was unable to control the aftermath of the Cuban Revolution in 1959, when initially, the USA sought imports from non-Cuban sources and drove the price up precipitously. By the mid-1960s the price had fallen dramatically as the USSR began to re-export large quantities of Cuban sugar. The 1968 ISA was unable to contain the 1973/74 sugar price boom. Similarly, the 1977 ISA – handicapped by

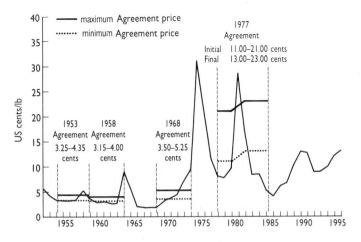

9.6   ISA price ranges and world sugar price, 1951–95 (source: ISO).

the non-membership of the EC whose burgeoning exports made ISA members reluctant to control theirs, and saddled with a cumbersome and over-complicated mechanism which left the agreement always running behind the market – could not prevent the 1980 price boom (or the subsequent collapse of prices).

However flawed ISAs proved to be, it should be recognized that they were a serious attempt to deal with a serious problem – extreme volatility. The boom-and-bust characteristic of the world free market up to 1980, while bringing short term windfall gains once every five to seven years to those exporters lucky enough to have sugar in years of shortage, was extremely destructive for sugar in the long term. Three principal destructive consequences can be cited:

- long post-boom periods when the world sugar price was less than the cost of production (sometimes less than half the cost of production) of even the most efficient producers, because of the over production encouraged by the boom prices;
- wasteful diversion of resources into un-needed expansion plans, particularly in capital-starved developing countries;
- the rapid expansion of HFCS production in the USA and Japan following the 1974 price boom and exacerbated by the 1980 price boom, leading, through the protective system put in place by the USA in 1981 (quotas for imports and guaranteed domestic price), to the sharp decline in US and Japanese imports noted elsewhere.

Since the 1977 ISA expired at the end of 1984 and negotiations in 1983 and 1984 failed to find an acceptable successor, there have been no further ISAs with economic clauses, and none is in prospect. The

1984, 1987 and 1992 ISAs have restricted the organization to providing information, statistics and analysis and a forum for intergovernmental policy discussion. There are two connected reasons why ISAs with economic clauses are no longer on the agenda. Most importantly, the changing economic and political philosophy from the early 1980s when the Keynesian ideas on which ISAs were based became increasingly discredited and were replaced by free market deregulatory ideas led ISAs to be labelled interventionist, and therefore bad.[3]

Secondly, the increased stability brought about since 1988 by the structural changes triggered by the 1974 price boom has rendered an economic ISA unnecessary. Currently, the world market is self-regulatory, with prices confined by the actions and responses of importers (and, to a lesser extent, exporters) to a range which any rational ISA would aspire to – a *de facto* ISA. Meanwhile, the International Sugar Organization aids this process by providing analysis, statistics and discussion, making the market more transparent and attempting to fulfil one of the conditions of a perfect market – freely available information.

Conclusion

This chapter has highlighted the main structural attributes of the world sugar market and pointed out where and when that structure has changed. There can be no doubt that the market has been structurally dynamic as well as volatile in price. From the Korean War price boom to the Cuban Revolution, and from the 1974 price boom to the 1980 price boom, down to the recent dissolution of the USSR, the world sugar market has been constantly changing. However, in terms of price, the change has been in the direction of more stability rather than less. All the factors cited have contributed to a more stable market, but undoubtedly the most important has been the increasing share of developing countries in imports. This is a consequence of the rise of HFCS since the 1974 price boom and the rise in developing country imports, particularly by oil exporting countries. However, all

---

3 This is a rather circular argument. ISAs were negotiated because the free market had failed sugar, and since they were never able to contain the worst excesses of the free market, the most valid argument that can be levelled against them is that they were flawed and to some extent naïve.

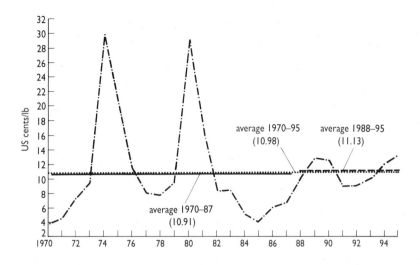

9.7 Evolution of raw sugar price and averages, 1970–95 (source: ISO).

the changes in structure, from the reduction in the share of special arrangements to the increase in the share of beet white sugar, have been in the direction of providing more stability. Figure 9.7, which shows the evolution of raw sugar prices from 1970 to 1995, confirms the increased stability since 1988.

10

Trends in world prices

Price volatility characteristics

It was established in Chapter 9 that the world sugar price has been the most volatile of all soft commodity prices rivalling even some of the non-ferrous metals in its volatility (see Fig. 9.1 and Table 9.1 in Chapter 9). Chapter 9 also explained the main reasons for the lack of stability. These may be summarized as follows:

- marginality of the market (only 22% of sugar production is traded);
- the traded portion is further reduced (to around 17%) by the existence of bilateral, intergovernmental trading arrangements, outside the price-setting free market;
- the free market has been a residual market where exporters have 'dumped' their excess sugar and importers who also produce have picked up, cheaply in the main, the difference between domestic production and consumption in any particular year;
- sugar cane is a perennial crop, requiring a large capital investment in field and factory – this makes cane sugar slow to react to shortages (and price rises) and then liable to have large quantities appearing on the market when prices are falling, driving prices down to extreme lows;
- sugar cane is a tropical or sub-tropical crop, subject to large swings in production due to weather (hurricanes, droughts etc);
- up to 1980, sugar imports were dominated by low price elasticity, high income importers (US, Japan and Canada) purchasing sugar

mainly as an input for sugar-containing products. High income, low (or zero) price elasticity purchasers, like soft drink manufacturers, have a tendency to protect market share when prices rise sharply, securing their requirements irrespective of the price, so as not to lose market share to their competitors. This behaviour, in aggregate, has a tendency to drive or chase the price up to very high levels when there is a shortage. This happened in the 1974 and 1980 world sugar price booms, when daily prices reached 64 cents/lb and 47 cents/lb, respectively. In 1974 and 1980, high income, low price elasticity developed country importers accounted for two-thirds of the world import market. (The structure of the world import market changed radically in the 1980s; by 1990 developing countries accounted for two-thirds of the world import market, bringing, with their high price elasticity, more stability to the market. Developments in the world sugar market and their consequences are discussed in more detail in Chapter 12.)

The long term volatility of raw sugar prices is clearly apparent in Fig. 10.1. Prices averaged 5.75 cents/lb in 1951 (the Korean War commodity price boom) and rose again above 5 cents/lb to average 5.2 cents/lb in 1957. From 1953 to 1963 the 1953 and 1958 ISAs were in operation, with price ranges of 3.25 cents/lb to 4.35 cents/lb and 3.15 cents/lb to 4 cents/lb, respectively. Although these were the most successful of all post-war ISAs, prices topped the agreed range in 1957 and fell below the floor price in 1961 (average 2.75 cents/lb) and 1962 (2.83 cents/lb). During this period world sugar trade was dominated by special bilateral trade arrangements: the US Sugar Act and the CSA,

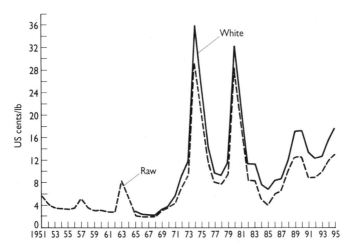

10.1   Raw and white sugar prices, 1951–95 (source: ISO).

and the price-setting free market accounted for only approximately 40% of world trade.

Following the Cuban Revolution in 1959, when the USA–Cuba trade flow was diverted to the USSR, raw sugar prices were initially depressed, but a combination of poor crops and US efforts to secure replacement supplies outside Cuba caused another sugar price boom in 1963 when raw sugar prices averaged 8.34 cents/lb. The inevitable reaction, in terms of increased world production, caused prices to decline sharply, and by 1966 the annual average was a post-war low of only 1.81 cents/lb. The low prices of 1966–69 caused world production growth to fall behind consumption growth, and prices climbed steadily to average 9.45 cents/lb in 1973. Poor crops in 1972 and 1973 set world stocks tumbling and in 1974 a record sugar price boom occurred. The average raw sugar price for the year was 29.66 cents/lb, still a record, and the daily spot quotation reached an all-time high of 64 cents/lb in October 1974. Although prices held up in 1975 (averaging 20.37 cents/lb) the inevitable reaction again set in. World consumption growth levelled off while production, inspired by the extraordinary prices of 1974–75, rose sharply. Prices averaged only 7.81 cents/lb in 1978. The 1968 ISA was in force from 1969 to 1973, with a price range of 3.5–5.25 cents/lb, but was quite unable to contain the rising price from 1971.

A new (1977) ISA entered into force in 1978, again with the objective of stabilizing the world sugar price (the target range was initially 11–21 cents/lb), and this time with stocks of 2.5 million tonnes to defend the ceiling price. The 1977 ISA was perhaps the least successful of all post-war ISAs (see Fig. 9.6). A sharp fall in world production, and consequently stocks, sent prices rising rapidly again to peak in 1980. Although the highest daily spot price attained, 47 cents/lb in October 1980, was considerably below the 1974 peak (64 cents/lb), the annual average registered for 1980 was 28.69 cents/lb, only 1 cent/lb below the average for 1974. Once more, world production reacted to the high prices by increasing much more rapidly than world consumption. Large stocks were built up and by 1985 the annual average raw sugar price had fallen to 4.06 cents/lb (the daily spot quotation fell below 3 cents/lb in 1985).

The immense stocks built up in the early 1980s were not cleared until 1988, because, although world production fell, world consumption grew only sluggishly, despite prices remaining extremely depressed from 1984 to 1987. From 1988 the world raw sugar price has begun a period of relative and absolute stability, compared to previous years. From 1988 to 1995, the raw sugar price averaged 10.2, 12.82, 12.55, 8.97, 9.06, 10.02, 12.11 and 13.28 cents/lb, with a mean of 11.13 cents/lb and variation about the mean of –2.16 and +2.15 cents/lb. The mean of the preceding eight years was 10.55 cents/lb, not much different, but the variation about the mean for 1980–87 was –6.49 and +18.14 cents/lb, different therefore by factors of –3 and +8 (see Chapter 12, Tables 12.1 and 12.2). This remarkable gain in stability is expected to continue into the indefinite future (see Chapter 12).

Several reasons for the volatility of world sugar prices were advanced at the beginning of this chapter. There is no doubt that the change that occurred during the 1980s leading to the post-1987 increase in stability, was the precipitous relative decline in the share of developed countries in world imports, from two-thirds in the 1970s to only 40% by 1990. It is the *quality* as well as the quantity of high income, low price elasticity developed country imports that is important. In the USA, which in 1974 imported 5.2 million tonnes (33% of the free market in that year), and Japan, which in 1974 imported 2.85 million tonnes (18% of the free market in that year), more than 80% of sugar is used in the manufacture of sugar-containing products. Therefore it is important to take account of the behaviour of individual corporate sugar users when prices begin to rise sharply. Product manufacturers' first concern as the price of one of their principal inputs rises is the maintenance of brand share. Substitution of an alternative input, such as HFCS, is a longer term solution, depending on availability. In the short term, the main concern is not to lose product share to competitors. So, in spite of rapidly rising prices, product manufacturers continue to purchase the quantities they need to keep their product flowing to their customers. In other words they have a low or zero price elasticity, failing to adjust their purchases downwards as the price rises.[1]

Between 1974 and 1980 two-thirds of the world free market was accounted for by developed countries, dominated by the USA, Japan and Canada. The sheer volume of imports coming from this category of sugar product oriented importers, with their policy of obtaining necessary supplies irrespective of prices, helped to drive prices up to peaks that are now almost unbelievable.

Although the declining import market share of developed

---

1 In fact, there is evidence that they actually buy more when prices are rising. In 1974, the price boom year, the USA imported 5.25 million tonnes, compared to 4.83 million tonnes imported in 1973 and 3.51 million tonnes imported in 1975. Japan imported 2.85 million tonnes in 1974, compared to 2.44 million tonnes in 1973 and 2.55 million tonnes in 1975. It appears that the expectation that prices will rise higher, combined with fears that they will not be able to keep their product flowing, leads product manufacturers to purchase more than they actually require for a given time period.

countries is the main factor behind the increased price stability since 1987, two other contributory factors can be identified. The first stems from the deregulation and movement towards freer trade that has been a feature of the world economy in general, both developed and developing, since the early 1980s. The world sugar economy has not escaped this change and, with the exceptions of the USA, the EU and Japan (see Chapter 4), all of the world's major sugar producers and consumers have freed and deregulated their sugar markets to some extent. In the 1960s and 1970s, the majority of world imports (and exports) were controlled by central, usually government, authorities issuing licences and setting quotas. By 1990 this situation had been reversed: in the vast majority of importing countries, with the exception of the USA, and Japan, there is now a connection between the domestic price and the world price of sugar, usually through a tariff. In exporting countries, with the exception of the EU and the ACP countries, farmers now receive signals, however imperfect, from the world price. In this process, the world market has been transformed from a residual, 'dumping' market to a 'real' market, where producer and consumer exchange signals via the world price. The increased price responsiveness that is associated with a more deregulated market has helped to improve the stability of the market price.

The second subsidiary factor promoting more price stability is the break-up of the USSR in 1991. This led to a reduction of almost two-thirds in Cuba's special bilateral arrangement shipments to Russia and Ukraine (and those that remain are now exchanged at the world sugar and oil prices) and, therefore, there was an equivalent increase in the size of the world free market, making it less marginal. But the changes due to the break-up of the USSR go deeper, as all imports of sugar are now made at the world price (raw sugar) or the world price plus a tariff (white sugar), instead of the highly subsidized price hitherto paid to Cuba. Also, the internal, domestic price is closely aligned to the world price, replacing the heavily subsidized price of the Soviet era. Not only is Russia now fully part of the free market, but it behaves in the market like a developing country, varying its purchases according to the price.

White sugar prices, shown in Fig. 10.1 from 1965,[2] have generally tended to follow raw sugar prices. The exception is during periods when raw sugar prices are rising rapidly, due to relative shortage of raw sugar. At these times the raw/white differential tends to narrow. Like the raw sugar price the white sugar price fell to lows in 1968

2 The Paris exchange started publishing a daily spot white sugar quotation in mid-1964.

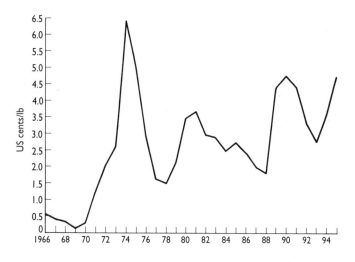

10.2 Unadjusted raw/white price differential (annual averages), 1966-95 (source: ISO).

(2.22 cents/lb), 1978 (9.3 cents/lb) and 1985 (6.8 cents/lb) and reached average peaks in 1974 (35.98 cents/lb) and 1980 (32.16 cents/lb). Like the raw sugar price it has been more stable from 1988, averaging 14.85 cents from 1988 to 1995, but with slightly more variation about the mean than raw sugar: -19% and +21% compared to -19% and +19% for raw sugar.

Figure 10.2 shows the unadjusted raw/white price differential between 1966 and 1995. (This is not a refining margin, as 100 tonnes of raw sugar makes only 92 tonnes of white sugar – in an efficient refinery.) The chart shows that the differential has been squeezed, relatively, in 1969, 1978, 1988 and 1993, but, discounting 1974 (a boom year), has followed a generally upward trend since 1970. From 1980, with the rise of EC production and exports, white sugar took an increasing share of gross world sugar trade, rising from around 30% in 1980 to above 50% in 1993 and 1994. The rising demand for white sugar (and the relative decline in demand for raw sugar) may explain the upward trend in the differential since 1980. The white/raw differential currently stands around 5 cents/lb ($110/tonne).

Deflated prices

Deflated prices are sensitive to the base year chosen for the deflator. Nevertheless, they do allow useful long term comparisons to be made.

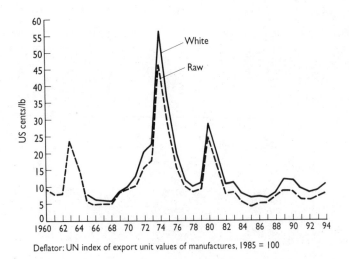

Deflator: UN index of export unit values of manufactures, 1985 = 100

10.3   Deflated raw and white sugar prices, 1960–94 (source: ISO).

Figure 10.3 shows raw and white sugar prices, from 1960 to 1994, deflated by the UN index of the export unit values of manufactures by developed countries with 1985 = 100. The average deflated raw sugar price for 1960–94 is 11.27 cents/lb, compared to an average over the same period for undeflated (nominal) raw sugar prices of 8.74 cents/lb. From 1965 to 1994 deflated white sugar prices averaged 13.81 cents/lb, compared to a nominal average over the same period of 11.95 cents/lb. The deflated average raw/white differential for 1965–94 was therefore 2.79 cents/lb ($61.50/tonne), illustrating the general upward trend in the differential mentioned earlier: the deflated average differential for 1995 was 3.25 cents/lb ($72/tonne). Table 10.1 shows decade average deflated white and raw sugar prices for 1960–94.

Table 10.1 confirms the long term decline in raw and white sugar prices, in real terms, since 1960. In spite of the increase in price

Table 10.1   Decade average deflated white and raw sugar prices, 1960–94, US cents/lb

	Raw sugar	White sugar
1960–69	9.26	
(1965–69)		(6.95)
1970–79	17.22	21.16
1980–89	9.27	11.81
1990–94	7.36	10.01

Note: Deflator: UN index of export unit values of manufactures, 1985 = 100. *Source: ISO.*

stability, the 1990–94 average real price of 7.36 cents/lb is 20% less than the average for the difficult 1980s (9.27 cents/lb), less than half of the average real price for the 1970s (17.22 cents/lb) and 20% below the real price for the 1960s. Figure 10.3 confirms that the lowest ever average real raw sugar price was recorded in 1985: 4.06 cents/lb.

Table 10.2 shows details of annual average raw and white normal and deflated prices for 1951–95.

Prices and stocks

Since sugar has a seasonal, 'lumpy' production pattern (see Chapter 5 and Fig. 5.1), and year to year production levels can be variable due to the effects of weather, the level of world stocks ought to be a good indicator of when prices are likely to rise or fall. Indeed it has been suggested that there is a critical level of stocks that will trigger a price rise or even a price boom. Because of its seasonal production pattern there is a question of when to measure stock levels. Clearly it is not correct, for this purpose, to measure stocks during or at the end of a major production period, since stock levels at that time will be inflated by sugar produced but not yet consumed or exported. Traditionally, the ISO measures stocks at end-December, but at this time the northern hemisphere beet crops have just finished and all the sugar produced in that season is in stock. Therefore, for the purpose of measuring the effect of stocks on prices, we follow F O Licht and measure stocks at end-August, when world stocks are at their lowest point, and as near as possible to carry over stocks.[3] Since the absolute size of stocks will rise with world production and consumption, it is important to define a relative measurement. Normally this is the stock/consumption ratio, because the purpose of holding stocks and maintaining a minimum carry over stock is to ensure that consumption needs can be met until sugar begins to flow from domestic production and/or imports. It is generally assumed that the supply 'pipeline' requires at least a minimum of two months consumption (17%) to keep supplies flowing without disruption.

Figure 10.4 and Table 10.3 show the stock/consumption ratio and

---

3 End-August is just before the northern hemisphere beet and the equatorial cane campaigns begin. Southern hemisphere cane crops start in June, but have not reached full production by August. There is no perfect time to measure world stocks, but end-August would appear to minimize the error.

Table 10.2 Annual average raw and white nominal and deflated prices, 1951–95, US cents/lb

	Raw sugar		White sugar		Raw/White differential	
	Nominal	Deflated	Nominal	Deflated	Nominal	Deflated
1951	5.75					
1952	4.22					
1953	3.46					
1954	3.31					
1955	3.29					
1956	3.51					
1957	5.20					
1958	3.55					
1959	3.02					
1960	3.12	9.18				
1961	2.75	7.75				
1962	2.83	7.86				
1963	8.34	23.17				
1964	5.77	15.81				
1965	2.08	5.58	2.90	7.79	0.82	0.98
1966	1.81	4.76	2.37	6.24	0.56	1.47
1967	1.92	5.05	2.32	6.11	0.40	1.05
1968	1.90	5.00	2.22	5.84	0.32	0.84
1969	3.20	8.42	3.33	8.76	0.13	0.34
1970	3.68	9.44	3.98	10.21	0.30	0.76
1971	4.50	10.59	5.71	13.44	1.21	2.85
1972	7.27	16.07	9.27	20.49	2.00	4.42
1973	9.45	17.83	12.05	22.74	2.60	4.91
1974	29.66	46.34	35.98	56.22	6.32	9.88
1975	20.37	28.00	25.38	34.89	5.01	6.89
1976	11.51	15.88	14.42	19.89	2.91	4.01
1977	8.10	10.19	9.71	12.21	1.61	2.02
1978	7.81	8.56	9.30	10.19	1.49	1.63
1979	9.65	9.32	11.77	11.37	2.12	2.05
1980	28.69	25.00	32.16	28.03	3.47	3.02
1981	16.83	15.48	20.50	18.85	3.67	3.37
1982	8.35	7.93	11.31	10.75	2.96	2.81
1983	8.49	8.36	11.37	11.20	2.88	2.84
1984	5.20	5.31	7.68	7.84	2.48	2.53
1985	4.06	4.06	6.80	6.80	2.74	2.74
1986	6.04	5.10	8.47	7.15	2.43	2.05
1987	6.75	5.27	8.74	6.83	1.99	1.55
1988	10.20	7.10	12.01	8.35	1.81	1.26
1989	12.82	9.12	17.21	12.25	4.39	3.12
1990	12.55	8.73	17.31	12.04	4.76	3.31
1991	8.97	6.27	13.41	9.38	4.44	3.10
1992	9.06	6.14	12.39	8.40	3.33	2.26
1993	10.02	7.20	12.79	9.18	2.77	1.99
1994	12.11	8.47	15.69	10.97	3.58	2.50
1995	13.28		17.99		4.71	

Raw prices: ISO daily price (average of New York No. 11 and London Daily Price or lowest +5 points, whichever lowest). White prices: 1965–85 Paris exchange; 1986–London Daily Price (Whites). Deflator: UN index of export unit values of manufactures from developed industrial economies, 1985 = 100. *Source: ISO.*

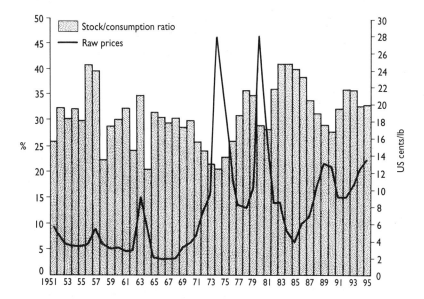

10.4 Raw sugar prices and the stock/consumption ratio, 1951–95 (sources: F O Licht and ISO).

Table 10.3 Raw sugar prices and the stock/consumption ratio, 1951–95

	Raw prices	Stock/ Consumption ratio, %		Raw prices	Stock/ Consumption ratio, %
1951	5.75	25.95	1974	29.66	20.42
1952	4.22	32.51	1975	20.37	22.88
1953	3.46	30.37	1976	11.51	25.96
1954	3.31	32.31	1977	8.10	30.98
1955	3.29	29.99	1978	7.81	35.77
1956	3.51	40.90	1979	9.65	34.80
1957	5.20	39.87	1980	28.69	28.79
1958	3.55	22.33	1981	16.83	28.13
1959	3.02	28.95	1982	8.35	36.05
1960	3.12	30.27	1983	8.49	41.02
1961	2.75	32.39	1984	5.20	41.00
1962	2.83	24.21	1985	4.06	40.00
1963	8.34	34.89	1986	6.04	38.39
1964	5.77	20.51	1987	6.75	33.80
1965	2.08	31.66	1988	10.20	31.19
1966	1.81	30.64	1989	12.82	29.03
1967	1.92	29.44	1990	12.55	27.72
1968	1.90	30.45	1991	8.97	32.25
1969	3.20	28.63	1992	9.06	35.96
1970	3.68	29.92	1993	10.02	35.86
1971	4.50	25.77	1994	12.11	32.64
1972	7.27	24.11	1995	13.28	32.86
1973	9.45	21.48			

Sources: FO Licht, ISO.

the raw sugar price from 1951 to 1995. Stocks are measured at end-August of each year, world consumption is for September–August of the appropriate year and prices are annual averages.

Figure 10.4 shows that there is indeed a relationship between declining stocks and rising prices. The price peak of 1957, when prices averaged 5.2 cents, coincided with a fall in the stock/consumption ratio to 22% in 1958. In 1964 the stock/consumption ratio had fallen to 20.5% and prices had peaked in 1963 at 8.34 cents/lb. In 1974 the stock/consumption ratio fell to 20.4% and prices averaged 29.66 cents/lb. This might have established 20% as the critical level, however, the next price peak in 1980, although associated with a fall in stocks, did not follow the pattern of earlier price peaks. The stock/consumption ratio fell to 28.8% in 1980 and 28.1% in 1981. This pattern was repeated in the next, much lower, price peak of 1989–90 (prices averaged 12.82 cents/lb in 1989 and 12.55 cents/lb in 1990, compared to 28.69 cents/lb in 1980) when the stock/consumption ratio fell to 29% in 1989 and 27.72% in 1990. Average prices exceeded 12 cents/lb in 1994 and 13 cents/lb in 1995, yet the stock/consumption ratio fell only to around 33% in both years.

Although a fall in the stock/consumption ratio to around 20% was a good indicator of a major price peak up to 1980, since then that linkage has been broken and the only conclusion that can be drawn is that a falling stock/consumption ratio is associated with rising prices.

An alternative approach to investigating the linkage between prices and stocks was developed by the ISO in 1988. The methodology involves removing the seasonal variation from stocks in individual countries so that they can be aggregated to a world total. From the deseasonalized stocks a constant, normal minimum carryover is subtracted. The resultant stock figure gives either surplus (positive) stocks or deficit (negative) stocks compared to 'normal' requirements.

Figure 10.5 shows world sugar surplus/deficit stocks and sugar prices from 1979 to 1996. It shows that surplus/deficit stocks have a strong negative relationship with prices. In 1979/80–1980/81 when prices were high, surplus stocks fell to low levels of 1.5 million tonnes in 1979/80 and 0.3 million tonnes in 1980/81. In 1982/83–1984/85 surplus stocks rose dramatically to over 9 million tonnes, and prices fell sharply to average only 4.05 cents/lb in 1983/84 and 4.39 cents/lb in 1984/85. By 1987/88 the surplus had been consumed and stocks went negative (deficit) to −1.45 million tonnes in 1988/89 and −2.16 million tonnes in 1989/90. Prices rose and averaged 13.91 cents/lb in 1989/90. In 1991/92–1992/93 surplus stocks again rose, to around 5 million tonnes, and prices fell back. From 1993/94 surplus stocks have fallen again and prices have firmed.

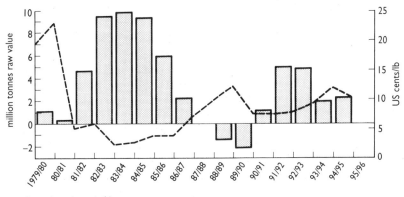

* stocks at the end of August
** September/August averages, 1994/95 – September/April average

10.5 World sugar surplus/deficit stocks* and sugar prices** (sources: F O Licht *International Sugar & Sweetener Report*; ISO records).

It is significant to note that from 1987/88 to 1989/90 surplus/deficit stocks fell to much lower levels than in 1979/80–1980/81, yet average prices were at 13.91 cents/lb, 10.75 cents/lb (44%) lower than in 1980/81. This illustrates the effect the structural change occurring during the 1980s had in lowering price peaks and making the world sugar price generally more stable than it has ever been. Table 10.4 shows world surplus/deficit stocks and raw sugar prices from 1979 to 1996.

Table 10.4 World surplus/deficit stocks* and raw sugar prices**

	Raw prices, US cents/lb	Surplus(+)/Deficit(−) stocks, million tonnes, raw value
1979/80	21.03	1.155
1980/81	24.66	0.299
1981/82	6.77	4.700
1982/83	7.60	9.500
1983/84	4.05	9.819
1984/85	4.39	9.354
1985/86	5.57	5.995
1986/87	5.62	2.281
1987/88	8.99	−0.011
1988/89	11.58	−1.454
1989/90	13.91	−2.156
1990/91	9.35	1.209
1991/92	9.17	5.019
1992/93	9.55	4.899
1993/94	10.99	2.015
1994/95	13.79	2.360
1995/96	12.00	

*stocks at the end of August. **September/August averages, 1995/96 September–December average. *Sources: F O Licht, ISO.*

CHAPTER

11

Futures markets

History

T he first futures markets were opened in Chicago around the middle of the nineteenth century to trade the main agricultural products such as wheat and soyabeans. The need arose from a desire on the part of farmers for an efficient and reliable method of hedging their production following some serious defaults on forward contracts by unscrupulous operators.

The great advantage that futures held over the old-style forwards was the lack of any counterparty risk; the futures markets themselves act as counterparty for both buyer and seller by guaranteeing the contract. Another advantage to users was the relatively cheaper outlay of only paying a small (usually around 10%, but negotiable) deposit followed by variation margins when and if the market moved against them. Quality guarantees were another feature introduced by the market operators which attracted trade and very soon the concept of futures trading was embraced enthusiastically by all sections of the trade and quickly flourished.

Futures trading in Europe, which was quick to follow the USA's lead, has enjoyed a chequered career. As with derivatives today, it suffered for years from a marked lack of understanding by many users and supervisors, with the resulting spectacular failure of several companies. This, coupled with some aggressive sales techniques on the part of crooked brokerage houses that simply churned a client's position until the entire sum invested had been swallowed up in commission, seriously hampered progress and it was not until the 1980s that futures trading became respectable and accepted as a serious investment vehicle. The boom in prices in 1994/95 gave it the impetus it needed to become recognized as an asset class in its own right.

The first sugar futures exchange was opened in Hamburg in 1880, followed by the London Terminal Market eight years later. The contract unit at that time was 400 tons of raw beet sugar FOB Hamburg. When the market was reopened after World War I, The contract was changed to white sugar ex bonded warehouses, London and the contract size was reduced to 50 tons. However, by 1929, tariff charges had virtually stopped the import of refined sugar, so the basis had to revert to raw sugar and the old white sugar one was de-listed in 1931.

All futures trading stopped again during World War II, and it was not until 2 January 1957 that the London sugar market reopened. Since then, with modifications and alterations, it has been trading to the present day.

Meanwhile, the Coffee Exchange of New York commenced operations in 1882 and, following the cessation of trading in Europe during World War I, added a sugar contract in 1916, changing its name to the New York Coffee and Sugar Exchange. It merged with the New York Cocoa Exchange in 1979 to become the New York Coffee, Sugar & Cocoa Exchange (CSCE) that we have today.

A white sugar contract was launched in Paris in 1988 and sugar futures are also traded in Tokyo and Rio de Janeiro. These three are very quiet and inactive.

When futures trading was resumed in London in 1957, it was known as the No.2 raw sugar contract and was a CIF contract, quoted in sterling. In 1979–80 this was replaced by the No.4 contract, denominated in US dollars. This lasted until 1984 when it was superseded by No.6 and changed to an FOB contract, but ceased trading in April 1993. In retrospect, the decision to change to a dollar-dominated contract can be seen as the beginning of the demise of raw sugar trading in London. This decision effectively wiped out arbitrage trading (see p. 161) which was the exchange's most lucrative income source and was followed by an inexorable decline in volume, from 155 875 lots in September 1989 to a low of 371 in January 1993.

Another decision, taken in 1991, put the No.6 contract briefly onto the London Commodity Exchange's Fast Automated Screen Trading (FAST) system. When this failed it reverted to open outcry, but confidence was not restored and the decline continued. After it ceased trading in 1993, brokers and traders still demanded a London raws contract, so, later the same year, the present No.7 contract was born. This has only minor modifications from the No.6 but was again placed on the FAST system. By this time, the traditional open-outcry method of trading had completely disappeared from the London sugar market. The FAST system enables orders to be matched up on screen and trades are executed in the brokers' offices. This has the advantage of being considerably cheaper than the former method and is becoming increasingly popular. It is considered by regulators to be quicker, safer and fairer than open outcry. A disadvantage of the system is the virtual disenfranchisement of the locals who are effectively excluded from trading sugar in London since their *modus operandi* entails eyeball-to-eyeball contact, making the market less volatile and less liquid than hitherto. It is not surprising, therefore, that the decision has had the opposite effect to that intended and has driven much business away from London. Indeed, apart from the spot month, the contract is seldom traded.

That, however, is not the case with the white sugar contract that was launched in 1987. Before that, during the 1970s, a differential contract was introduced but that was very short-lived as it failed to win the support of the refiners. The present contract (known as the No.5 white sugar contract) has proved far more successful and enjoyed soaring volumes in 1994 with prices reaching a four-and-a-half year peak in early January 1995. That contract now enjoys 65–75% of the market.

Current contracts

The London Daily Price

Every day a special committee, appointed by the market, establishes a London Daily Price (LDP) for raws and whites. These prices represent the value of prompt physical sugar as reported to the committee, with the general tone of the futures market taken into account. The LDP is a basis on which the fixing of physical contracts can be achieved and it is widely used by the trade; indeed, many deals are struck months and even years before delivery is due and are settled on the basis of the LDP on delivery. They are also widely used by governments and other bodies for other purposes, such as the fixing of subsidies by the EU. However, the introduction of Cuba as a permitted delivery country of origin caused problems with US operators who are not allowed by law to deal in Cuban sugar. This also had serious implications for investors and, as a result, a great deal of business was switched onto the No.11 contract, where Cuban sugar is not deliverable, to London's detriment.

Because sugar is so susceptible to supply problems, it attracts a large speculative interest. Speculator activity in sugar has always been very popular and this leads at times to violently fluctuating prices, subjecting the market to temporary distortions. For that reason, therefore, it is important to have a daily fixing-price that overrides technical squeezes and speculator-induced distortions and can be used as a yardstick by physical traders.

Contract specifications

There are, therefore, just two sugar contracts trading in London, the No.5 white sugar contract and the No.7 premium raw sugar contract. The latter is known as premium because it trades at a variable premium to the New York No.11 contract. However, the situation is academic since it is virtually tradeless; indeed the contract was suspended on 27 March 1996, having not traded since June 1995.

The specifications of the two contracts are as follows:

	No. 7 raw	*No. 5 white*
Contract size:	50 long tons	50 metric tonnes
Quotations:	US currency per lb FOBS, designated port	US currency per tonne FOBS, designated port
Minimum price fluctuation:	0.01 cents/lb	10 cents/tonne
Contract terms:	Raw sugar from current crop with min polarization of 96° and max of 98.99° shipped in bulk from specified origins**	White beet or cane crystal or refined sugar of any origin from current crop*
Delivery months:	January, March, May, July and October	March, May, August, October and December
Trading hours:	10.00–19.01 London time	09.45–19.00 London time
Last trading day:	12.00 hours on the last market day prior to commencement of the relevant delivery month	19.00 hours, 16 days prior to final market day of delivery month
Trading method:	FAST	FAST

* Following origins are tenderable: Argentina, Australia, Barbados, Belize, Brazil, Colombia, Costa Rica, Cuba, Dominican Republic, El Salvador, Ecuador, Fiji, French Antilles, Guatemala, Guyana, Honduras, India, Jamaica, Malawi, Mauritius, Mexico, Mozambique, Nicaragua, Peru, Philippines, Réunion, South Africa, Swaziland, Taiwan, Thailand, Trinidad, USA and Zimbabwe.

** Sugar to be stowed at one of the following designated ports: Amsterdam, Antwerp, Bangkok, Bilbao, Bremen, Buenos Aires, Cadiz, Delfzijl Dunkirk, Eemshaven, Flushing, Gdansk, Gdynia, Gijon, Guangzhou, Hamburg, Huangpu, Imbituba, Immingham, Inchon, Le Havre, Lisbon, Lixoes, Maceio, Matanzaz, New Orleans, Penang, Port Kelang, Recife, Rostock, Rotterdam, Rouen, Santander, Santos, Savannah, Shekou, Singapore, Stettia, Ulsan and Xiamen.

Polarization provides an indication of the purity of the sugar. The origin of the term lies in the behaviour of a beam of polarized light when passing through a solution of sugar. A solution of sucrose will turn such a beam to the right, whereas a solution of invert sugar will turn it to the left. The extent of the movement is a measure of the strength of the solution.

Options

Options, which are explained in detail later in the chapter, are also available on the white sugar contract, specifications of which are as follows:

Option type:	American
Contract size:	50 metric tonnes
Strike price increments:	$10/tonne
Minimum price fluctuations:	5 cents/tonne
Trading months	Same as futures
Trading hours:	Same as futures
Expiry date:	Close of first business day of the preceding month. Instructions to be given to Clearing House within one hour
	All options that expire in-the-money will automatically be exercised

The New York market

Four sugar contracts are traded on the CSCE, the No.11, or world, contract, a new white sugar one, the No.14 domestic and a white sugar contract. The last two are purely domestic contracts which are traded only intermittently and are highly illiquid. The No.11 contract, on the other hand, is truly a world contract and the only viable international vehicle for hedging raw sugar. It calls for the delivery of sound raw centrifugal cane sugar of 96° average polarization, FOBS in bulk in any one of 28 foreign countries as well as the USA itself. The No.14 domestic contract requires delivery of US origin raw centrifugal cane sugar, CIF duty paid, in bulk, at named Atlantic or Gulf ports while the white contract specifies delivery of refined cane or beet sugar. Specifications for the three oldest contracts are as follows:

	No. 11	*No. 14*	*White*
Contract size:	112 000 lbs (50 long tons)	112 000 lbs (50 long tons)	50 metric tonnes
Quotations:	Cents/lb	Cents/lb	Dollars/tonne
Minimum price fluctuation:	0.01 cent ($11.20/contract)	0.01 cent ($11.20/contract)	20 cents/tonne ($10/contract)
Contract terms:	Raw centrifugal cane sugar based on 96° average polarization	Raw centrifugal cane sugar based on 96° average polarization	Refined or white beet or cane sugar based on minimum 99.8° polarization
Delivery months:	March, May, July and October	January, March, May, July, September and November	January, March, May, July and October
Trading hours:	10.00–13.43 Closing calls start at 13.45	09.40–13.43	09.45–13.43
Last trading day:	Last business day of month preceding delivery month	Eighth, or next business day of month preceding delivery month	Fifteenth, or next business day of month preceding delivery month
Trading method:	Open outcry	Open outcry	Open outcry

The following origins are deliverable against the No.11 contract: Argentina, Australia, Barbados, Belize, Brazil, Colombia, Costa Rica, Dominican Republic, El Salvador, Ecuador, Fiji, French Antilles, Guatemala, Honduras, India, Jamaica, Malawi, Mauritius, Mexico, Nicaragua, Peru, Philippines, South Africa, Swaziland, Taiwan, Thailand, USA and Zimbabwe.

Deliverable growths against the No.14 contract are: cane sugars of US origin, duty free or foreign origin duty paid, and delivered in bulk.

To be deliverable against the world white sugar contract, parcels must be manufactured in the country of the delivery port (EU nations count as one country). However, this contract is now dormant and tradeless.

The New York CSCE also sets a daily spot price; this is posted a few minutes before the market closes for the day and is set by the exchange which rings around its members beforehand. This can lead to some anomalies if an important member is unavailable but, like the LDP, the price is widely used for settling maturing physical contracts.

The CSCE imposes position limits in all its contracts with options forming a part of that position if held. The actual limits are variable and subject to change at short notice. At present the limits on the No.11 contract are 4000 lots of any one month and 6000 lots in total. Straddles and arbitrage positions can usually be netted and there are exemptions for genuine hedging operations. At present, the CSCE, where the US futures contracts are traded, has no plans to convert to screen-based trading, preferring to stick to the well tried open-outcry method.

In June 1996 the CSCE launched a new white sugar futures contract to cater for those active in trading refined sugar and needing a more efficient hedging mechanism than the No.11 raw contract. It has never been satisfactory for refined operators to hedge on the raw sugar contract as the variability of price between the two gets more and more unpredictable as time goes on, making such a practice unacceptably risky.

The new contract calls for the delivery of 50 metric tonnes of white sugar processed from either cane or beet, allowing direct hedging of white sugar commitments by refined sugar processors, merchants and users throughout the world. Investment capital and speculative interest should be attracted to the new contract and, if it is successful, there will be many arbitraging possibilities.

The specifications of the new contract are as follows:

Contract size:	50 metric tonnes
Quotations:	Dollars/tonne
Minimum price fluctuation:	20 cents/tonne ($10/contract)
Contract terms:	White refined or crystal beet or cane sugar, in new woven polypropylene bags of 50 kg net, based on a minimum 99.8° polarization with a maximum moisture content of 0.08%
Delivery months:	March, May, July, October and December
Trading hours:	09.15–13.20 (New York time)
Last trading day:	Fifteenth of the month preceding the delivery month
Trading method:	Open outcry

Delivery points consist of 80 ports* worldwide which may be added to or deleted as circumstances dictate. The sugar must be manufactured in the country of the delivery port and there are solid restrictions on Cuban sugar which is not deliverable under any circumstances. EU delivery ports may take sugar from any EU nation.

---

* The deliverable ports are:

Argentina – Buenos Aires; Australia – Sydney, Mackay, Melbourne, Fremantle, Brisbane, Bundaberg and Townsville; Belgium – Antwerp; Brazil – Recife, Maceio, Imbituba/Itajai, Santos, Paranagua and Rio de Janeiro; Canada – Montreal and St John; China – Shanghai, Dalian and Huangpu; Colombia – Buenaventura; Costa Rica – Punta Morales; Dubai – Dubai; Egypt – Alexandria, Damietta and Port Said; El Salvador – Acajutla; Finland – Porkkala and Helsinki; France – Dunkirk, Rouen, Calais and Le Havre; Germany – Hamburg, Bremen and Rostock; Guatemala – Quetzal; India – Bombay, Kandla, New Mangalore, Tuticorin and Madras; Korea – Pusan, Inchon and Ulsan; Malaysia – Penang; Mexico – Vera Cruz/Tampico, Manzanillo and Mazatlan; Mozambique – Nacala, Beira and Maputo; Netherlands – Rotterdam, Flushing, Amsterdam, Delfzijl and Eemshaven; Nicaragua – Corinto; Pakistan – Karachi; Philippines – Manila, Iloilo and Ormoc; Poland – Gdansk/Gdynia; Portugal – Lisbon; Russia – Novorossiysk; Saudi Arabia – Jeddah; Singapore – Singapore; South Africa – Durban; Sweden – Malmo; Thailand – Bangkok, Kosichang and Laem Chabang; Turkey – Mersin; Ukraine – Odessa and Nikolayev; United Kingdom – Immingham; United States – Galveston, New Orleans, Savannah, Baltimore, New York and Crockett.

Sugar from Malawi is deliverable at Nacala and Beira. From Swaziland at Maputo and from Zimbabwe at Maputo and Beira.

Other markets

In 1988, a white sugar contract was launched on the Paris Bourse, by the Marché à Terme International de France (MATIF). Originally denominated in French francs, it was converted to US dollars in 1990 although instant conversion into French francs and/or Deutsche Mark is available to local traders. The specifications for that contract are as follows:

Contract size:	50 metric tonnes
Quotations:	US dollars/tonne
Minimum price fluctuation:	1 cent /tonne ($5/contract)
Contract terms:	White crystal sugar, beet or cane, from any origin; min polarization 99.8°; max moisture 0.06%; FOBS, trimmed, customs cleared and in approved port during delivery and following month
Delivery months:	March, May, August, October and December, 16 months forward
Trading hours:	10.45–13.00 and 15.00–19.00
Last trading day:	Fifteenth day of month preceding the delivery month
Trading method:	Open outcry

Approved ports are nominated by a specialized exchange committee.

The only other active sugar futures market is in Tokyo. It has a whites and a raws contract but is very small. Trading takes place only during four calls per day with none permitted outside those times. Prices are quoted in yen/kg and overseas traders are virtually excluded from taking delivery from the spot month as the necessary certificates are not available to them.

Options

In 1982, the CSCE, with its launch of sugar options on the No.11 contract, was the first US exchange to sanction these since 1936 when they were prohibited by law following a massive fraud perpetrated in the 1930s. Since then volume has grown steadily and traded options were launched in London in 1985.

Options are a very useful risk management tool for both the trade and speculators. In return for the payment of a premium (often but by no means always, around 10% of the strike price), the right but not the obligation is granted to buy or sell on the market on a given day in the future. If the price on that day is not acceptable, the trader simply abandons the option, losing only his premium. The main advantage is that one's losses are known, while profits can be quite considerable if the price continues to move in the right direction.

If the price is expected to rise, a call option is bought and if to fall, a put option is purchased. If by the exercise date the price has moved in the wrong direction or in the right direction but by less than the amount of the premium, the option is abandoned. Options are fully tradable in the market and there is always a thriving market in the most popular months.

Trading in sugar options has grown substantially in the last 10 to 15 years and is now a useful, popular and highly flexible hedging tool. Options are also very useful in ironing out violent price movements that speculative activity can sometimes generate.

Sellers, or granters, of options are usually in the trade, as it is necessary to have the physical sugar to back up the sale. Without such back-up, a seller is said to be writing a naked option, as he is completely uncovered and is consequently liable to substantial losses, even unlimited losses in extreme cases. For double the premium, it is also possible to purchase a double option. This is both a put and a call to each for a movement in either direction.

There are many option strategies available to the trader and many books have been written on the subject; another advantage of options is not having to pay variation margins. This is particularly helpful to fund managers who thereby gain extra gearing for further trading opportunities.

Uses of the futures markets

Hedging

It tends to be forgotten in today's jungle of trading strategies, that the original purpose of setting up a futures market in a commodity was to provide a vehicle which would enable the trade to hedge its exposure to significant adverse price fluctuations by taking a contrary position on it. Hence producers could protect their forward sales by buying futures and consumers could protect their forward purchases by selling them, with speculators, as often as not, taking the inherent risk.

Nowadays, risk has become an unacceptable operation on futures markets. So many futures transactions are now inter-linked with other, similar operations, all designed to beat some obscure index without losing money, that true hedging strategies have become extremely difficult, if not impossible. Since the greater part of such activity is now, in any case, largely concerned with protection from currency fluctuations, most hedging operations are now done on the currency markets.

Arbitrage

Arbitrage operations have been similarly affected. These operations entail buying sugar in one currency and selling in another, or on a different exchange. When the London market switched to a dollar-denominated contract in 1979, arbitrage operations virtually died out for a number of years. Hitherto, arbitrage had been an extremely lucrative source of revenue for both the exchange and its members, but it was not until the launch of the No.5 white sugar contract in 1983 that it was revived. Arbitrage trading between the No.5 contract in London and No.11 in New York is currently very active. These contracts, of course, also have to take account of the premium that

11.1 White sugar premium basis London Daily Price, 1986–96 (source: E D & F Man (Sugar) Ltd).

white sugar enjoys; this premium can fluctuate violently in certain circumstances and there are also times of temporary shortages, etc., so these operations can be quite exciting. The whites premium has ranged from almost $200/tonne in September 1989, to around $20/tonne in June 1993 (see Fig. 11.1).

AAs and EOs

Against Actuals (AAs) and Execution Orders (EOs) are two specialist trading operations between producers and consumers involving large deals of 10 000 tonnes or more that would not otherwise be possible to hedge satisfactorily.

AA deals are essentially a straightforward hedge; the difference is that both parties have agreed to the operation, from start to finish, for exactly the same reason that a smaller operator hedges his deals. Both sides take opposite action in physicals and futures; the producer selling futures to protect himself from a fall in the price and the consumer buying them against a rise in the price and to safeguard his sales up to the time the physical sugar becomes available to ensure continuity of supplies to his customers. Once the sugar does become available, the futures deals are liquidated at a price acceptable to both parties. The producer delivers the physical sugar in exchange for the same amount of futures.

The price at which the futures side is traded is usually by agreement and does not necessarily bear much resemblance to the prices paid on the market on that particular day, since both prices have to be the same to make the operation work and to eliminate any risk from hedge lifting or any unforeseen and sudden price movements. A member of the exchange has to act as middleman to register the futures transaction on the terminal market. To distinguish the trades from the day-to-day business of the exchange the letters AA are placed against the deal and this explains any discrepancy in the price.

EOs are a variation of AA deals but with a higher profile played by the exchange members. Essentially, an AA becomes an EO when both sides use different brokers or trade operators who therefore have to go on to the open market to set up the futures side of the operation. In this case, the price of the physicals would be the average of the futures selling price for the producer and the average of the futures buying price for the consumer. After the rest of the deal, such as premium or discounts, quantities and shipment period, etc. have been agreed, a small financial adjustment might need to be made.

The advantages to the physical operators of a scheme such as this is that they can fix the price of the actual sugar at any time they like during the period of the open futures position and in that way can benefit from any premium or discounts previously agreed. However, one drawback is that they would be liable for any margin call that may arise but it is not difficult to turn it into a fixed sale. Physical operators do not have to pay commissions on the futures side of such deals, only the actuals.

Brokers can, of course, do simultaneous transactions for both parties; any losses on the futures market would lead to adjustment to the physical invoice. It is a safe hedge.

Speculation

The speculator buys and sells futures purely for capital gain. Without this most maligned of participants, futures markets simply would not be able to function. It is the speculator who provides the risk and the liquidity that makes the market work.

These days, in order to spread that risk, speculators often use commodity funds to obtain added gearing for their operations. These funds constitute a large pool of money that is invested in a basket of commodities, spreading the risk across several markets. Because of this diversification the chances of success are that much greater. Trading strategies of commodity funds vary considerably, depending on the methods of the manager. The decision to enter a certain market is often determined by its trend; once the fundamentals signal a rise in price and the rise has started, the trend is established and in come the funds.

The tremendous growth in commodity fund investment during the 1980s and 1990s has had a profound effect on sugar futures prices – often to the disadvantage of hedgers. These machine-like trades have no interest in the fundamental position of a market – simply its price movements and the level of its liquidity and volatility. Once a trend has been established funds will pile into a market, seriously distorting the price for a short time and often pushing prices too far, too fast. Even when a bull move is entirely justified, funds will push prices to a level that bears no relation to the true market situation, simply through the sheer weight of orders. In addition, such actions can often trigger off yet more buy signals, pushing prices even higher.

Such self-fulfilling price actions seriously disrupt the activities of genuine trade users of a market and sugar is no exception. Much hedging activity is now done on the currency markets. The sugar market has always been very popular with speculators; such popularity could possibly be because it was one of the first London futures market to be re-opened after World War II.

Most commodity funds are not permitted to sell short on any market so it is only a bull market that attracts them. However, the individual speculator is not so constrained and has an equal opportunity of making (or losing) money whether the price moves up or down. A straight buy or sell trade is only one of a number of transactions available to a speculator: spreads,[1] straddles[2] and arbitrages are three others but with today's increasingly sophisticated derivative strategies the opportunities are manifold.

One result of fund activity is the speed with which the market falls back once the buying dries up. Once that happens, because there are no fundamental reasons to substantiate the high price levels, they fall back very fast – often too fast to enable the fund managers to take any decent profits. These price distortions have become a fact of life

---

1 A spread is a simultaneous deal in two different futures contracts such as raw and white sugar, buying one and selling the other, anticipating a change in the relationship between the two.

2 A straddle is a similar deal to a spread but in different trading positions, such as March and October, in the same futures contract where an alteration in the difference in the two is expected.

and tend to make life very difficult for the genuine trade operator. Nevertheless, the phenomenon is not going to go away – indeed it is likely to grow further and, although financial markets attract the lion's share of fund money, soft commodities such as sugar will continue to get a substantial slice of it.

Forecasting techniques

All users of futures markets, particularly the speculators, want to be able to forecast future price movements in order to make a profit on transactions. There are two main methods of forecasting – fundamental and technical. The former analyses the supply and demand situation – crop prospects and weather conditions play an important part in these calculations, as do stock levels, price elasticity and shipping conditions. It is a truism to say that if the fundamentals are right and properly assimilated, making a profit is a certainty. Unfortunately, there are so many imponderables, such as political events and sudden acts of God, that such is never the case.

A speculator, therefore, tends to rely more heavily on technical analysis. Since it is calculated that around 85% of speculator trades are losing ones, such analysis is more straightforward, even if it isn't any more accurate. Technical analysis is the science of trying to forecast future price trends from past ones. By plotting a graph of prices to date and identifying perceived support and resistance levels, one can build up a position of what might happen in both the short- and long-term future.

The techniques of such trading methods are both many and complicated and it is not appropriate here to go into details of their finer points.

Managed funds are also very fond of the technical analysis method and every commodity trading adviser (CTA) has his or her own pet scheme. CTAs stand or fall by their methods and failure is not tolerated for long.

Although this speculator-induced volatility sometimes turns the serious business of trade into something of a gamble, the sugar trade has to live with it. Despite the problems facing hedgers and other genuine trade operators, futures markets will continue to try to function for their benefit. However, with speculators assuming the risk, the prospect of huge profits will continue to attract both them and system traders. Without them, one must remember, futures markets would virtually cease to exist.

Regulation

Back in 1975, US market regulation was considerably tightened by the formation of the Commodity Futures Trading Commission (CFTC). This organization took over the duties of regulation from the US Department of Agriculture following the launching of new financial futures contracts. One of its chief functions was (and is) to ensure that futures trading meets its underlying purpose, i.e. to ensure there is a genuine trade-driven need for a new market. All new markets have to be approved by the CFTC and that includes approval of their rules. It also monitors traders' positions and imposes position limits on them to prevent any market manipulation. In addition, the CFTC imposes minimum training and capital adequacy standards on brokers and demands the total segregation of clients' funds from those of the company.

All this was widely resented by many US market operators and London benefited from a consequent influx of business. However, it wasn't long before stricter regulation came to London. Following the Gower report and the Financial Services Act of 1986, the Securities & Investments Board (SIB) was formed to set up self-regulatory organizations (SROs) for all financial services.

Under the SIB, the futures industry originally came under the auspices of the Association of Futures Brokers and Dealers (AFBD) but was later merged with the Securities Association to form the Securities and Futures Association (SFA). This oversees all the regulatory aspects of the industry. Its rulebook is very complex and detailed but this is not the appropriate place to discuss it in depth. However, amongst the more important requirements for members is the segregation of clients' funds, as mentioned above.

After many instances of investors losing large sums of money to unscrupulous traders, public opinion demanded adequate protection from such people, so now anyone wishing to work in the industry must show himself to be a 'fit and proper' person to do so. Unfortunately, there are at present no guidelines as to what exactly constitutes a fit and proper person – authorization by the SFA appears quite arbitrary. Much of the SFA's work is unobtrusive – a word here, a suggestion there – and, as far as the sugar market is concerned, seems to work very well.

Regulation in today's business climate is essential; the financial rewards for cutting corners and circumventing rules can be immense. Unregulated markets, as well as unsupervised staff, lead to unsociable behaviour. If the confidence of investors and speculators is to be retained, the markets must seem to be doing everything possible to ensure that the markets are honestly and openly supervised.

IV

The future

CHAPTER

12

▨ ▨ ▨

Key issues for the future

Structural change

A s we have seen in earlier chapters the world sugar market underwent a profound structural change in the 1980s and 1990s. Before 1980 it had been dominated by developed country importers like the USA and Japan. The high income countries with extremely low price elasticities followed or even drove price rises by pursuing their required supplies irrespective of the world price. This tendency was exacerbated because in both the USA and Japan more than 80% of sugar is used in products and large manufacturers are more concerned with maintaining product share than with the price. From 1980 developed country imports declined sharply as large HFCS industries developed, encouraged by the price booms of 1974 and 1980, in the USA in particular and in Japan and their consumption of sugar fell. At the same time, imports by developing countries rose, partly because of the rise in oil prices from 1973 (oil exporting sugar importers were the major source of import growth from 1973 to 1980), and partly because of the very low sugar prices in the mid-1980s.

The result of these trends was a reversal of the situation in the 1970s. By the late 1980s two-thirds of world sugar imports were accounted for by high price elasticity developing countries. Their reaction to rising prices was to purchase less, bringing more stability to world sugar prices. By the late 1980s the world raw sugar price had

Table 12.1 Annual average world raw sugar prices, 1988–94, US cents/lb

1988	10.20
1989	12.82
1990	12.55
1991	8.97
1992	9.06
1993	10.02
1994	12.11

Notes: Mean = 10.82. Variation about mean +2, −1.85. *Source: ISO.*

Table 12.2 Annual average world raw sugar prices, 1980–86, US cents/lb

1980	28.69
1981	16.83
1982	8.35
1983	8.49
1984	5.20
1985	4.06
1986	6.04

Notes: Mean = 11.09. Variation about mean +17.6, −7.03. *Source: ISO.*

stabilized around 10 cents/lb. Table 12.1 shows that in the seven years from 1988 to 1994 the annual average of the world sugar price varied only between 8.97 cents/lb and 12.82 cents/lb. The actual (daily) price was confined to a range of 7–16 cents/lb, which may not appear to be stable but compared to a range from 47 cents/lb in 1980 to less than 3 cents/lb in 1985, this is relative stability indeed.

The relative price stability coming to the market in the late 1980s to mid-1990s is emphasized if we make the same calculation for the seven years from 1980 to 1986. Table 12.2 shows annual average world raw sugar prices from 1980 to 1986.

Although the means are quite similar, 10.82 for 1988–94 and 11.09 for 1980–86, the variations about the mean speak for themselves: +2 and −1.85 for 1988–94 compared to +17.6 and −7.03 for 1980–86. Up to 1988 both importers and exporters had to wrestle with wild swings in prices which made forward planning extremely difficult. The new stability is welcomed by both sides.

There is no reason to think that the price stability seen since 1988 will not continue. The HFCS industries in the USA and Japan are well established and will continue to be able to operate under the umbrella of higher, supported, sugar prices – the GATT Uruguay Round agreement having had relatively little impact. In general, developed country consumption is stable, growing only with population growth, which itself is slow. Per capita consumption in the FSU is falling from the former subsidized level of around 50 kg and will probably stabilize at 30–35 kg, near the Western European average. Therefore, growth in sugar consumption and imports will be confined to developing countries, continuing the structural change of the 1980s and the first half of the 1990s towards greater domination of the import market by developing countries. World sugar market prices are therefore likely to become more stable as the share of developing countries in imports grows.

Perhaps unsurprisingly, because of its complexity, few comprehensive studies have been devoted to the future of the world sugar market. The best available was published jointly by FAO/ISO in 1992.[1] This study developed a 60 sector model to predict world production, consumption, trade and prices for the year 2000.

The model predicted that the growth rate of world sugar consumption in the 1980s will be almost maintained through the 1990s provided there is sustained income growth in developing countries. The growth rate estimated from 1990 to 2000 was 1.76%, compared to 2.07% from 1980 to 1990. Total world consumption is predicted to reach 128.3 million tonnes by 2000, a growth of 20.5 million tonnes over the base year, 1990, and compared to world consumption of 113.8 million tonnes in 1994 (exactly on track). Of the 20.5 million tonnes growth over the decade, 18.6 million tonnes (90%) occurs in developing countries, representing a growth rate of 2.7%.

According to the model, world production, weather permitting, has no problem keeping pace with the growth in world consumption. No capacity problems were identified. Normal, endemic, annual increases in mill or factory capacity run at almost the rate of consumption growth, and new mills or factories are constantly being constructed. The model estimated that world production in 2000 would be 127.3 million tonnes, a slight (1 million tonnes) deficit on consumption, but this was not the result of under capacity but rather a normal cyclical imbalance, which higher prices would be expected to correct in the following year.

The model predicted a healthy growth in world net imports of 3.9 million tonnes from the base year (1990) to 2000. World net imports were estimated at 25.5 million tonnes in 2000, compared to 21.6 million tonnes in 1990 and 22.9 million tonnes in 1994. Declines in imports by developed countries (mainly FSU countries) were more than offset by growth in developing country imports of 4.3 million

---

1 *The World Sugar Market: Prospects for the Nineties*, ESC/M/92/3, FAO, Rome, 1992.

tonnes over the decade. The share of developing countries in world net imports is expected to grow to 65% in 2000, compared to 57% in 1990. Virtually all the growth in developing country imports occurred in white sugar importers. However, any optimism that these results might engender in exporters should be tempered by two considerations:

1 The prices at which the growth in the market takes place are either below or equal to current prices in real terms.
2 An important part of the overall growth – about 2 million tonnes – comes from developing countries with low incomes.

The predicted growth in sugar trade would be seriously jeopardized unless all developing economies grow at a rate similar to that predicted by the UN which was used in this study. For example, a low income growth rate used as an alternative reduced the increase in total imports for 2000 by almost 1.5 million tonnes, or 40%.

The price predictions derived from the model confirm the stability discussed at the beginning of this chapter. The annual average raw sugar price for 2000 was estimated at 10.16 cents/lb in real, 1990 terms. Allowing for inflation and changes in the value of the dollar this would give a nominal price of around 12 cents/lb in 2000, close to current values. Table 12.3 gives a summary of FAO/ISO projections for 2000.

When first published in 1992 the FAO/ISO predictions were characterized in one press report as 'gloomy'. However, growth of almost 4 million tonnes in market size cannot be pessimistic. The gloomy tag arose for two reasons. First, the prices at which this growth can take place are similar to current prices (in the region of 10–12 cents/lb for raw sugar). This will clearly favour large, low cost, efficient exporters and may cause a further restructuring of exports in favour of countries like Australia, Brazil and Thailand. Secondly, such growth is consequent on income growth in developing countries –

Table 12.3 Summary of FAO/ISO projections for 2000, million tonnes, raw value

	1990	2000	Annual growth rate, %, 1990–2000
Consumption	107.8	128.3	1.76
Production	108.4	127.3	1.63
Imports	21.6	25.5	1.66

Sources: FAO, ISO.

something not obvious in the context of the recession of the early 1990s, when the study was published. Income growth at less than the average UN predictors used by the study would severely restrict growth in the market size. Overall, the study suggested that the maintenance of price stability would provide adequate growth in the world sugar market, but that exporters would have to make every effort to increase their efficiency and reduce their production costs in order to compete successfully in the market place.

The break-up of the USSR

Just when the world sugar market looked like beginning a period of consolidation after the upheavals of the 1980s the world's largest cohesive net importing region exploded politically in 1991 with immense consequences for the world sugar market. The USSR, through heavy subsidization of both domestic production and Cuban imports had raised consumption levels to almost 50 kg/person, among the highest in the world. Readjustment towards a market economy and free market prices for sugar led to a steep decline in consumption – to 30 kg in Russia by 1994 – and imports. Net imports in 1991, the last year of the USSR, were 4.83 million tonnes. Total net trade of the FSU in 1994 had fallen to 1.72 million tonnes. USSR consumption in 1987 was 14.95 million tonnes, by 1994 FSU consumption was down to 10.07 million tonnes, a drop of one third. Clearly the brunt of the precipitous drop in imports was felt by Cuba. In 1991 Cuba exported 3.83 million tonnes to the USSR, in 1994 Cuba exported only 1.03 million tonnes to the FSU. But the loss of consumption which caused world consumption to fall in 1993 is irreversible – it is highly unlikely that Russia will return to the heavy subsidies of the Soviet era. As already mentioned, Russian consumption will probably consolidate at around the Western European average of 35 kg/person.

If most of the impact of the loss of imports and consumption due to the break-up of the USSR has already been absorbed by the world sugar economy, there remains one area where the effects will continue through the 1990s: sugar production. This concerns the autarkic tendencies of Russia and the position of Ukraine as a sugar exporter. Under the Soviet system Russia was a major producer of sugar, producing up to 2.5 million tonnes. With the shortage of inputs since the break-up, Russian production fell to 1.65 million tonnes by 1994. However, experts in Russia believe that with relatively small capital inputs, a management attitude revolution and adequate credits to growers, the situation could be restored without the necessity of large inputs of capital. There are even ambitious plans to raise production to 3 million tonnes. In Russia 12% of GDP comes from the agricultural sector (compared to less than 3% in Western Europe) and it is unlikely that the rural sector will be abandoned to market forces, for social as well as economic reasons. Therefore some increase in production and a further decrease in imports can be expected.

Ukraine was the major producer of sugar under the Soviet system, producing up to 5 million tonnes and exporting 2–2.5 million tonnes to Russia, as well as refining most of the Cuban imports. Ukraine is an agricultural rather than industrial country and sugar is the major agricultural product of the country. In Ukraine the agricultural sector makes up more than 10% of GDP. Sugar production has also fallen in Ukraine since the break-up of the USSR. In 1994 it was down to 3.63 million tonnes. But the same arguments apply as in Russia – experts believe that with a revolution in management attitude and a concentration on making processing more efficient plus better yields from using Western European beet varieties, a relatively small input of capital can revitalize the industry. Since the Ukraine is even more rural than Russia, and has a higher proportion of the population in rural areas, it is again unlikely that the sugar economy will be abandoned entirely to market forces. Therefore an increase in Ukraine's production and exports is likely. Ukraine's natural market is Russia, and if Russia also expands production there is the prospect of meeting all its import requirements from Ukraine, closing the Russian market to other exporters.

Outside the FSU, Cuba suffered most in both general economic and sugar terms from the break-up of the USSR. The loss of the heavily subsidized export market provided a general economic crisis and the consequent shortage of inputs like fertilizer and spare parts for its highly mechanized sugar industry led to a steep drop in production. In the last years of the USSR, 1990 and 1991, Cuba produced 8.1 and 7.2 million tonnes, respectively. By 1994 output had fallen to 4 million tonnes and exports to 3.2 million tonnes from 6.8 million tonnes in 1991. However, sugar is vitally important to the Cuban economy. Since 1995 Cuba has permitted foreign investment in its sugar industry and this has been forthcoming. As a result, most of the sugar producing provinces are receiving fertilizer for the first time in three years. Allowing foreign investment should bring an improvement in production and efficiency and while Cuba may never return to production levels of 7–8 million tonnes it can be expected to achieve, in the future, 5–6 million tonnes depending on market conditions.

Because of the severe curtailment of its former main market, Russia, the resurgence of a new, more efficient Cuba can be expected to provide strong competition for other major raw sugar exporters – such as Australia and Thailand – particularly in the Far East.

Enlargement of the EU

Enlargement of the EU towards the east is becoming a political reality. In sugar terms it poses an immense problem for the policy makers. There is no doubt that the current level of the intervention price would cause an explosion of production if Poland, Hungary, the Czech Republic, Romania and Turkey acceded to the EU. It is doubtful if a substantial lowering of the intervention price would be politically acceptable to current EU members – but would a two-tier price system be acceptable to acceding members? A large increase in the world export availability from Eastern Europe could have severe consequences for the world sugar price.

Other key players

India and China can also be considered as key players. India, because it is the world's larger producer and consumer, will always interact with the world sugar market. As discussed in previous chapters, the Indian sugar cycle can produce such large swings that within the space of two years India can change from being a large importer to a large exporter (e.g. in 1994 India imported 2.65 million tonnes and in 1996 it may export 1 million tonnes). Sometimes India's imports can help to boost low prices (e.g. 1986), at other times they can exacerbate an already tight situation (e.g. 1994). But the relationship between the Indian sugar cycle and the world sugar market price cycle always needs to be monitored carefully.

China has been regarded as the potential saviour of the world sugar market in many quarters. With per capita consumption of only 6 kg and a huge population, there is clearly potential for growth. Yet there is no statistical evidence that sugar consumption would be allowed to keep pace with demand. Whenever China has been forced to import large quantities of sugar because of poor crops steps have been taken immediately to increase production. Consumption growth overall has kept pace with production growth. Nevertheless the Chinese economy, including the sugar sector, continues to be liberalized and it may be that the goal of self-sufficiency of the late 1980s, achieved briefly in the early 1990s, will be modified. Undoubtedly, China has the largest potential for growth in the world import market, but the outcome will depend on further modifications of policy.

White versus raw sugar

From the emergence of the EC as a major exporter in the late 1970s through the 1980s, growth in sugar imports was largely in the form of white sugar. The severe curtailment of the FSU market was another loss for raw sugar, borne by Cuba. Further losses could occur if Ukraine becomes the major supplier to Russia. And the FAO/ISO model quoted earlier in this chapter suggested that all the growth in imports up to 2000 would be in the form of white sugar. Prospects for raw sugar could be characterized as 'gloomy'. However, in the mid-1990s the opening of two new efficient super refineries in the Middle East (one in Saudi Arabia and one in Dubai), taking advantage of the lower transport cost of raw sugar in bulk, may offer a way forward for raw sugar in the late 1990s. Since the Saudi refinery will supply the whole of the domestic market, raw sugar will effectively replace white sugar in a 500 000 tonne market. Only time will tell if these ventures are successful, but certainly in the Eastern Mediterranean/Middle East region traditional white sugar suppliers such as EU and Turkey will face strong competition from refined raw sugar.

Alternative sweeteners

Twenty years have elapsed since the appearance of HFCS as an important calorific sweetener and although it has entered the sweetener markets of many countries it has made significant inroads in relatively few, namely the USA, Japan, Canada, Korea and Argentina. In most of these countries domestic sugar prices have been significantly above world sugar prices and this played a major role in the expansion of the HFCS industry from the mid-1970s onwards. Research by FAO/ISO has shown that expansion of HFCS production is largely a function of price.[2] In countries with high domestic sugar prices HFCS substitution for sugar is at or near its technological limit. The new (since 1988) stability of the world sugar market price, which is predicted to continue through the 1990s, should ensure that no new impetus is given to HFCS production in countries where domestic sugar prices are related to the world price. However, with HFCS production costs thought to be 12–14 cents/lb, if the world sugar market price was sustained above 15 cents/lb for a significant length of time, further investment in HFCS productive capacity could be expected, and this could, like the 1970s, present immense danger to the world sugar market. However, the gradual penetration of HFCS into developing countries seen from the 1980s is likely to continue, based on market or raw material niches in particular countries.

From the 1980s a boom occurred in high intensity sweeteners, led by aspartame, which will continue through the 1990s. So far they have not made significant inroads into the traditional sweetener market but rather seem to have retarded the rate of growth of HFCS and other non-sucrose sweeteners, as well as creating or expanding the 'diet' market. Despite the growth of alternative sweeteners during the last two decades, sucrose still dominates the global market and should continue to do so through the 1990s. In 1990 starch based sweeteners (HFCS and glucose) accounted for about 9% of the total sweetener market and high intensity sweeteners about 4%. By 2000 their combined share is expected to rise modestly from 13% to 17%, with sucrose accounting for the other 83%. However, as more research is carried out on new, improved high intensity sweeteners with heat resistance so that they can be used in cooked products, and with developed countries' preoccupation with diet, it can be expected that high intensity sweeteners will begin to encroach on sucrose and HFCS, rather than remaining confined to the diet market.

Vertical diversification

Sugar by-products (mainly bagasse and molasses) have always been partially used. But with the prospect of sugar prices confined to a

2 *Prospects for Alternative Sweeteners,* ISO MECAS (91) 26, London, 1991.

narrower range in future there is more of an incentive to, for example, make cane mills more energy efficient so as to produce more surplus bagasse. Bagasse can be used to make paper fibre board, animal feed and ethanol, etc. Surplus bagasse can be used for the co-generation of electricity for sale. Molasses can be fermented to produce alcohol – potable or industrial. From alcohol many derivatives, such as plastics or chemicals, can be produced. Vertical diversification offers a way to increase the returns on sugar cane cultivation and broaden revenue so that countries are less reliant on the sugar market price. With sugar prices unlikely to rise in the future, vertical diversification will become increasingly important.

Diversified end-uses

The sugar industry has always searched for non-food uses of sugar to supplement revenues from normal food use. Sucro-chemistry appeared to offer the possibility of beginning a hydro-carbon chain with sugar leading to plastics and other hydro-carbon products. But the falling oil prices of the 1980s made the use of sugar to produce these products uneconomic. Another possibility involves taking the production process one step backwards and using cane or beet juice to produce ethanol. This has been done on a large scale in Brazil and the possibilities have been investigated in the EU. The discovery of a new, non-food use for sugar could help to improve demand for the product.

I

Sugar and the environment

(A) Introduction

T he growing, processing and transporting of sugar is taking place in a rapidly changing regulatory context due to increasing environmental concerns. The extent to which current and prospective environmental legislation will affect consumer behaviour and the location and cost of production can barely be described let alone assessed. Much information is lacking in what – particularly from an international perspective – is a new subject. Much of the evolving national legislation reflects considerable scientific as well as economic uncertainty.

National legislation, by incorporating environmental cost considerations into sugar sector activities may well be changing the comparative advantage of producers and regions in sugar production. Possibly premature concerns have been expressed that in view of national differences (in legislation, ecology, stage of economic development) that a new round of government distortions will emerge and affect the functioning of the sugar and sweetener markets. Similarly, possibly premature hopes have been expressed that the concept of sustainable development will yield a rational process for the evolution of behaviour by governments, companies and individuals so that future generations will inherit, among other things, a more eco-friendly sugar sector.

A field of cane or beet or a sugar factory poses a variety of risks to an eco-system and so ecological management choices have to be made. Similarly in a national or the global context, sugar industry activities involve ecological management choices. This brief note attempts an overview of such issues in a context of the natural resources used (energy, air, water, soil, and land and biological), some of the costs of which are beginning to be included in the current economic calculus.

(B)   Global issues

Energy

While the extent to which the sugar industry in global terms has a positive energy balance is not clear, as life-cycle energy and emission accounts are not available, there is every likelihood the outcome would be positive. A feature of the relative efficiency of sugar cane and to a lesser extent sugar beet in transforming solar energy into plant materials is the energy potential. Bio-fuels for transport, notably an alcohol – ethanol – can be derived from sugar, while thermal energy – increasingly used for electricity generation – can be derived from bagasse – the residue from sugar extraction from cane. The amount of bagasse available has an energy value greater than the needs of the cane sugar industry. The 700 million tonnes or so available each year are equivalent to 90 million tonnes of coal or 50 million tonnes of petroleum (an amount equivalent to over 4 per cent of the petroleum needs of developing countries).

Air

The sugar sector makes positive and negative contributions to emissions of global significance. The practice of burning cane as means of reducing harvesting costs adds to carbon dioxide emissions. The burning of a tonne of cane waste produces 680 kg of particulates and dust. The 1992 UN Framework Convention on Climate Change and the objective of stabilizing carbon dioxide emissions at the 1990 level by the year 2000 is expected to contribute to the pressure on limiting this practice. Harvesting the cane green may well be in the interest of those holding the land rights as it can contribute to soil conservation. The sugar industry also contributes to global emission reductions as the addition of ethanol to petrol extends petrol supplies and contributes to less vehicle emissions.

Biological resources

Certain eco-systems, unique in global terms, including the Everglades wetlands in Florida USA and the Great Barrier Reef off Queensland, Australia are under pressure from sugar industry practices. Ecological concerns in the Everglades include the reduction in the size of the system, the organic soil loss (about 3 cms a year) and water pollution by nutrients (especially phosphorus).

From a global perspective insight into a variety of biological resource risks involved in growing cane and beet (dependency on a few varieties, adequacy of gene banks, extent of genetic erosion, decline in on-farm bio-diversity) is very limited. The 1992 UN Convention on Biological Diversity is designed to strengthen activities for in-situ on-farm and ex-situ conservation.

(C) National issues

Energy

While there are common pressures on the sugar industry in terms of energy conservation (and related emissions) the national circumstances and policy context in which the industry contributes to energy production vary a great deal. Alcohol production from cane is a feature of development in some Latin American countries that have limited domestic supplies of petroleum, notably Brazil. Similarly the development of the production of thermal energy from bagasse is taking place in varying regulatory and economic contexts. While some developing countries have been handicapped by their lack of capital in developing this energy source, in some developed countries – Australia and the USA (notably Hawaii) – the handicap has been the regulated nature of the electricity market.

In many cases the efficiency of the sugar sector in energy use is by no means clear. In addition to direct energy uses (diesel on farms, electricity in factories), certain inputs (fertilizers) can be relatively energy intensive (a tonne of nitrogen requires 1.8 tonnes of oil equivalent).

Air

A range of local air pollution risks are associated with the growing and processing of sugar. Safety concerns for the health of farm and factory workers are often the starting point for much of the regulatory controls. Farms can be a local source of pesticide spray problems, while if cane is burnt there may be local smoke and photo-oxidant problems. Factories can be a source of odour problems, while smoke from burning bagasse, and dust in waste gas can also be of concern to those living in the vicinity.

Water

The growing and processing of sugar, and the manufacture of alcohol are very water intensive processes that involve considerable pollution risks and conservation opportunities. Water management policies are often primitive, not least in terms of water pricing for agriculture. Though much of the world's sugar production is irrigated, little is known as to whether this involves adequate resource accounting. For example in Europe the recourse to spray irrigation for beet is typically in the summer season when rainfall and riverflow are lower so the additional stress on water resources can be significant and may not be captured in average historical pricing practices. Water pollution is a major problem. Sugar production involves the risk that runoff from rainfall and irrigation will carry pollutants such as sediment, minerals, nutrients and pesticides into rivers, lakes, ground water, estuaries and coastal waters. Nitrates from inorganic fertilizers are a major pollutant. In Europe, partly as a result of greater awareness of the issue, application rates on beet have fallen significantly with little impact on yields. Factory wastes can be a problem, production of alcohol leaves a residue – vinasse – in the proportion 13 litres per 1 litre of alcohol.

Soil

The farm sector of the industry has responsibilities for a significant share of soil resources in some countries. Though for farm families the maintenance of soil quality has long been an index of intergenerational equity the idea that governments have broad responsibilities for the stewardship of soil resources is relatively recent so explicit soil policies are still rare. Certain issues such as off-farm costs of soil erosion have prompted legislation. Cane growing offers higher value production opportunities than other enterprises (i.e. timber production) on sloping ground, though there are soil conservation risks if production techniques are not sound. Irrigation involves soil salinity risks. The heavy machinery used can compact soils. The practice of burning cane before harvest can damage or destroy micro-organisms important for fertility contained in the surface layer of soil. Beet production can be associated with some soil loss, as soil on the beets when they arrive at the factory is not returned to the field in which the beet was grown. In most cases it is not clear whether the soil degradation (physical, chemical, biological) and loss associated with the industry is outweighed by the soil conservation and creation also linked to the industry.

Biological resources

Greater accountability for the stewardship of biological resources used in the industry is a current feature of many national sugar industries; due often to a mix of self-interest and regulatory pressure. Again there are positive and negative features mostly associated with sugar growing, though some biological resources (yeasts) are directly employed in the processing sector. Further expansion of sugar production may involve the destruction and fragmentation of increasingly scarce habitats. The simplified agro-ecosystems, whether based on cane or beet in conjunction with cereals, provide very limited habitats and accelerate pest and disease evolution and thus resistance. The recourse to biological control techniques involves risks. With the benefit of hindsight it has become apparent that some introductions – such as cane toads into Queensland, Australia – were mistaken. As a science based industry with a strong research tradition the industry is well positioned to make better use of biological resources as well as respond to the challenges of biological resource conservation; however the policy signals are confusing. Better use of interactive biological values (between crop species, plant density, rotations, nutrients, moisture pests, temperature, etc.) is hampered by policies. Government research (typically focused on yield improvements by breeding) and regulations (i.e. pest control) and commodity specific producer assistance (payments per tonne) do not add up to a package focused on interactive biological values.

Land

National land resource situations – in terms of surface area (a non-renewable resource and landscape, a partly renewable resource) – vary. Such differences underlie the important role of trade in the sector. Within countries competitive pressure from urban needs is leading, for example, to a reduction in the scale of Hawaiian sugar industry and a re-location of some of the industry in Thailand; while general land use pressures are leading to rapid changes in the distribution of production in China. In many developed countries with stable consumption patterns the spatial requirements of the industry are declining as yields rise. This substitution by technology for land in the sugar sector results in the availability of arable land for alternative uses, including conservation uses.

(D) Industry-wide approach

Environmental progress in the sugar industry has largely been a fragmented and often defensive reaction to the enactment of environmental legislation and growing public awareness. The South African sugar industry decided to approach the problem head on and develop an environmental plan covering the whole industry. This plan is reproduced below as an example of this approach:

The sugar industry and the environment

Environmental mission

The South African Sugar Industry will use its best endeavours to set an example of sound environment resource management and protection of the Sugar Industry's natural resources.

In the light of this Mission, the following Environmental Plan will be undertaken by the Sugar Industry.

Objectives

- To conserve and protect the environment within the territorial boundaries of the Sugar Industry.
- To coordinate all environmental work for the Sugar Industry.
- To win respect and credibility for the preservation and correct use of natural resources within the Sugar Industry.

Key issues

- The need to coordinate all environmental effort within the Sugar Industry.
- The need to conserve catchments within the Sugar Industry, including all rivers, streambanks, and wetlands.
- Alien plant control.
- The need to minimize atmospheric pollution created by cane burning, factory emissions, and the use of pesticides. Also control impact of mill effluent from sugar cane factories and other associated processing plants.
- Cane spillage.
The need to maintain contact with research and environmental bodies and to be aware of and stay abreast of other environmental projects.

Strategies

To achieve the stated objectives, the Environmental Management Plan will employ the following strategies:
- Continuously monitor and analyse threats and opportunities arising from the industry's activities and simultaneously suggest and advise appropriate action.
- Educate and inform internal stakeholders (partners, employees) about environmental issues that affect the industry in order to optimize the coordination of internal action.
- Concentrate resources on issues that fall within the industry's sphere of influence and responsibility.
- Continue to acquire a database of facts on geographic, topographic, agronomic, climatic, and other attributes for scientific research.
- Regularly measure our progress against scientific criteria in order to maintain credibility and momentum.

– Effectively communicate the achievements of the industry in order that the special interest and public groups will acknowledge and endorse the industry's Environmental Management Plan.

Audiences

Millers, growers, the Sugar Milling Research Institute and South African Sugar Association Experiment Station, the general public in growing areas and in non-growing areas, the Republic of South Africa government, the KwaZulu government, the KaNgwane government, local governments, special interest bodies such as the South African political groups, environmental writers, universities and other academic bodies, and the South African Police.

Method and time span

Present an action plan defining responsibility and setting time boundaries. The plan will be reviewed quarterly by management and the Environmental Sub-Committee.

Action plans

Assign responsibilities for and execute the following:

– **Coordinate activities of the Industry Environment Committee.** Liaise with committee representatives and sections to set up a coordinated structure, with three joint meetings a year. Overall, endeavour to enhance the environmental awareness in the industry. Every farmer, miller, and staff member will be encouraged to participate in the Environmental Management Plan.

– **Map and record relevant industry data.** Continue the present soil and water research programmes involving runoff plots, catchment projects, rainfall simulation, and computer modelling. Continue to promote the implementation of sound agricultural practices (Land Use Plan's farm assessments, drainage lines, wetlands). Establish the status of wetlands in the industry and provide guidelines for the preservation and correct utilization of existing wetlands. Develop a Wetland and Resource Register, using a geographic information system.

– **Alien plant control.** Liaise with Cedara Weeds Laboratory to undertake an alien invasive plant control programme.

- **Cane burning.** Educate growers and the public about burning, using industry guidelines and South African Sugar Association Experiment Station data.

- **Cane spillage.** Influence growers, millers, transport companies, and traffic authorities in an awareness campaign in order to reduce cane spillage.

- **Continue to develop strong contact with environmentally active groups.** For example, the Departments of Agriculture representing all three houses of Parliament, the Department of Water Affairs, Earthlife Africa, Wildlife Society, Department of Environmental Affairs, etc.

Provide a technically competent representative to sit on the Council for the Environment or its sub-committee who can respond to any queries with regard to sugar cane agriculture. Continue with representation on the Wetlands of Natal and KwaZulu Steering Committee. Continue cooperation with governmental units, and continue to liaise with the conservation bodies, both nationally and regionally, seeking awareness and respect from these bodies for the Industry's environmental programmes.

Internal awareness and education

Concentrating our resources on issues that fall within our sphere of influence and responsibility among the industry by informing and educating members on all previously identified issues, and specifically:

- Set aside a 'green page' in each edition of the *Sugar Journal* on environmental issues, along with ongoing education about cane burning, strip cropping, etc.

- Initiate industry-wide presentations on environmental subjects, with speakers visiting mill group areas. Involve environmental committees, the local growing community, and bodies such as the Agronomists' Association.

- Commission a video illustrating achievements within the industry relating to agricultural practices and conservation for distribution to growers and millers.

Internal/external awareness

- Extend the South African Sugar Association Study Kits to include environmental posters.

– Assist with communication for regional industry efforts at highlight events, e.g. farmers' days, conservancy meetings, awards.

– Institute a planned programme of bringing specialist audiences face-to-face with growers through farm visits – with emphasis on environmental practices.

Direct publicity

Prepare general editorial material on all major achievements in the broad environmental field (soil conservation, Small Growers' Financial Aid Fund, KwaZulu Water Development Fund, etc.) and place these strategically. Prepare advertising, including endorsements by conservation organizations. Use industry facilities for conservation themes at exhibitions, tour centres and visit programmes.

(E) The ISA and the environment

The 1992 ISA is the first agreement to contain a reference to the environment. The text of article 30 reads as follows 'Members shall give due consideration to environmental aspects in all stages of sugar production'.

While an agreement without sanctions can have little direct influence and the wording of the article is very general, there are indirect ways, apart from discussion and debate, that the ISO can influence environmental matters. For example, through its role as an ICB to the Common Fund for Commodities the ISO can promote environmentally friendly projects. Indeed all the projects approved or under active consideration by the CFC have a positive environmental element. The GEPLACEA project approved in 1993 and sited in Cuba involves the treatment of waste at factories producing alcohol from molasses to yield biogas and yeast; the GEPLACEA project for promoting alcohol fuel programmes, approved in 1994, will investigate the addition of alcohol to gasoline which can reduce automobile emissions; and the Indian integrated pest management project as designed to reduce pesticide use.

II

Sugar and health

The role of sugar in the diet

In foods sugar plays many roles, as a taste enhancer, a bulking agent, providing texture, preserving, elevating the boiling point and depressing the freezing point and as an antioxidant. Its value in the diet, however, is in providing energy (calories) and in making a variety of foods palatable.

In developed, industrial countries population growth rates are declining and the average population is ageing at the same time as labour is shifting from manual to sedentary occupations. Average daily energy requirements are falling. All elements of the diet providing energy therefore come under pressure as diets slowly adapt. But sugar remains an important source of energy in developed country diets (see Chapter 6, Table 6.1) with shares of total energy intake varying from 9% to 17%, and the average for all developed countries in 1988–90 standing at 12%.

In developing countries there are wide variations in sugar consumption according to culture, income levels, availability, etc., but in many, particularly large sugar producers and exporters, sugar is an important source of cheap energy. According to Viton (1990),[1] in Colombia 100 calories in the form of white sugar cost 0.86 US cents, in the form of bread 5 cents, 2.6 cents in the form of potatoes and 10 cents in the form of rice. In El Salvador and Guatemala 100 calories in

---

1 Viton, A (1990) 'Sugar and the WHO Study Group. The battle continues'. F O Licht, *International Sugar and Sweetener Report*, Vol. 122, No. 36.

the form of sugar cost slightly less than 1 cent, and 2–5 times as much in the form of bread, corn, rice or potatoes.

Table 6.1 in Chapter 6 illustrated the wide variations in sugar consumption and sugar's share of energy intake in developing countries. Latin American countries, generally sugar surplus countries, have high levels of consumption and the share of sugar in the provision of energy reaches high levels in Brazil (18%), Guatemala (19%) and Cuba (21%). The average for South America is 16%. In sub-Saharan Africa levels are low, mainly for economic reasons, and the average for the whole of Africa is 6%. The average for Asia is also relatively low, partly for cultural (dietary) reasons, at 5%. Overall, in developing countries sugar accounts for 7% of energy intake with an annual average per capita consumption of 15.2 kg. Because of the greater contribution of developed countries the world average is higher, with sugar supplying 8% of world average energy intake at a per capita consumption level of 20.8 kg/year.

A review of attacks on sugar for health reasons

Having survived unscathed for centuries, first as a prized luxury and then as a common, harmless, household food, sugar first felt the weight of scientific criticism almost 50 years ago.

Sugar and obesity – late 1940s

It was proposed that excess sugar intake led to obesity which is linked to conditions such as hypertension, coronary heart disease, diabetes, gallstones and other gastrointestinal diseases. Changes in body fat are governed by the balance between energy intake and expenditure. Many factors cause the variations, such as physical stature, age, weight and physical condition, i.e. obesity can occur in subjects as they grow older as a result of decreasing exercise leading to reduction in muscle mass resulting in a declining basic metabolic rate, and failure to adjust eating habits. Other factors at work may include genetic (hereditary) or psychological (reaction to anxiety, depression, boredom, etc) problems. On the other hand, several eminent scientists (e.g. West) concluded that on balance the evidence is against any connection between sugar consumption and obesity. Fat is more fattening than carbohydrate because it costs less energy to store dietary fat than to store dietary carbohydrate and *even when carbohydrate is consumed in excess very little is converted to body fat.*

Dental caries – from 1950s

Sucrose is involved in the mechanism of dental caries in that it provides an energy source for cariogenic bacteria. However, good dental hygiene, and especially fluoride, effectively controls and even eliminates caries.

The use of fluoride in drinking water has had a marked effect in reducing caries. In developed countries in recent years the increasing use of fluoridated toothpaste has significantly reduced rates of dental caries, independently of any changes in sugar consumption. Fluoride acts principally by strengthening the enamel and by having an effect on the dental plaque. Writing in the WHO publication *World Health* Marthaler (1994)[2] states that, 'while the daily practice of tooth brushing with a dentifrice relies on the individual, the users are in fact the largest community to benefit from fluoride. Their number exceeds a thousand million, which is far above the numbers reached by other fluoridation methods. The beneficial effect has been proved, both on the experimental and the population level. Fluoride dentifrices are the only common cause of the dramatic decline in the prevalence of dental caries which is evident in many highly industrialized countries.'

Sugar and cardiac diseases – late 1960s

Yudkin (*Pure White and Deadly*)[3] showed that large doses of sugar caused arterial disease in rats. He proceeded to write the ubiquitous book condemning sugar. He maintained that the correlation with heart disease rates was stronger with consumption of sugar than with that of fats.

As well as being refuted by many individual pieces of research several expert committees have published reports expressing doubts about a causal relationship between sucrose intake and heart disease and none have made specific recommendations for reducing sugar consumption. For example, in 1975 the *World Review of Nutrition*

2 Marthaler, TM (1994) 'Fluoridation at Community Level'. WHO *World Health*, Vol. 47, No. 1.

3 Yudkin, *Pure White and Deadly*, Davis-Poynter, London, 1972.

and Dietetics concluded that the evidence available did not support the view that sugar in the amounts present in diets, such as the USA was a causative factor in the development of cardiac heart disease. In 1976, the Royal College of Physicians and the British Cardiac Society concluded that there was no firm evidence linking sugar intake and coronary heart disease. In 1976, also, the Federation of American Societies for Experimental Biology, in a statement prepared for the FDA, stated that, with regard to cardiovascular disease 'There is no evidence in the available information on sucrose that demonstrated a hazard to the public when used at the levels now current and in the manner now practised'. In 1981, the UK Department of Health stated 'not one of the expert committees has specifically recommended cutting down on the amount of sugar in the diet as a direct way of preventing cardiac heart disease.' In 1984, the UK Department of Health reported the findings of an expert committee (COMA) which considered diet and cardiovascular diseases. The panel recommended that the intake of simple sugars should not be increased further but pointed out that any reduction of sugar intake was not based on cardiovascular health grounds.

It is clear from the work of these committees and expert groups that the data does not support a causal link between refined sucrose consumption and heart disease.

'Empty calories' – 1980s

Refined sugar stood accused of supplying only calories and no other nutrients, vitamins, mineral or proteins. The function of sugar in the diet is to make many foods palatable and to keep the diet varied. Because appetite is geared to the control of energy, it has been claimed that consumption of foods rich in sucrose might reduce the desire for other sources of energy. Sucrose intake at the expense of other carbohydrate such as starch was of particular concern since starch, when obtained from cereals, pulses and vegetables, is accompanied by a wide range of health promoting micro-nutrients. Additional sugar consumption might therefore add to micro-nutrient dilution. But sugar stands as an energy source in its own right and brings to food consumption many desirable properties like taste, texture, preservation, etc. Other necessary nutrients can be obtained from other sources. No evidence that sugar leads to a significant reduction in micro-nutrient intake has been forthcoming. The only clear evidence is that sugar consumption seems to discourage consumption of fat.

A feature of recent decades has been the decline in direct ('table-top') consumption of sugar and the increase in indirect consumption incorporated into food products. In Western Europe around 65% of sugar consumption is in the form of products, in the USA and Japan more than 80%. Sugar intake in association with other foods affords the opportunity for the intake of micro-nutrients contained in these foods.

WHO report – 1990

In 1990 a WHO Study Group on Diet, Nutrition and Prevention of Noncommunicable Diseases published its report entitled 'Diet, Nutrition, and the Prevention of Chronic Diseases'[4] which set out population nutrient goals. Their goal for free sugars was: lower limit 0% of energy, upper limit 10% of energy. Although the Group, in its explanation, first cited dental caries as a reason for limiting free sugar intake, it went on to admit that fluoride (including fluoride in toothpaste) and oral hygiene practices had 'confounded' the positive correlation between increasing sucrose use by the population and increasing dental caries rates. The Group also cited the empty calorie argument: 'The other concern relating to excessive use of free sugars is that they provide energy without associated nutrients and hence displace nutrient-containing foods.' The Group favoured energy intake through complex carbohydrates rather than free sugars because of beneficial effects on intestinal function and recommended a lower limit of 50% energy, setting the upper limit at 70%. Thus sugar found itself squeezed by the Group's preference for other, complex carbohydrates. Elsewhere in the report the Group referred to concerns expressed about sugar causing the development of obesity and thereby diabetes and cardiovascular disease, but went on to say that 'there is little evidence that sucrose or other free sugars have specific effects that would warrant a lower intake than that recommended to minimize the problem of dental caries. Any greater intake, however, could be disadvantageous in that free sugars in the diet displace other energy sources such as starches which, when obtained from cereals, pulses and vegetables, are accompanied by a wide variety of micronutrients.' No evidence, however, was cited in support of statements that sugars displace more 'useful' foods in the diet.

4 'Diet, Nutrition, and the Prevention of Chronic Diseases', 1990. Report of a WHO Study Group, Technical Report Series 797, WHO, Geneva.

The publication of such goals by an authoritative body like the WHO provoked great concern in the sugar industry, especially since the upper limit was significantly lower than sucrose intake in most developed countries and many developing countries. It was seen by the industry as part of a campaign against sugar and that such goals and views, with the weight of the WHO behind them, could severely damage the reputation of sugar and even the industry itself. Viton (1990)[5] calculated that the implementation of the goals would mean a reduction in consumption of 19 million tonnes (17% of world consumption), a reduction of 6–6.5 million tonnes in imports (one quarter of world imports) and the loss of 1 million jobs, without taking into account the consequences of a sharp fall in the world price because of initial oversupply. Although it is unlikely that the WHO goals would be formally implemented, they have already influenced government sponsored guidelines in some developed countries and there is no doubt that they have provided strong ammunition for campaigns against sugar.

Positive reports

Not all the institutional enquiries into sugar have been negative. Perhaps the most exhaustive was that of a Sugars Task Force established by the Federal Drug Administration (FDA) in the USA which made its report in 1986 entitled 'Evaluation of Health Aspects of Sugars Contained in Carbohydrate Sweeteners'. Some of its conclusions were: on diabetes 'There is no evidence to support a change in the . . . conclusion that the consumption of sugars is not related to diabetes other than as a non-specific source of calories'; on hypertension 'No evidence was found to support the contention that the current dietary intake of sugars contributes to the development of hypertension'; on arteriosclerosis and heart disease 'No new epidemiological or clinical survey evidence has emerged [since 1976] which indicates a link between sugars intake and cardiovascular disease for the general population' and 'there is no conclusive evidence that dietary sugars are an independent risk factor for coronary artery disease in the general population'; and on obesity 'The available data support the conclusions that sugars do not have a unique role in the biology of obesity.'

5 Viton, A (1990) 'Sugar: That which we all love, some love to hate'. F O Licht, *International Sugar and Sweetener Report*, Vol. 122, No. 4.

The overall conclusion of the Task Force was that 'Evidence exists that sugars as they are consumed in the average American diet contribute to the development of dental caries. *Other than the contribution to dental caries there is no conclusive evidence that demonstrates a hazard to the general public when sugars are consumed at the levels that are now current and in the manner now practised.'*

In the UK a similar exercise, in 1989, by the Committee on Medical Aspects (COMA), reached almost the same conclusions. The report confirmed the role of sugar in dental caries but largely exculpated sugars from being a direct cause of diabetes or coronary heart disease, and sugar calories were judged as no more implicated in obesity than calories from other foods.

Conclusion

Although sugar has been blamed for causing and contributing to many diseases, nothing has been proved against it except for its role in the development of dental caries. But even this case against sugar has been weakened by the substantial reduction in the prevalence of caries achieved by the increasing use of fluoride toothpaste, while sugar consumption is static or grows in most countries. Moreover, it should be borne in mind that recent data shows that cooked starches and all sugars, not just sucrose, are potentially cariogenic.

The most damaging consequence of the attempts to implicate sugar in the development of specific diseases, and the recommendations of expert groups like the WHO to reduce sugar intake, is the public perception that sugar is in some way a harmful constituent of the diet. Hence it is possible to advertise 'sugar free' as a positive selling point.

Another damaging perception is that sugar is fattening, when there is strong evidence that a high fat intake is more likely to be associated with excess energy intake leading to obesity than a high intake of sugars. Recent research indicates that excess carbohydrate is burnt off and not converted to fat. Within populations, intake of sugars is inversely related to the prevalence of obesity. Likewise, within populations, Body Mass Index (BMI)[6] and intake of carbohy-

---

6 An internationally recognized measurement of the body's condition; the ratio of weight (kg) divided by the square of height (m). The higher the value received, the more overweight the subject.

drates are inversely related, whereas BMI and percentage of energy from fats are positively correlated. Fat is more likely to promote the development of obesity, and metabolic studies support this association for several reasons: fats have a higher energy density than carbohydrates, the ability to store excess energy from carbohydrate is limited, whereas the ability to store excess energy from fats is large. Carbohydrate intake in excess of energy needs promotes an increase in oxidation, and is not converted efficiently to fat. In contrast, excess energy from fats does not promote lipid oxidation and can be stored directly as lipid.

The studies briefly reviewed here also indicate no scientific justification for associating sugar with cardiac disease or nutrient dilution.

It is significant that the FAO/WHO Rome International Conference on Nutrition (December 1992) deliberately deleted a reference to sugar with diseases in the 'Plan of Action' it prepared, which could have led to an association of sugar with diseases.

But the continuation of damaging propaganda and perception makes it necessary to continue scientific research on all nutritional aspects, and to disseminate the information on the findings. Also, there is evidence from various parts of the world that nutrition officials working on the preparation of national Plans of Action, in implementation of the International Conference on Nutrition recommendation, are promoting the '10% maximum, 0% minimum' guideline, although not approved by the International Conference on Nutrition, in view of the importance that nutrition policies should be based on the best medical findings, not fads and fashions.

It is quite clear that sugar plays a valuable role in the diet of developed and developing countries both as an important energy source and a taste enhancer making other foods more palatable. The scientific objections to sugar were all hypothetical, and none of them, except for dental caries, have been proven. The question of what is a reasonable level of consumption of sugar has been raised by the debate, and it has not been satisfactorily answered. No conclusive evidence has been produced of what the limit for sugar intake should be, and therefore there is no evidence that current levels of consumption, anywhere in the world, should be reduced.

The ISO invites members to make suggestions for further activities of the Organization in the field of sugar and health. The secretariat intends to develop closer relations with the Sugar Bureau and the WSRO in the UK, and with sugar associations in other countries with a view to providing more information to members on campaigns to improve the image of sugar and rebut specific attacks.

Members should consider whether periodic reviews of the latest medical and nutritional research on sugar would be useful and what additional international action would be appropriate.

III

The Brazilian alcohol programme

The Brazilian sugar and ethanol industry: performance and prospects[1]
by
Peter Buzzanell and John C Roney

S ugar, from beets or cane, is produced in virtually every country on the globe. Yet Brazil's sugar industry is unique, and its role among the world's producers is singularly important.

Brazil is either first or among the world leaders in sugarcane, sugar and ethanol (fuel alcohol) production, and in sugar consumption and exports. In addition, it is among the most efficient of all the major sugar producers and its sugar export products are the most diverse.

Because global sugar stocks are declining and world prices are rising, attention is focusing on Brazil as the country that could respond most rapidly to a potential world sugar shortfall, since less than half its cane is currently ground for sugar. Brazil's sugar and ethanol industry will, however, face new challenges in the late 1980s in servicing the nation's growing domestic food and fuel requirements. Meanwhile, the government must cope with large public-sector

1 Reprinted from *Sugar and Sweetener,* USDA, Washington, July 1988.

debt problems that threaten its subsidization of the sugar and ethanol industries.

Giant of the south

Brazil is by far the world's leading producer of sugarcane, currently producing close to 250 million metric tonnes from over 4 million hectares. Only India comes close, with 185 million tonnes from 3.3 million hectares. Cuba, the third largest producer, turns out about 68 million tonnes of cane from 1.5 million hectares. Brazil has tripled production since the mid-1970s, largely by expanding sugarcane acreage while investing in milling capacity and ethanol distilleries (Table III.1).

Even though about 60% of Brazil's cane is ground for ethanol, it is consistently among the world's top three sugar producers (Figures III.1 and III.2). Its most recent three year production average of 8.4 million tonnes, raw value, trails only the Soviet Union and India.

Table III.1 Brazil: sugar cane production for sugar and ethanol

| Year | Area Million ha | Sugar cane production | | | Production | |
| | | for sugar | for ethanol | Total | Raw sugar | Ethanol |
		Million metric tonnes			Million litres	
1975/76	1.969	68	0	68	6.200	0.580
1976/77	2.093	88	0	88	7.500	0.642
1977/78	2.270	99	7	106	8.863	1.388
1978/79	2.391	87	23	110	7.740	2.359
1979/80	2.537	80	37	117	6.990	3.437
1980/81	2.608	92	40	132	8.547	3.746
1981/82	2.826	91	42	133	8.393	4.211
1982/83	3.084	102	65	167	9.300	5.647
1983/84	3.479	105	93	198	9.400	7.986
1984/85	3.656	97	105	202	9.300	9.165
1985/86	3.912	83	141	224	8.100	11.800
1986/87	3.946	95	132	227	8.525	10.500
1987/88[1]	4.314	90	133	223	8.500	11.600
1988/89[2]	4.500	95	136	231	8.100	12.500

[1] Preliminary.

[2] Forecast.

Sources: Brazilian Institute of Sugar and Alcohol (IAA); US Agricultural Office, Rio de Janeiro.

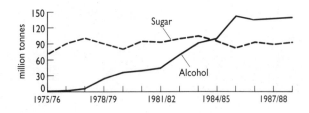

III.1   Brazil: sugar cane production for sugar and alcohol.

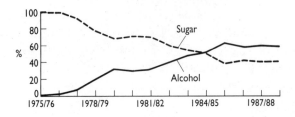

III.2   Brazil: shares of sugar cane production for sugar and alcohol.

In addition, Brazil (in particular the Centre-South region which accounts for about two-thirds of production) is one of the world's lowest-cost sugar producers. Production costs in the Centre-South continue to decline, reflecting efforts to improve efficiency in all phases of the production process.

Domestic sugar appetite

The world's fifth-largest population and a long tradition of high per capita sugar consumption have made Brazil one of the world's leading sugar-consuming countries. With annual consumption of 6.0–6.7 million tonnes, about 6% of global use, Brazil ranks behind only the Soviet Union, India, China, and the United States. Per capita consumption averages about 45 kg, compared with a world average of about 20 kg (Table III.2).

Brazil's sugar consumption fluctuates from year to year, reflecting economic conditions and changes in government policy. For example, under the Sarney government's Cruzado Plan in 1986, wages were raised sharply while prices were controlled. Consumption of sugar shot up nearly half a million tonnes in 1986/87, while sugar exports fell to 20% of production, down from 30% in 1985/86 (Table III.3). As the

Table III.2 Brazil: sugar consumption, total and per capita

Year	Population,[1] millions	Sugar consumption, million metric tonnes	Per capita sugar consumption, kg
1970/71	95.6	3.74	39.1
1975/76	108.7	5.18	47.7
1980/81	123.2	6.11	49.6
1985/86	140.0	6.30	45.0
1986/87	143.5	6.70	46.7
1987/88	147.1	6.40	43.5
1988/89[2]	150.7	6.50	43.1
1989/90[2]	154.3	7.00	45.4
1990/91[2]	157.9	7.20	45.6
1991/92[2]	161.7	7.40	45.8
1992/93[2]	165.6	7.50	46.0

Sources: [1] *World population by country and region, 1950–86 and projection to 2050 by F Urban and P Ross, USDA/ERS/ATAD, March 1988.* [2]*USDA projections.*

Table III. 3 Brazil: sugar production and consumption[1]

Year	Sugar production	Domestic consumption	Consumption as % of production	Exports	Exports as % of production
	Million metric tonnes			Million metric tonnes	
1975/76	6.200	5.177	83.5	1.263	20.4
1976/77	7.500	5.148	68.6	1.700	22.7
1977/78	8.863	5.165	58.3	2.497	28.2
1978/79	7.740	5.508	71.2	1.850	23.9
1979/80	6.990	6.098	87.2	2.296	32.8
1980/81	8.547	6.107	71.5	2.305	27.0
1981/82	8.393	5.832	69.5	2.984	35.6
1982/83	9.300	6.178	66.4	2.615	28.1
1983/84	9.400	6.300	67.0	2.700	28.7
1984/85	9.300	6.300	67.7	3.439	37.0
1985/86	8.100	6.300	77.8	2.690	33.2
1986/87	8.525	6.700	78.6	1.720	20.2
1987/88[2]	8.500	6.400	75.3	2.000	23.5
1988/89[3]	8.100	6.500	80.2	1.500	18.5

[1]All sugar data converted to raw value. Consumption and export shares may not add to 100% because of stock changes. [2]Preliminary. [3]Forecast. *Sources: IAA, USDA.*

Cruzado Plan collapsed and the economy deteriorated in early 1987, consumer purchasing power shrank and sugar consumption fell nearly 5%. The contraction was, however, not as great as for many other items, reflecting the high level of sugar in the Brazilian diet.

Noting the economic importance of sugar in the national diet,

Brazilian governments regularly have given priority to ensuring that domestic production is sufficient to cover consumption needs. Sugar for export, while also vital to the national economy, has been secondary. This long-standing priority is unlikely to change. With Brazil's high birth rates and increasing industrialization, even greater supplies will be needed in the future.

Sugar exports: a versatile power

Despite the fact that sugar exports are a secondary priority, Brazil is consistently among the world's top four sugar exporters, along with Cuba, the European Community (EC), and Australia. Since 1970 Brazil has averaged 2.2 million tonnes of annual exports, raw value, with record sales of 3.4 million in 1984/85 accounting for 11% of global exports. While Brazil has maintained its traditional position as a leading raw sugar supplier, it has also diversified sales to include plantation white or semi-refined sugar (known as crystal sugar in Brazil) and refined sugar (Figure III.3).

According to the Foreign Trade Office of the Bank of Brazil (CACEX), raw sugar exports in calendar 1986 totalled about 904 000 tonnes to widely varied destinations, with two-thirds going to the Soviet Union.

Semi-refined exports totalled about 331 000 tonnes, raw value equivalent, with Egypt and other developing countries the major markets. Refined sugar exports, second only to the EC's, totalled 1.2 million tonnes, going largely to oil-exporting countries such as Iran, Iraq and Nigeria which lack sufficient refining capacity to import raw sugar. Brazil's refined exports surpassed its raw exports in volume in 1985, and the refined share of Brazil's total has climbed to nearly one-half from less than 15% in the mid-1970s. Thus, Brazil has positioned itself well in the refined segment of global sugar trade in which many sugar analysts foresee considerable growth potential.

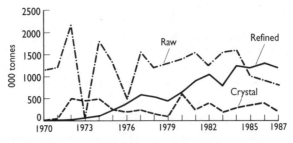

III.3   Brazil: sugar exports, 1970–87.

The evolution of a diverse export capability, unique in the world at this volume, provides Brazil with considerable flexibility to serve a wide range of markets as well as the varied needs of individual importers. For example, Brazil in 1986 shipped Algeria 111 300 tonnes of raw sugar, 24 600 tonnes of semi-refined, and 65 000 tonnes of refined sugar – an order no other country in the world could fill.

Brazil's diverse sugar export portfolio also has enabled the industry to buffer, to some extent, the effects of low world prices and the contraction of the US market. Sales to the USA fell from 30% of Brazil's total sugar exports in 1981 to 5% in 1986.

Sugar export earnings have continued to be important to the economy, though their share of total earnings has shrunk as Brazil's exports of minerals, manufactured products, and other agricultural commodities have grown and world sugar prices have fallen from earlier peaks. In 1987, sugar exports of $400 million provided only 2% of Brazil's total export earnings of $26.2 billion, compared with the boom of 1975 when sugar exports of $1.1 billion represented 12.6% of the total of $8.7 billion. Nonetheless, sugar exports, which have averaged close to $0.5 billion over the past five years, are important to the debt-ridden Brazilian economy, especially the impoverished Northeast where roughly two-thirds of exports originate.

Sugar-powered cars

Brazil is by far the world's leader in ethanol production. Output in 1988/89 is forecast at 12.5 billion litres from 136 million tonnes of sugarcane. No other country comes close. US ethanol production, the world's second largest, is expected to total a record 3.2 billion litres in 1988.

Influenced by the run-up in world oil prices in 1974, Brazil launched the world's first major fuel ethanol programme, in 1975. This decision was reinforced by the further rise in oil prices that began in 1979 and peaked in 1981. Drawing on the country's vast resources of land and rural labour and its highly favourable conditions for sugarcane growth, Brazil has more than doubled its sugarcane area and more than tripled its sugarcane production since 1975. Through a programme of adding distilleries to existing sugar mills, and constructing more efficient distilleries devoted strictly to converting cane to fuel-ethanol, Brazil increased its ethanol production from half a billion litres in 1975/76 to 11.6 billion in 1987/88 (Table III.1, Fig. III.1 and III.2).

Brazil's ethanol programme subsidized distillers and consumers, and has come under considerable criticism for its cost, particularly given the sharp downturn in world oil prices since 1986. The programme's future, however, seems assured. Of Brazil's automobile fleet of about 10 million, more than half the cars run on pure ethanol and the remainder use a 'gasohol' blend of 22% ethanol and 78% gasoline. The Brazilian government has been subsidizing the production and marketing of ethanol-powered cars, which now comprise more than 90% of the new cars manufactured and sold in Brazil and are unable to run on gasoline.

As the number of ethanol-powered cars increases, Brazil will need additional funds to finance the ethanol programme. The rate of economic growth will continue to have a major effect on ethanol demand and the price of ethanol to consumers may play an increasing role. There has been no major change in the pricing policy since the national ethanol programme began in 1975, but changes are being considered. Ethanol use is subsidized with prices at the pump set at 65% of gasohol, reflecting ethanol's fuel efficiency relative to gasoline when the programme was started. Improvements in the motors built for ethanol cars have raised ethanol's relative efficiency to 80–85%. Citing that improvement and soaring subsidy costs, government officials are pressuring Brasilia to raise the ethanol price to 70–75% of gasohol. Such an increase, though modest, would almost certainly dampen the rapid growth in ethanol demand.

Attainable goals?

To protect its domestic sugar consumption at the recent average per capita level of about 45 kg, and maintain exports at about 2 million tonnes, Brazil would need to produce about 9.5 million tonnes of raw sugar in 1992/93, not much above its peak production year of 1983/84. At recent extraction rates, the cane requirement for that much sugar would be about 102 million tonnes (Table III.4).

The government has projected ethanol demand in 1992/93 at 20 billion litres. Current distillery capacity is estimated at less than 16 billion litres, so a 25% expansion is planned. At recent extraction rates, about 236 million tonnes of cane would be needed to produce 20 billion litres of ethanol, more than a 70% increase over the tonnage currently devoted to ethanol. This would put Brazil's total cane requirement for sugar and ethanol in 1992/93 at 338 million tonnes, from over 6 million hectares, nearly 50% above current production and area levels.

Brazilian industry sources suggest, however, that a 20 billion litre goal for 1992 is not realistic, given the recent pace of growth in ethanol demand, and that a more reasonable expectation would be 16–17 billion. Such a level would not require any significant further expansion in distillery capacity and would call for 42 million fewer tonnes of sugarcane than the 20 billion litre plan.

Still, production of 296 million tonnes of sugarcane in 1992 will require that 1 million more hectares of cropland be devoted to cane than were harvested this past year.

The government has received considerable criticism in the past for cane acreage expansion that has been perceived as occurring at the expense of food crops. A further large increase could put added pressure on traditional farming areas in both the South and Northeast regions. Expansion of sugarcane area, particularly for ethanol production, most likely would occur in the Centre-South and Centre-West portions of the country, for several reasons:

1 both areas contain significant amounts of pastureland or land that is relatively open, but currently uncultivated;
2 their climate and topography are better suited to cane production than the dry Northeast, where yields are lower, costs are higher, and cane cultivation is largely limited to coastal areas;
3 the Centre-South, in particular, is close to existing mills, roads, and population centres where ethanol is demanded.

However, with rising input costs and relatively low producer prices, and with many mills, particularly in the Northeast, reportedly facing bankruptcy, there is little incentive for cane producers anywhere in Brazil to expand production.

Brazil's flexibility in sugar and ethanol production – implications for the world sugar market

With its state-regulated milling industry and varied regional harvest schedules, Brazil has the technical flexibility to shift cane between sugar and ethanol production fairly quickly. This flexibility is most pronounced in the Centre-South, which accounts for about 80% of ethanol production. Brazil's quantity of cane is so large that even marginal shifts could have important effects on the world sugar market.

Ethanol absorbs a quantity of sugarcane sufficient to produce over 10 million tonnes of sugar, or more than one-third of world exports. With sugar milling capacity estimated at 12 million tonnes, Brazil would appear to be able to lift sugar production to that level from current levels around 8 million tonnes, by diverting 40–45 million tonnes of cane from ethanol. This additional 4 million tonnes of cane sugar would be more than enough to sustain domestic per capita sugar consumption at current levels as Brazil's population tops the 150 million mark by the end of the decade. Part or most of this tonnage could be placed on the world market in the event of a price surge resulting from a sharp jump in sugar export earnings.

While this scenario would have Brazil providing greater stability to the world sugar market in the event of global shortages, such a large volume of adjustment is highly unlikely. Brazil will have to continue to assure the security of ethanol supplies to service its growing pure-ethanol-dependent motor fleet. This, along with the long-standing commitment to satisfy domestic sugar needs, could mitigate Brazil's ability to take advantage of higher sugar export prices. National security requirements could override the pursuit of short-term profits.

Brazil does, however, have some options open to it to reduce the rapid rate of growth in ethanol demand without undermining the overall programme. It could:

1 raise ethanol prices – a move recently postponed but still being hotly debated;
2 reduce the amount of ethanol in gasohol from the current 22% to some proportion closer to the USA's 10% at the same time providing a market for Brazil's surplus gasoline supplies;
3 put some future limits on the number of ethanol cars produced.

Consideration of these options will be influenced by the outlook for world oil prices and by Brazil's prospects for increasing its own oil production.

It would appear, in any event, that if Brazil is to be all things in all markets, another round of heavy investments – like those of the last 15 years – in the sugar and ethanol industry is required. However, with its huge foreign and internal debts it is unclear where the funding for such a program could emerge. Brazil, consequently, is facing some hard choices.

20 years of Proalcool:
Is a shortage going to spoil the birthday party?[2]

Since its launch in November 1975 the Brazilian government's Proalcool programme has weathered all kinds of storms. But despite all the criticism it has received it seems to be firmly in place and could probably even experience a new spring if recent reports are to be believed, according to which the government is planning to boost the ailing sales of alcohol powered cars. The front line between those who are for the programme and those who are against is clearly defined. The critics' camp primarily emphasizes the distortionary effects of the alcohol policy as it affects the energy sector. Hence, it is not surprising that the state oil company, Petrobras, is one of the staunchest attackers of the programme. Its view is that imports and domestic production of oil are much cheaper than the manufacture of cane-based ethanol which only attracts customers because of the enormous subsidies that are provided by the government. State support is granted by fixing both the price of imported petroleum and the domestic prices of sugar cane so that these are favourable to ethanol production. A further incentive was given to motorists to use 100% ethanol in vehicles by differential taxation. Furthermore critics charge that sugar cane will be used inefficiently under the current regime as world market prices would indicate that a higher proportion of the cane should be used for the manufacture of sugar than is presently the case. In fact, the Proalcool programme was premised on the beliefs that oil prices would remain around the record highs of the 1970s, that Brazil's economy would be vulnerable to a shortage of automotive fuels and that the price of sugar would remain low. In the meantime quite a lot has changed: oil prices have fallen considerably and Brazil has discovered significant oil reserves of its own. When Proalcool was launched in the 1970s the country produced only 30% of its petrol requirements from domestic sources. Today, with a much increased consumption of petrol this ratio has improved to 50%. Finally, sugar prices are still reasonably attractive for efficient producers such as Brazil. It seems that the economic environment has changed

---

2 Reprinted from F O Licht, *International Sugar and Sweetener Report*, Vol. 127, No. 35, Ratzeburg, November 1995.

fundamentally while the Proalcool programme in its present form is not capable of accommodating all of these changes. But one must not forget the social and environmental achievements which accompanied Proalcool. Tens of thousands of jobs were created in the rural area thus curbing the exodus to the cities and air pollution could be contained in the major cities by using a mixture of anhydrous alcohol and gasoline, the so-called gasohol mixture. Moreover the Brazilian sugar and alcohol producers are a powerful industrial grouping which will not easily give in to calls for quick reform of the sector. Finally it is not hard to forecast what would happen to the sugar price on the international markets if Brazil were to concentrate primarily on the production of sugar at the expense of alcohol. Any shift away from the current production ratio of roughly 60:40 (60% of the cane is processed into alcohol, 40% into sugar) would seriously depress sugar prices and this cannot be in the interest of either the industry or the government.

The economics of the sugar/alcohol complex

The sugar and alcohol industries in Brazil are inextricably intertwined. Quite a lot of sugar factories have a distillery annexed but there is also a growing number of distilleries which are able to produce sugar after some technical adjustments. Besides these locational connections, the economics of sugar and alcohol production are closely related. When setting up the Proalcool programme one of the major targets of the government was to have a secure source of energy which was independent from the vagaries of the world market. Therefore the authorities had to produce the right set of incentives which would guarantee sufficient supplies of alcohol to the domestic market. This obligation resulted in complex technical parities between all cane-based products (sugar, alcohol, molasses) which were designed to convince sugar factories that no particular advantage could be obtained from the production of sugar. The administrative price structure for the various products aimed at equalizing the returns to all cane-derived products, linking them ultimately to the price of alcohol. This together with the master production plan for the whole industry was to ensure stable and sufficient supplies to the domestic markets. But no pricing formula can work flawlessly as it will have to be based on average values as reported by the factories/distilleries. Consequently the variety across the industry as a whole had to be neglected. However, sugar cane is an agricultural crop and as such shows a large range as to sugar content, ash content, fibre etc. Likewise technical performance in various factories can differ even if the machinery employed is the same. All these factors have resulted in a situation where some plants are better at producing sugar and others excel in the manufacture of alcohol. A considerable strain for the system as a whole originated from the fact that the administrative price structure had nothing to do with the relative prices of sugar and alcohol on the world markets. If price regulation had not existed Brazil would have continuously favoured the production of sugar over alcohol. Nevertheless some cracks have developed in the system in recent years. Ever since the demise of the Brazilian Institute for Sugar and Alcohol (IAA) in 1990 the marketing freedom of the sugar producers has grown. While prices at the wholesale level are still set administratively, retail prices are more or less determined by market forces. Because restrictions in the alcohol sector still apply the attractiveness of producing sugar has been greatly enhanced. Therefore it does not come as a surprise that overall increases in alcohol production have recently been smaller than the industry capacity available and that an increasing number of distilleries have started to produce sugar as well. In order to avoid the complete dismantling of the system Brazil allowed mills to swap sugar for alcohol on the international markets. Given the relative price structure of these two products on the world markets *vis-à-vis* the ratio in Brazil it has proved extremely profitable for the mills to engage in large scale swaps. Although factory productivities vary the generally accepted rule of thumb says that one tonne of cane can produce either 88 kg of crystal white sugar or 53 litres of ethanol. Considering that one tonne of crystal white sugar fetches around US$340 while one cubic metre (1000 l) of imported ethanol costs around US$350 the profit for swapping sugar against alcohol works out at US$11.30 per tonne of cane. This is no small margin indeed given the fact that total Brazilian cane production amounted to 241 million tonnes in 1994/95. But one must not forget that Brazil's thirst for ethanol as well as its potential to flood the world market with sugar are so vast that even marginal shifts in the present pattern of production would have significant effects on prices. If world market prices for ethanol/sugar would simultaneously rise/fall by 10% the profit per tonne of cane would shrink to US$6.43 and it would be down to virtually zero if the increase/decrease margins would be 20% respectively. As the past has shown such price swings are not completely beyond imagination. Leaving the Brazilian potential aside for a moment, the outlook for the world markets for ethanol and sugar in 1995/96 seems to exacerbate the above calculation: while the former seems to be rather tight with looming plant closures and high input costs currently pressing US producers the latter is generally believed to be in a big surplus with expectations of record breaking crops in India and Thailand. This suggests that any bigger deviation from the current production pattern could very quickly backfire and therefore there is much to say in favour of keeping up the status quo. Nevertheless, other factors have to be taken into consideration.

Trends in consumption: a recent survey

The most important outlet for ethanol in Brazil is the market for fuel alcohol. In 1995/96 12 billion litres are estimated to be used by motorists while a little bit over 1 billion litres is expected to go in other uses, mostly in the chemical industry. Consumption of fuel alcohol has been on the rise over recent years although the market share of alcohol powered vehicles has dropped. Basically there are three explanations for this phenomenon. First, the number of cars sold is rising rapidly. Overall growth in car sales in 1995 is expected to be around 40% which puts the loss in absolute terms somewhat into perspective. For example, the number of alcohol powered vehicles sold in December 1994 amounted to 3664 which corresponded to a market share of 3.70%. In May 1995 4052 ethanol cars were sold (+11% as against the December figures) but the market share dropped to 1.71%. Secondly, taking into account the fact that an estimated 17 000 alcohol powered vehicles are scrapped per month the total number of ethanol cars in use is only slightly down on 1994 at 4.286 million units against 4.364 million. Thirdly, the Brazilian economy is booming and this implies that longer distances are travelled thus pushing up the demand for ethanol.

Despite increasing demand for ethanol the industry for producing alcohol powered cars is clearly in trouble. Total sales in 1994 amounted to 142 000 units compared to almost 700 000 in 1986. 1995 will be another dismal year with sales up to August 1995 amounting to no more than 24 503 units, a result which is unmatched in the entire history of the market for alcohol powered cars. The alcohol and sugar industries are clearly concerned about this development and in order to arrive at a first assessment they asked the Gallup Institute to conduct a survey on the car market in the state of São Paulo, the biggest producer and consumer of alcohol in Brazil.

The results of the survey showed that 23.7% of all car owners would prefer an alcohol powered vehicle while 58.3% would rather have one with a gasoline engine; 18% had no opinion. According to the Gallup study, the major advantages of the alcohol car were its lower purchasing price, its positive effect on employment and the economy in Brazil and its ability to reduce pollution in urban areas. Major drawbacks of alcohol engines were their lower miles per gallon performance as compared to gasoline engines, the lower life expectancy of the engine and its lower performance characteristics. What this boils down to is that alcohol engines seem to be held in lower esteem by motorists as far as their technical performance characteristics are concerned while other aspects (environment, economy, lower purchasing price) seem to speak in favour of it. The alcohol industry as well as the car industry continues to reiterate that there is still much scope for technical improvements both in terms of the quality of the alcohol fuel and in the performance characteristics of the engine.

Turning to the proposals for the future shape of the alcohol policy in Brazil the results of the study show that the Proalcool programme has the firm backing of the public. Almost 75% are in favour of stimulating the production of alcohol powered cars via fiscal means whereas only 45% would like to see similar measures for gasoline cars; 82% believe that alcohol is of strategic importance for Brazil while 72% are critical of the proposal that it would be better to import more oil than to produce more alcohol. Although the outcome of the survey may be a little distorted due to the fact that it was restricted to São Paulo State where the pollution problem (São Paulo City) as well as the employment effect (largest sugar and alcohol producing state) was the biggest the message seems to be clear: the Proalcool programme is not in danger of being dismantled. On the contrary, it is seen as an important sector of the Brazilian economy which should receive further promotion by the government.

Despite this nice birthday present by the São Paulo public to the Proalcool programme, the scheme is clearly in need of fundamental reform. Looking at the figures for 1995/96 there is an acute need to act. The system as a whole is in a state of disintegration after the partial liberalization of the sugar markets which spurred the production of sugar at the expense of alcohol. What is the point of rallying broad public support for alcohol when there is simply not enough of the fuel around to keep the fleet of ethanol cars going? One only has to recall that the total number of alcohol powered cars in 1995 will probably drop by 2% as against the 1994 figure. At the same time the number of miles travelled has certainly risen by a much bigger margin thus exacerbating the supply crunch which is reflected in the lower than planned alcohol production figures for the Centre/South. Brazilian motorists relying on alcohol will certainly not be amused if the 20th anniversary ends with an alcohol shortage which would revive the memory of the traumatic events of the late 1980s. So what options are there for policymakers, industrialists and consumers to ensure the birthday party is still a success despite the gloomy outlook?

The likely strategy: flexibility in fuel mixtures

There can be no doubting the fact that the government is committed to continuing the Proalcool programme even though the terms of managing it might change. Only recently Industry and Commerce Minister Dorothea Werneck said there was a consensus that the programme should be reactivated for economic and environmental reasons. Therefore an interministerial committee will meet at the end of this month to discuss details of reformed scheme. One of the major aims of this policy initiative is to stem the decline in market share of alcohol powered cars. According to Mrs Werneck, the share of ethanol cars should be boosted to 20% by the year 2000. At the same time the proportion of anhydrous alcohol is to be reduced to 12% from 22% at present. It is clear that Mrs Werneck has to balance a variety of interests and this proposal clearly seems to be a viable compromise. Of course, environmentalists are outraged by this shift in fuel policy as they fear a drastic deterioration of the air quality in big cities. On the other hand, Brazil's auto industry needs to be cheered up and nothing can achieve that better than the promise of higher sales of domestically produced cars. But one must not forget that the announced measures are nothing but a mini-reform which cannot conceal that the whole mechanics of the Proalcool programme is due for an overhaul.

For quite a number of years it has been Brazil's policy to shift production towards anhydrous alcohol as this sort of fuel can be mixed with other components (gasoline, methanol) to give gasohol. Hydrous alcohol on the other hand is primarily used for 100% ethanol powered cars. In this respect 1995/96 will be no exception: the production of anhydrous alcohol for the use in the country's fuel pool is planned to rise to 3.447 billion litres from 2.869 billion litres actually produced in 1994/95. The production of hydrous alcohol is scheduled to amount to 8.627 billion litres compared to 9.277 billion litres planned for 1994/95 and 9.827 billion litres actually achieved in that year. Although the planned figures will hardly be reached the shift in policy is clear: the flexibility in the composition of the nation's fuel pool is to increase. By enlarging the scope for quick adaptations in fuel mixtures, shortages like the ones seen in the late 1980s can certainly be avoided but politicians would have to cope with a problem of credibility. The public will find it hard to understand that the government is still committed to its environmental goals if gasohol compositions can be changed almost *ad libitum* subject to the alcohol/sugar economics on the world markets. For the moment the strategy of the government is probably the only choice to save the programme as a whole but for the formulation of a coherent policy it will certainly take more than that.

Table III.4 Brazil: sugar cane needs in 1992

Year	Cane for sugar				Cane for ethanol						Total cane production		Total cane area	
	Cane prod.	Sugar prod.	Sugar cons.	Sugar exports	Ethanol prod. Scenario		Cane prod. for ethanol Scenario				Scenario		Scenario	
					I	II	I	II			I	II	I	II
	Million metric tonnes				Billion litres		Million metric tonnes						Million hectares	
Average 1983–88	94.0	8.8	6.4	2.5	10.2	—	120.8	—			214.8	—	3.9	—
1988/89	85.0	8.1	6.5	1.5	12.5	—	136.0	—			231.0	—	4.5	—
1989/90	96.4	9.0	7.0	2.0	14.0	13.5	165.1	159.2			261.5	255.6	4.7	4.6
1990/91	98.5	9.2	7.2	2.0	16.0	14.5	189.7	171.0			287.2	269.5	5.2	4.8
1991/92	100.6	9.4	7.4	2.0	18.0	15.5	212.3	182.8			312.9	283.4	5.6	5.1
1992/93	101.7	9.5	7.5	2.0	20.0	16.5	235.8	194.6			337.6	296.3	6.1	5.3

Projections assume most recent 5-year average (1983/84–87/88) cane yields (55.73 tonnes/ha) and recovery rates for sugar (9.34%) and ethanol (8.48%). Scenario I: Produce 20 billion litres of ethanol in 1992. Scenario II: Produce 16–17 billion litres of ethanol in 1992. *Sources: 1983/84–87/88 data: IAA, USDA; 1988/89–92/93 data: USDA projections.*

Table III.5 Production plan sugar/alcohol, 1995/96

| | Alcohol, metres³ | | | | | Sugar (tonnes) | | |
| | Fuel alcohol | | Other uses | | | | | |
	Anhydrous	Hydrous	Anhydrous	Hydrous	Total	Internal sales	Exports (estimate)	Total
Total	3 447 040	8 627 486	100 200	941 157	13 115 881	7 427 752	4 032 500	11 460 252
Centre South	2 982 597	7 245 138	100 000	900 000	11 227 597	5 897 000	2 612 500	8 509 500
North/Northeast	464 443	1 382 348	200	41 157	1 888 284	1 530 752	1 420 000	2 950 752

Table III.6 Centre/South: supply and demand of alcohol 1994/95, 000 metres^3

	Anhydrous	%	Hydrous	%	Total	%
Supply	2.767	100	9.551	100	12.318	100
Production	2.576	93.11	8.571	89.74	11.147	90.49
Imports by Petrobras	150	5.42	0	0	150	1.22
Imports by Copersucar	41	1.47	182	1.91	223	1.81
Methanol	0	0	798	8.35	798	6.48
Demand	2.704	100	9.363	100	12.067	100
Alcohol fuel	2.579	95.38	8.418	89.91	10.997	91.13
Other	105	3.88	880	9.40	985	8.16
Transfer	20	0.74	65	0.69	85	0.70

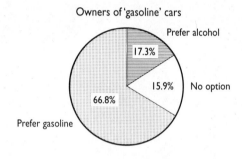

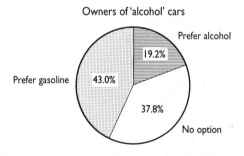

III.4 The image of alcohol powered cars (source: AIAA).

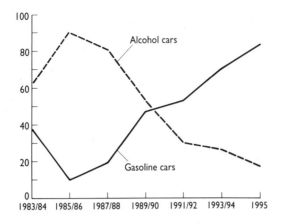

III.5 Development of market shares (source: AIAA).

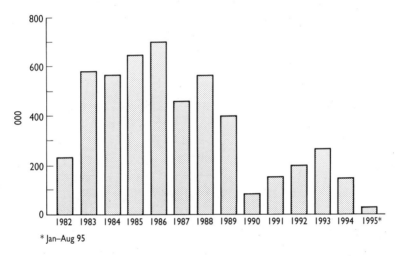

III.6 Sales of new alcohol powered cars (source: AIAA).

International sugar agreements

(Reprinted from *Food Policy*, 1994 19 (1) 1–10, with kind permission from Elsevier Science Ltd, The Boulevard, Langford Lane, Kidlington OX5 1GB, UK)

Summary

Sugar has been the subject of multilateral intergovernmental commodity agreements intermittently since 1864, although inherently unsuited for international market regulation. Obtainable from tropical and temperate plants grown over a wide range of natural conditions (and now vulnerable to replacement by alternative sweeteners), it invites countries to seek self-sufficiency on the supply side, while its role as a staple food encourages autarkic impulses from the demand side. A secular decline in the ratio of international trade to global production has been accompanied by the compartmentalization of markets and a dispersal of power both among exporters and importers, eroding the basis for consensus among a heterogeneous population of market participants. In addition to structural obstacles, asymmetric and conflicting supply and demand responses stand in the way of effective international market management. Since 1985, the International Sugar Organization has existed by virtue of administrative agreements without regulatory clauses. While a return to market controls is unlikely, the organization fulfils monitorial and investigative functions not provided by commercial information services, all the more needed owing to developments which may upset the current relative stability of the market.

Ironically, the aphorism that everything is sweetened by risk does not apply to sugar. Growers of sugarbeet and sugar cane, cost-intensive crops with relatively long production cycles, need certainty of adequate returns perhaps more than most agricultural producers. Nations dependent on sugar for a significant portion of their export earnings seek price stability in the interest of sustained development. Yet, until recently, the world market price of sugar was far more volatile than those of other major primary commodities (House of Lords, 1977; Gordon-Ashworth, 1984). And the very commodity characteristics which made the world sugar price so unstable and fostered the desire for order, hindered its fulfilment. Although sugar gave rise to the world's first multilateral intergovernmental commodity agreement in 1864 and to a series of treaties since, it was frustratingly unsuited from a technical viewpoint for the kind of international market controls to which it was subjected. Now, structural changes in the sugar market and the spread of alternative sweeteners may have made traditional regulatory instruments altogether obsolete, calling for a new approach to the quest for order.

International sugar agreements have been shaped and their effectiveness determined by the nature of the market they sought to influence. The first impulse towards international cooperation to regulate the world trade in sugar arose precisely out of what had become its dominant feature and, for the chances of successful control, its main defect: with the advent of beet sugar two centuries ago, sugar ceased to be an exclusively tropical product and became obtainable from two quite different agricultural raw materials, capable of being produced over a wide range of natural conditions. Neatly stated by Timoshenko and Swerling (1957): 'The beet sugar industry of Europe in the nineteenth century provides the earliest example of the market for an important tropical product being seriously eroded by the application of modern scientific methods in relatively advanced countries.' With few exceptions of any consequence (Korea, New Zealand, Norway), virtually all countries eventually established domestic sugar industries to cover at least part of their requirements: and since World War II, Bolivia, Chile, Ethiopia, Greece, Honduras, Malawi, Morocco, Pakistan, Swaziland, Zambia and Zimbabwe, among others, have joined the ranks of centrifugal sugar producers, with Malawi, Swaziland and Zimbabwe going on to become sizeable exporters. Although production is fairly concentrated – the six largest producers (European Community, India, Brazil, China, Cuba, and USA) accounted for 54.5% of world output in 1992 – sugar does not lend itself to the formation of a producer cartel. On the other hand, international market management is unlikely to be effective without agreement among this heterogeneous group of major producers. Data in this paper refer to centrifugal sugar, as defined in international sugar agreements, and exclude open-pan sugars still produced in significant quantities by small enterprises for local consumption in Asia and parts of Latin America and Africa. Unless otherwise noted, all figures stem from Food and Agriculture Organization (1961), International Sugar Council (1963), and International Sugar Organization (1972).

Amenable to self-sufficiency on the supply side, sugar engendered strong autarkic impulses also from the demand side. Its dual role as a source of energy and sweetener – not to mention its functions as a preservative, flavour enhancer, bulking agent, and stabilizer – made it a staple food in one country after another. Highly responsive to rises in low-level incomes, demand for sugar went hand in hand with economic development (Viton and Pignalosa, 1961). At the same time, governments found import substitution comparatively easy, with the added benefits of contributing to the intensification of agriculture and stimulating rural development. From early days an object of taxation and means of fulfilling mercantilist aspirations, sugar grew in political and strategic relevance the more it became an article of mass production and consumption, which could only make governments less inclined to regard international market regulation as other than supplementary to domestic controls. Not surprisingly, international sugar agreements tended to play second fiddle to single-regimes and the securing of bilateral trade flows.

In consequence of the secular movement towards self-sufficiency, world sugar trade, though grown in absolute volume, declined in relation to production. Gross exports represented only 26% of world production in 1986–90, against 70% in 1921–25 and 42% in the first half of the 1950s. Gross export figures must not be interpreted too closely: net trade was always smaller, since much sugar enters the market twice, first raw and then refined, and the goal posts have been shifted to some extent, mainly because shipments between countries now part of the European Community no longer count. But they show the trend.

Special arrangements and free market

A shrinking proportion of production, the sugar that does enter world trade is not subject to uniform rules. Since colonial days, markets have been compartmentalized, and from the International Sugar Agreement of 1937 onward, the regulatory reach of the agreements has been limited by the division of world trade into two distinct segments: free market and outside the free market. Classifications have varied over the years, but basically the free market was defined as that part of world trade to which special trading arrangements did not apply (and which for this reason bore the brunt of changes in the supply/demand situation). Under the 1937 agreement, the free market comprised all exports except those to the USA, certain exports by the USSR to neighbouring countries, and movements between French territories and between Belgium and Luxembourg. The 1953 and 1958 agreements excluded from the free market imports by the United States and Soviet imports from Czechoslovakia, Hungary and Poland, trade between member exporting countries and their overseas departments, territories and associated states, and some movements between adjoining territories or islands covered by the Commonwealth Sugar Agreement of 1951. Trade under the latter was then formally part of the free market, but in fact subject to special conditions. The 1968 agreement introduced the concept of 'special arrangements', under which it recognized exports to the UK covered by the Negotiated Price Quotas of the Commonwealth Sugar Agreement, exports by Cuba to socialist countries with certain restrictions, exports covered by the Guaranteed Price Quota of the African and Malagasy Sugar Agreement, and exports to the United States. This approach was continued with some modifications in the 1977 agreement which recognized as special arrangements the exports to the EEC under the Lomé Convention and related acts, and Cuban exports to socialist countries, again with certain restrictions.

Since the free market embraced only a minor portion of world production, it has long been labelled a 'residual market' (e.g. Rowe, 1965). On the principle of leverage or gearing, such a market is held to be liable to wide price fluctuations, and price stabilization 'is *a priori* likely to be an extremely difficult problem' (Rowe, 1965). A further, altogether depressing effect on prices is ascribed to the compartmentalization of the world's sugar trade, in that the normally higher prices paid under preferential arrangements allowed favoured participants to cover their overhead costs of production and to export to the free market at prices that met variable costs alone (Timoshenko and Swerling, 1957).

What the world sugar trade lost in relative size, it gained in complexity, probably also becoming more unstable in the process. Owing to the increased number of producers, more countries could be expected to switch from the importer to the exporter column and back again. Regulation of the market was complicated by a dilution of power on the exporter side. Cuba and Java alone furnished 32% of gross world exports (including all shipments from overseas territories to metropolitan countries) in 1935–39. Together they accounted for 53% of the total export quotas under the 1937 agreement and held 34.5% of the exporter votes in the International Sugar Council (Debus, 1976). During 1951–55, Cuba on its own was responsible for nearly a third of gross world exports; in the first agreement after World War II, it had nearly 5% of basic export entitlements subject to quota adjustment and cast 245 of the 1000 exporter votes (Debus, 1976). But by 1976–80, Cuba's share of world exports had declined to 25%, and its basic export tonnage under the 1977 agreement was not much larger than those of Australia and Brazil. In terms of net exports to the free market, as defined in the respective agreements, Cuba's share fell from 28% in 1954–58 to just over 10% in 1978–82, and the spotlight had shifted to the European Community.

A similar diffusion of power took place on the importer side. The two main centres in earlier days, the United Kingdom and the United States, accounted for 57% of gross imports (including shipments from offshore areas) in 1935–39 and 53% in 1951–55. In the International Sugar Council, each had 17 of the total 45 importer votes in 1937, and 245 out of 1000 votes in 1953. Presiding over their respective 'sugar empires' (Rowe, 1965), neither represented purely importer interests (Debus, 1976). The five years following conclusion of the 1977 agreement, however, saw quite a different distribution, with the top places now occupied by the Soviet Union (19%), the United States (15%, excluding shipments from offshore areas), Japan (8%), and the European Community (6%). In net imports from the free market, the United Kingdom, the former linchpin of the system, no longer figured at all.

Whatever common ground between exporters and importers, developed and developing countries, could be constructed for what remained essentially an export restraint agreement, the prerequisite for the sort of supply management and market control attempted in the past – an adequate base of fundamentally similar interests among the major players (cf. Khan, 1982) – was fatally eroded. Even narrowed down to net exporters, wide differences in the outlet structure and national importance of the various sugar industries now stood in the way of international consensus. In the matter of export dependence, for instance, whereas roughly 75% of Brazil's production in 1980 was consumed at home, 90% of Cuba's output was exported, and whereas sugar accounted for under 7% of Brazil's merchandise exports in value, it made up over 80% of Cuba's export earnings.

Supply and demand and economic forces

Structural problems aside, attempts to regulate the sugar market come up against the hurdle of asymmetric and contrary supply and demand responses. Subject to the vagaries of nature in addition to economic forces, sugar production is considerably less stable than consumption even in global aggregates. Since 1960, the upward trend of world production was interrupted five times (in 1962, 1966, 1979–80, 1983, and 1985), declining by as much as 6.4% from 1961 to 1962. World consumption fell only three times from one year to the next (in 1964, 1975, and 1980), by at most 3.7% (from 1974 to 1975), and marked time from 1982 to 1983 and from 1987 to 1988. In the other direction, the largest year-to-year increase in world production was one of 14.3% (from 1963 to 1964), against a maximum rise of 8.1% in world consumption (from 1960 to 1961).

The global supply response of sugar is more mobile in the upward than in the downward direction. Overall, there is usually enough slack in the system to expand output quickly in response to attractive prices. On the other hand, unremunerative prices do not cause a commensurate contraction of supply. One reason for this is the increasingly heavy capital investment in specialized equipment, and the fixity of assets which is particularly marked in the cane sugar sector because of its perennial crop cycle. Although Timoshenko and Swerling (1957) disputed the notion that growers will respond to low prices by perversely increasing output, the volume and fixity of the assets committed, coupled with institutional factors and a not uncommon immobility of production factors (e.g. apparent lack of more profitable or less risky alternative land uses), may in the short run lead to a backward-sloping supply curve as long as greater output reduces unit costs because of the often high ratio of fixed to variable costs in sugar production (e.g. when the marginal cost of harvesting the full crop is less than marginal revenue). Moreover, as in other commodities, income stabilization may be more compelling than price stabilization and cause both private producers and governments to react perversely to falling prices.

The demand response to prices, on the other hand, tends to be skewed in the opposite direction, expanding relatively less in reaction to lower prices than it contracts in response to higher prices. The most obvious reason is that much of the world has reached saturation in the per caput food demand for sugar. Another reason is that poor importing countries with unsaturated demand may be unable to increase consumption in line with the decline in prices because of foreign exchange constraints. For their part, importing countries possessing sugar industries have been prone to react to cheaper foreign sugar not by increasing imports but by raising the margin of protection to domestic producers (Timoshenko and Swerling, 1957).

Changed economic conditions and trends

From first to last, international sugar agreements have been very much children of their time. The topical issue to which the governments of Belgium, France, The Netherlands, and the United Kingdom addressed themselves in the Paris Sugar Convention of 1864 was the growth of bounty-fed beet sugar exports. In the interests of their treasuries they agreed to suppress protective duties and bounties so as to put sugar production and trade on an equal competitive footing. The agreement failed, partly because of technical difficulties of accurately determining the refining quality of different raw sugars, and subsequent international conventions of similar design in 1875, 1877 and 1888 were not ratified.

By the end of the century, however, the European sugar industries had matured and governments of exporting countries had grown tired of escalating subsidies. On the importer side, Britain, while enjoying the supplies of beet sugar at subsidized prices, was concerned about the effect this competition had on its cane sugar producing overseas possessions and domestic refiners. Export bounties were effective only as long as importers did not impose countervailing duties. The tariff policies of Great Britain, the United States and British India allowing the entry of subsidized sugar had been the necessary counterpart to the export-promoting measures of the Continental countries.

Out of this consensus emerged the Brussels Convention of 1902 between the governments of Austria, Belgium, France, Germany, Hungary, Italy, The Netherlands, Norway, Spain, Sweden, and the United Kingdom. Except for Russia, the convention encompassed all significant beet sugar exporters, as well as the United Kingdom, then with the United States the leading sugar importer. In addition to other measures for the protection of domestic sugar producers and refiners, the United States since 1890 imposed a countervailing duty on bounty-fed sugar imports (Ballinger, 1971).

In order to equalize the conditions of competition between beet and cane sugar from different parts of the world and promote consumption, the parties undertook to eliminate all direct and indirect production and export subsidies on sugar, to bar entry to or impose countervailing duties on sugar imports from countries granting such bounties, and to limit surtaxes (the difference between imposts on foreign and domestic sugar). Luxembourg, Peru, and Switzerland joined later, while Spain failed to ratify the convention. Russia became a member under special conditions in 1907, at the same time as a new Liberal administration in Britain declared itself unable to continue implementing the commitment to penalize bounty-fed sugar. Extended in 1908 and 1912 (now without Italy and the United Kingdom), the agreement was rendered inoperative by World War I and formally annulled in 1920.

Abolition of the bounties did not lead to reduction of European beet sugar production. Among the larger producers, Austria, Germany and Russia all registered considerably higher levels in 1910/11, compared with 1900/01, and only France a decline. Western and Central European beet sugar exports actually appear to have been slightly higher in the decade following the Brussels Convention than in the ten years before, despite poor harvests in 1909/10 and 1911/12, while Russian exports increased substantially from 1908 on (Debus, 1976). Nor did the convention achieve a significant increase in world prices. But since exports no longer needed to be subsidized, consumption taxes could be reduced and internal prices fell, which together with rising incomes boosted domestic demand on the Continent.

The somewhat chequered history of the Brussels Convention foreshadowed the experience of subsequent international sugar agreements. They could formalize convergent views, smooth over differences, codify a set of rules that governments had come to recognize to be in their mutual interest, and establish a balance of rights and obligations. But they could not alter fundamental economic conditions and trends.

World War I severely disrupted European beet sugar production. When output finally regained the prewar level in the second half of the 1920s, both the patterns of world sugar production and trade as well as the economic and political climate had drastically changed.

Large investments of foreign capital in Cuba, Puerto Rico, Hawaii, the Philippines, Java, Japanese-occupied Taiwan, and other tropical areas had initiated a phase of rapid expansion in the cane sugar industry at the turn of the century, which was to continue until the Great Depression. Corporate enterprises combined cheap land, low-wage labour and large-scale processing techniques to turn out great quantities of relatively low-cost sugar. Whereas in the 30 years preceding World War I a substantial part of the sugar crossing national borders had come from beet-growing countries, international trade in the interwar period was increasingly taken over by cane sugar.

A coincidence of good crops in various parts of the world in 1924/25 suddenly raised supplies far above immediate demand and pushed prices back to prewar levels, signalling the onset of the interwar crisis in the world sugar economy. Cuba, which had produced a record harvest of 5.3 million tonnes, roughly a quarter of the global outturn, unilaterally restricted its three subsequent crops and tried to persuade other major producers to exercise similar restraint. In what became known, after the Cuban negotiator, as the Tarafa Action of 1927/28, the sugar industries of Czechoslovakia, Germany and Poland agreed to support Cuba's adjustment policy, although only Czechoslovakia took a tangible step and reduced its beet area. More seriously, echoing Russia's intransigence in 1902, the Dutch interests in control of Java's industry now refused to play. The market east of Suez had not yet deteriorated to the same extent as that west of Suez, and Java was riding the crest of a revolution in cane yields thanks to the introduction of the famous POJ 2878 variety. On the importer side, the United Kingdom undermined the Tarafa Action by revising its sugar duties in order to protect British refiners against white and refined sugar imports.

World prices drop

New peaks of world production in 1927/28 and 1928/29 brought a further buildup in stocks and drop in prices – and an inquiry by the Economic Committee of the League of Nations. This saw the solution in an output freeze (whether by all important producers or just by the major exporters was left open) to be dealt with at an industry rather than governmental level. Much of the thinking of the day was still imbued with the notion of the 'battle between beet and cane sugar' –

portrayed as a fight against an unfair, and indeed immoral, attempt to replace a product of innate natural superiority by the artificial creation of protectionism – which obscured the autarkic impulses and imperial preferences mainly responsible for the excess of both. Without waiting for the committee's report, from which they evidently expected little, Cuba, Czechoslovakia, Germany, and Poland, now joined by Belgium and Hungary, negotiated a new accord at a quasi-official level in the summer of 1929, setting themselves export limits on the assumption that their production would also keep within certain agreed amounts. It was recognized, however, that supply and demand could not be wholly balanced without the cooperation of others, particularly Java, the Dominican Republic, Peru, and the Philippines. The report of the Cuban delegation concluded that 'the conditions in which the world's cane and beet sugar is produced are too diverse, and the natural, economic and political factors involved so opposed, that the interests of the various countries are in practice irreconcilable' (Pérez–Cisneros, 1957).

Cuban initiatives thus far had formed part of a package of measures motivated also by a domestic concern to ensure that the older, smaller and more vulnerable Cuban-owned mills survived the adjustment process alongside the fitter American-owned sector. The Wall Street crash in October 1929, followed by the Hawley-Smoot Tariff Act of 1930, which raised the US duty on Cuban sugar to 2 cents a pound, equivalent to an *ad valorem* rate of 160% of that year's world market price, augured the imminent collapse of all. Significantly, a New York lawyer, Thomas L. Chadbourne, became the central figure in the ensuing negotiations, and the agreement concluded in Brussels in 1931 bears his name.

The Chadbourne Agreement reunited the participants of the 1929 accord. The important addition was Java, at last willing to join, since current world prices put even most of its sugar companies in the red. Peru and Yugoslavia subscribed later. The pact was signed by producer organizations, but clearly could not function without government cooperation and national legislative backup. Formally respectful of the aversion to state intervention shown by the League's Economic Committee, it was an odd hybrid: neither a commercial treaty between governments nor strictly a cartel of private producers. In essence, the signatories agreed to keep their exports within specified amounts during the five years to 1 September 1935 and to limit production so that segregated surplus stocks would be gradually cleared. An International Sugar Council was established in The Hague to administer the pact.

Judged against its aim of restoring world sugar prices to a 'normal' level, the Chadbourne Agreement failed utterly. Far from rising, prices fell further, despite the fact that members actually exported considerably less than their quotas, drastically cut total output over the period of the agreement, and substantially reduced their stocks, though not as much as hoped. But the agreement could do nothing about the real problems. Consumption stagnated or declined in many parts of the world, owing to the Great Depression. Lower production in the Chadbourne countries was partially offset by higher output in the rest of the world. The growth under tariff protection of a centrifugal sugar industry in India virtually put paid to Java's Indian market, and its Japanese market shrank owing to increased production in Taiwan. Cuba had to cede ground on the US market to mainland beet sugar producers and the Philippines. For all their sacrifices, the Chadbourne countries appear to have received little benefit, unless they gained something from apportioning market shares among themselves. It is hard to imagine that unbridled competition could have driven world prices lower and protective barriers higher, and the argument that the situation would have been much worse without the scheme begs the question – for whom?

Not surprisingly, the Chadbourne Agreement was not renewed. In any event, the deliberations on coordination of production and marketing of primary products, including sugar, during and after the World Monetary and Economic Conference of 1933 had created the climate for a broader approach. Moreover, conditions were ripe to bring the centres of the two great sugar empires into an international arrangement. With the Jones-Costigan Act of 1934, new ground rules were established for domestic and foreign suppliers of the US market, while in Britain, the Sugar Industry (Reorganization) Act of 1936 set a limit on the volume of subsidized domestic beet sugar. Meanwhile, on the world sugar market, the fundamental situation had improved by the mid-1930s, as far as consumption and stocks were concerned, but prices remained relatively low in the presence of huge excess capacities.

This was the setting for the International Sugar Agreement of 1937, the direct lineal ancestor of the sugar agreements since World War II. Later instruments replicated its basic characteristics, although like the progeny of intensive breeding in other fields, they became more highly strung. Illustrating the increasing complexity of international sugar agreements, the number of articles in the 1968 and 1977 agreements, the last with economic provisions, increased from 72 to 85, and annexes from two to five. Henceforth they would be formally negotiated between governments, not producer associations, and would include importers as well as exporters. They would distinguish between the free market and preferential markets. Their main operational objective would be to promote an orderly relationship between supply and demand in the free market. The main mechanism to this end would be the regulation of exports through adjustable quotas, supplemented by provisions concerning stocks. And they would set a price objective, defined in 1937 as 'a reasonable price, not exceeding the cost of production, including a reasonable profit, of efficient producers', and 40 years later as 'remunerative and just to producers and equitable to consumers'. There was even a foretaste in 1938, in connection with the German occupation of Czechoslovakia, of the possible effect of outside events on quota allocations (Khan, 1982), experienced some 20 years later following the rupture of relations between the United States and Cuba.

Implicit in the 1937 agreement was a concern to guard against further shrinkage of the free market, and this was met by British and American pledges to maintain the *status quo*. Short-term perceptions of the balance of costs and benefits determined governmental attitudes towards international sugar agreements, and that the United Kingdom and United States were willing to give such undertakings reflected the mixture of their interests as exporters as well as importers and as centres of large trading blocs. Concern over the size of the free market also illustrated another lasting behavioural trait: the seemingly overriding preoccupation of exporting countries with volume rather than value, which then and later gave negotiations about basic export tonnages and quota adjustments an exclusively quantitative flavour, although a narrow, essentially static approach to quotas and the extent to which they could be cut in the face of surpluses may not have maximized average revenues.

Postwar sugar agreements

How well the 1937 agreement might have worked will never be known because its economic provisions had to be suspended after only two years on the outbreak of World War II. After the war, assimilation into the General Agreement on Tariffs and Trade of the parts of the Havana Charter of 1948 relating to commodity agreements resulted in a uniform procedure for the negotiation of commodity control schemes by intergovernmental conferences under United Nations auspices and established certain general principles, including equal voting power of exporters and importers as proxies for producers and consumers (the 1937 accord gave exporting countries 55 votes and importing countries 45). This does not mean that subsequent sugar agreements covered net exports to and net imports from the free market to an equal extent. The membership increased, but there were always notable absentees, which at one time or another included Brazil, China, Peru, Thailand, the European Community, and the United States.

Within this framework, four international sugar agreements with economic provisions were negotiated in the last 40 years, those of 1953, 1958, 1968 and 1977. Although each was concluded for a period of five years, they did not fully operate the entire time. Quotas and all other limitations on exports were suspended during the greater part of 1957 as a result of a price spike occasioned by bad harvests in most of Europe and international tensions. All economic provisions of the 1958 agreement went into abeyance after three years owing to the failure of the UN Sugar Conference of 1961 in the wake of the closing of the US market to Cuban sugar to provide for the regulation of exports in 1962–63. The only economic provision of the 1968 agreement to function in the last two years of its life was the supply commitment whereby exporting members were obliged to sell sugar to traditional importing members at a specified price below the prevailing market price. Quotas under the 1977 agreement were suspended from the beginning of 1980 to May 1981 as a result of another price boom, and although extended to 1984, the agreement was impotent for the last two years. In effect, the free market has been unregulated for the greater part of the time since 1953, and nations have relied more on domestic than international means to provide stability.

Postwar sugar agreements added various refinements to the basic ingredients of the 1937 model. The 1953 agreement introduced a target price range to guide the operation of the regulatory mechanisms. Initially, this was a narrow band of 3.25–4.35 US cents per pound of raw sugar, reduced to 3.15–4.00 cents in 1956, and continued in that form in the 1958 agreement; it was widened to 3.25–5.25 cents in 1968 and further to 11–21 cents in 1977, and ended up at 13–23 cents. Stockholding provisions were progressively reinforced to give greater assurance of supplies to importing countries in times of shortage. Rules were made to limit the amounts of sugar members could import from non-members. The 1968 agreement added a supply commitment provision, not repeated in 1977, which allowed importing members to purchase certain quantities from traditional sources at a fixed price when the actual free market price rose above that level. In its place, the 1977 agreement obligated the large exporting countries to accumulate special stocks of uncommitted sugar totalling 2.5 million tonnes for the defence of the upper part of the price range.

In the interval between the breakdown of the 1958 agreement and conclusion of the 1968 agreement, the United Nations Conference on Trade and Development of 1964 widened the terms of reference of international commodity agreements from dealing with the special problems of a particular commodity to the role commodity trade should play in stimulating the economic development of developing countries. In compliance with this normative principle, the first objective of the International Sugar Agreement became 'to raise the level of international trade in sugar, particularly in order to increase the export earnings of developing exporting countries'. (Inflation of the objectives of international commodity agreements engendered a need for classification. Thus Khan (1982) distinguished between primary, secondary and tertiary categories: 'Primary objectives are those which have corresponding instruments for their implementation, Secondary objectives are either expected to be achieved as an indirect consequence of the operation of the main instruments, or measures for their achievement are left for future negotiation; and the tertiary objectives are at best aspirations.')

Not to be overlooked today in the case of sugar, however, are the interests of less-developed importing countries. Just half a dozen low-income countries – Bangladesh, China, Gambia, Ghana, Pakistan, and Sri Lanka – accounted for nearly a fifth of estimated net imports from the free market in 1988, for example, even though that year's average world price was the highest since 1981.

In essence, international sugar agreements addressed the problem of supply management by a combination of quantitative regulation and stockholding. Applied to sugar, supply management to stabilize prices in the first instance involves smoothing crop fluctuations of considerable magnitude, for which sugar is not very suitable, at least at the global level. One difficulty with the quantitative regulation of supplies is that current output cannot be controlled with sufficient speed in order to stabilize prices. Also, sugar is a high-volume product of relatively low unit value. At free market prices, raw sugar has often been cheaper than rice or soyabeans. Moreover, though storable, raw sugar is subject to deterioration. Consequently, stocks of the magnitude required for international price stabilization would present serious physical and financial problems. By way of comparison, the International Cocoa Agreement of 1980 provided for a buffer stock of up to 250 000 tonnes, the International Natural Rubber Agreement of 1979 a buffer stock of 550 000 tonnes, the International Tin Agreement of 1980 total buffer stocks of 50 000 tonnes, whereas the International Sugar Agreement of 1977 required exporting members to accumulate 'special stocks' of 2.5 million tonnes.

At best, stockholding of sugar can moderate price fluctuations, but in a residual market prone to more frequent and greater upsets from the supply than from the demand side, stockholding alone could neither cope with what the Havana Charter called 'burdensome surpluses', nor defend the upper end of a price range against the effect of a temporary shortage. The volatility of free market prices confirmed the observation that 'market demand and market supply often increase the fluctuations of price arising from changing final demand and current production' (Rowe, 1965).

The record of international sugar agreements also demonstrates the incapacity of a static and restrictionist approach to commodity control to deal with the problem of outsiders. In 1978, the then non-member European Community became the largest net exporter to the free market and its internal sugar regime a prime factor influencing world trade. One consequence of this – not contemplated in the agreement – was that direct-consumption white sugar again made up a significant portion of international trade, as it did in the last quarter of the 19th century. In 1991, while sugar accounted for 40% of gross world sugar exports, with Thailand, Brazil and India, in addition to the EC, in the ranks of major primary sources. Though influenced by the same fundamentals as the raw sugar market, white sugar prices march to a distinct tune of supply and demand, to the extent that occasionally the purer article is cheaper than the less pure.

Had the agreement survived beyond the early 1980s as a regulatory instrument, its weaknesses would soon have been exposed in the face of another form of the outsider problem challenging existing positions – this one created by technical progress. Until the early 1970s, substitutes did not materially affect the demand for sugar, except in North America and Japan, and even there were only a minor factor. The starch and artificial sweeteners then available differed sufficiently from sucrose to limit competition. The subsequent development of high fructose corn syrup or isoglucose gave food manufacturers and other industrial users a technically acceptable starch-derived replacement for sucrose in liquid applications, usually at lower cost. US consumption of HFCS has trebled since 1980, and since 1985 consumption in the US of all types of corn sweeteners exceeds total sucrose consumption (US Department of Agriculture, 1993). HFCS has advanced farthest in the United States and Japan under the umbrella of protection for home-grown sugar, a textbook illustration of the proposition that administrative schemes to raise prices tend to stimulate product development outside their jurisdiction. High free market prices for sugar now would simply encourage HFCS expansion in various parts of the world, to the lasting detriment of the sugar industry.

In addition to HFCS, new synthetic high-intensity sweeteners, such as aspartame, are now on offer, which do not have the drawbacks of saccharin and other older products of this kind and which cater to the growing demand in developed countries for a sweetener with little or no caloric value. The arrival of adequate sucrose substitutes means that sugar producers have to revise their traditional attitude towards the sugar cycle: the brief boom that so often in the past sustained them through several years of depressed prices would in future bring not just the longed for bonanza but also an invitation to the competition.

A stable and self-regulating market

Since 1985, the International Sugar Organization has existed by virtue of administrative agreements without economic clauses, with the objective of fostering international cooperation in sugar matters. The political winds of recent years were not propitious to the philosophy underlying multilateral commodity management schemes. In the case of sugar, moreover, the pattern of international trade had changed radically during the life of the four functional postwar agreements. The share of developing countries in world net imports rose from 25% in 1960 to 57% in 1990, while their share in world net exports dropped from 88% to 67%. Always skewed towards the exporter side, ISO membership fell from 44 exporting countries and 15 importing countries in 1982 to 34 exporters and eight importers in 1992. In the absence of regulatory tasks, the secretariat concentrated on the collection, analysis and dissemination of information, on the principle that the market works better with greater knowledge and understanding. A reconstituted Market Evaluation, Consumption and Statistics Committee provided an active forum for discussions among the members.

A new administrative agreement came into force at the beginning of 1993. Though it participated in the negotiations, the United States refused to sign the accord, after its proposal to reduce the ISO to a study group failed to win sufficient support. In the operational sense, however, this is what the ISO has become. Defaults in subscription payments triggered a financial crisis in 1992 that brought the organization to the brink of liquidation and led to cuts in staff and activities that went beyond the non-essential.

To be sure, management of the free market is, for the time being, unnecessary. Since 1988, free market prices have moved within a narrow range, which even a fall in Cuban export availabilities by perhaps as much as 45% within three years failed to shatter. Owing to the structural shift of the bulk of imports from wealthy to lower-income countries, whose demand is more price-elastic, the market is more self-regulating and stable. The price responsiveness of developing countries is reinforced by the new Russia which, without the gold and oil resources that allowed the USSR to act like a rich importer, now behaves like them. Happily for free market price stability, moreover, the precipitous drop in Cuban export capability coincides with a reduction in ex-Soviet consumption and import requirements as a result of internal price rises. Turning to the global supply side, current prices appear high enough to keep efficient producers on a course of modest expansion. At least for now, the market is mimicking the effects of a successful international sugar agreement.

Equally apparent, on the other hand, are the potentially destabilizing ingredients of the present situation. The end of special arrangements between Cuba and former socialist countries, as defined in the 1977 International Sugar Agreement, enlarges the free world market and makes it less residual; but it does not necessarily increase the total volume of world sugar trade. On the contrary, looking beyond the current depression of effective import demand caused by presumably transitory difficulties international trade would shrink if – free from the political constraint of their previous links with Cuba – Russia and other former Soviet republics seek to become more self-sufficient in sugar, as China has done. One argument advanced in recent times against agreements to regulate international commodity markets was that they were incompatible with the trade liberalization objectives of the General Agreement on Tariffs and Trade. Yet hearing the clamour for protection on the lines of the EC's Common Agricultural Policy emanating from East European sugar industries, it cannot be ruled out that a reduction of supports, and hence of the degree of sugar self-sufficiency in industrialized Western countries could be offset by contrary tendencies elsewhere in the world.

For the present, the quantitative expansion of the free market is coupled with a palpable loss in quality. The immediate result of the breakup of the Soviet Union and the transition to market economies in the region is the entry of a multitude of new operators, public and private, to the detriment of market transparency. Independently of whether or not the International Sugar Organization ever again acquires regulatory functions, its official status gives it a monitorial and investigative role beyond the capacity of commercial information services. Governments and sugar industries around the world would eventually have cause for regret were the organization to receive less than adequate support in recognition of this fact.

References

Ballinger, R A (1971) *A History of Sugar Marketing*, US Department of Agriculture, Economic Research Service, Agricultural Economic Report No 197, Washington, DC

Debus, L (1976) *Vorraussetzungen für die Wirksamkeit internationaler Rohstoffabkommen, abgeleitet aus den Erfahrungen mit den Weltzuckerabkommen*, Agrarwirtschaft, Sonderheft 66, Alfred Strothe Verlag, Hannover, Germany

Food and Agriculture Organization (1961) *The World Sugar Economy in Figures 1880–1959*, Commodity Reference Series No. 1, FAO, Rome

Gordon-Ashworth, F (1984) *International Commodity Control: A Contemporary History and Appraisal*, Croom Helm/St Martin's Press, London/New York

House of Lords (1977) *Report of the Select Committee on Commodity Prices*, HMSO, London

International Sugar Council (1963) *The World Sugar Economy: Structure and Policies, Vol II: The World Picture* ISC, London International Sugar Organization (1972) *Sugar Yearbook*, ISO, London

Khan, K (1982) *The Law and Organization of International Commodity Agreements*, Martinus Nijhoff, The Hague

Pérez-Cisneros, E (1957) *Cuba y el Mercado Azucarero Mundial*, Ucar Garcia SA, Havana

Rowe, J W F (1965) *Primary Commodities in International Trade*, Cambridge University Press, UK

Timoshenko, V P and Swerling, B C (1957) *The World's Sugar: Progress and Policy*, Stanford University Press

US Department of Agriculture (1993) *Sugar and Sweetener Situation and Outlook Yearbook*, Economic Research Service, SSRV18N2 (June)

Viton, A and Pignalosa, F (1961) *Trends and Forces of World Sugar Consumption*, Commodity Bulletin Series No. 32, FAO, Rome

V

World sugar situation 1955–94

Year	Production	Consumption	End year stocks, 000 t, raw value	Exports	Imports	Per capita consumption, kg	ISA daily price, cents/lb
1955	38 040	38 760	16 003	14 281	14 494	14.3	3.24
1956	39 808	41 757	14 230	13 917	14 093	15.1	3.47
1957	43 583	42 469	15 511	15 293	15 460	15.0	5.16
1958	47 225	44 979	17 721	15 580	15 544	15.5	3.50
1959	49 647	46 404	21 013	14 664	14 713	15.7	2.97
1960	51 945	49 282	23 698	17 512	17 534	16.1	3.14
1961	53 769	53 208	24 083	20 306	20 130	17.1	2.70
1962	52 281	53 607	22 642	19 049	18 934	17.3	2.78
1963	52 601	54 801	20 397	17 467	17 422	17.3	8.29
1964	60 192	55 711	24 125	17 204	16 451	17.2	5.77
1965	63 725	59 056	28 597	19 051	18 854	18.0	2.08
1966	62 930	61 127	30 773	18 715	19 088	18.3	1.81
1967	64 592	63 019	32 421	20 216	20 291	18.5	1.92
1968	65 158	66 260	30 124	21 284	20 089	19.1	1.90
1969	68 042	68 425	29 939	18 469	18 667	19.3	3.20
1970	72 891	71 856	30 446	21 766	21 238	19.9	3.68
1971	73 950	74 477	29 437	21 018	20 536	20.3	4.50
1972	75 724	75 822	28 595	21 875	21 131	20.4	7.27
1973	77 792	78 346	28 101	22 369	22 429	20.7	9.45
1974	76 004	77 249	26 275	22 099	21 518	20.0	29.66
1975	78 842	74 438	30 578	20 604	20 503	18.9	20.37
1976	82 390	79 250	32 791	22 757	21 830	19.7	11.51
1977	90 352	82 594	38 942	28 474	26 867	20.2	8.10
1978	89 832	86 356	42 151	25 072	24 805	20.7	7.81
1979	89 402	90 288	40 341	25 985	25 061	21.2	9.65
1980	83 946	88 647	35 506	26 826	26 692	20.2	28.69

Year	Production	Consumption	End year stocks, 000 t, raw value	Exports	Imports	Per capita consumption, kg	ISA daily price, cents/lb
1981	92 764	89 910	37 436	29 135	28 211	19.8	16.83
1982	101 812	93 066	45 349	20 430	29 597	20.2	8.35
1983	96 972	93 964	47 115	28 983	27 741	20.2	8.49
1984	99 222	96 774	49 126	28 495	28 058	20.4	5.20
1985	98 355	97 857	48 436	27 755	26 567	20.3	6.04
1986	101 177	101 316	48 191	27 202	27 096	20.6	6.04
1987	103 822	106 171	45 131	28 373	27 662	21.1	6.75
1988	104 591	105 863	43 562	27 420	27 123	20.7	10.20
1989	107 184	107 298	43 252	27 956	27 760	20.7	12.82
1990	110 894	108 417	44 877	28 474	27 622	20.6	12.55
1991	112 100	108 865	47 002	27 394	26 284	20.4	8.97
1992	117 564	112 803	50 724	31 801	30 762	20.9	9.06
1993	112 376	111 754	50 987	29 573	29 214	20.3	10.02
1994	110 286	113 798	47 508	30 038	30 071	20.4	12.11

Source: ISO.

240

References

Ahlfeld H: *World Sugar Trading – Analysis and Outlook of World Sugar Markets*, Agra Europe European Outlook Conference, London, 1995.

Ahlfeld H and Hagelberg G: 'Statistical Problems in World Sugar Balance Calculations', *Sugar, Essays to Mark the 125th Anniversary of F O Licht*, F O Licht, Ratzeburg; 1988.

Buzzanell P and Roney J: 'The Brazilian Sugar and Ethanol Industry: Performance and Prospects', *Sugar and Sweetener,* July 1988, Washington, 1988.

Deerr N: *The History of Sugar,* Chapman and Hall, London, 1950.

Early T and Westfall D: *The International Dynamics of National Sugar Policies,* Abel, Daft, Early and Ward International, Washington, 1994.

FAO: *Production Yearbook*, various issues; *Trade Yearbook*, various issues.

Sugar: Major Trade and Stabilization Issues in the Eighties, Economic and Social Development Paper No. 50, Rome, 1985.

The World Sugar Market, Prospects for the Nineties, ESC/M/92/3, Rome, 1992.

Fry J: *Cost-Competitiveness and Price Trends in the Asian Sugar Market,* Asia International Sugar Conference, Delhi, 1995.

Hagelburg G B: *The Caribbean Sugar Industries: Constraints and Opportunities,* ARP Occasional Paper No. 3, Yale University, 1974.

Hagelburg G B and Hannah A C: 'The Quest for Order: A Review of International Sugar Agreements', *Food Policy* 1994 19 (1), Elsevier Science Ltd, Oxford, 1994.

Hannah A C: 'Surplus Stocks', *International Sugar Economic Yearbook and Directory,* F O Licht, Ratzeburg, 1986.

'The Sugar Cycle, Structural Change and International Sugar Agreements', *International Sugar Report,* Vol. 119 No. 14, F O Licht Ratzeburg, 1987.

REFERENCES

The Dynamics of the World Sugar Market and International Co-operation, ABARE Outlook Conference, Canberra, 1990.

'World View on Sugar Trade and Prices', *Sugar and Sweetener,* December 1991, Washington.

International Sugar Trade: A Demographic Analysis of Major Trade Zones – The Past Present and Future, Asia International Sugar Conference, Delhi, 1995.

Hobhouse H: *Seeds of Change,* Sidgwick & Jackson, London, 1985.

Hugill A: *Sugar and all that – A History of Tate & Lyle,* Gentry Books, London, 1978.

IMF: *International Financial Statistics,* various issues.

ISO: *Sugar Yearbook,* various issues.

Monthly Statistical Bulletin, various issues.

World Sugar Statistics, 1955–94, London, 1996.

The Importance of Sugar in Export Earnings, MECAS(89)6, London, 1989.

Sugar Prices and HFCS Production, MECAS(90)2, London, 1990.

The Cost of Production of HFCS in the US, MECAS(90)18, London, 1990.

White Sugar Production and Trade (1956–1988), MECAS(90)45, London, 1990.

World Sugar Calendar, MECAS(91)1, London, 1991.

Evolution of the White Sugar Trade, 1970–89, MECAS (91)12, London, 1991.

Instability in the Sugar Market, an Overview, MECAS(91)14, London, 1991.

The Influence of National Policies on International Sugar Price Instability, MECAS(91)15, London, 1991.

Prospects for Alternative Sweeteners, MECAS(91)26, 7, London, 1991.

Sugar Trade and Changes in the World Economy 1960–90, and *Prospects for the 1990s,* MECAS(92)8, London, 1992.

The Role of Developing Countries in World Sugar Trade, MECAS(93)5, London, 1993.

Ecological Management Issues in the Sugar Sector, MECAS(94)8, London, 1994.

Sugar and Health, MECAS(94)17, London, 1994.

A Survey of Developments in Self-Sufficiency in Sugar from 1970 to 1993, MECAS(95)7, London, 1995.

Prospects for the Sugar Industry and Sugar Market in Eastern Europe, Proceedings of the 1st ISO Seminar, London, 1993.

The Far East Sugar Market, Proceedings of the 2nd ISO Seminar, London, 1994.

The Middle East and North African Sugar Market, Proceedings of the 3rd ISO Seminar, London, 1995.

Implications of the Uruguay Round for Sugar, Proceedings of the ISO Workshop, 1994.

Latin American and Caribbean Sugar Economies and Related Trade Pacts, Proceedings of the 4th ISO Seminar, London, 1996.

The World Sugar Economy – Structure & Policies, London, 1963.

Janes H and Sayers H J: *The Story of Czarnikow,* Harley Publishing Company Limited, London, 1963.

Mintz S W: *Sweetness and Power – the Place of Sugar in Modern History,* Viking, New York, 1985.

Perez-Lopez J: 'Cuban-Soviet Trade: Price and Subsidy Issues', Bulletin of

Latin American Research, Vol. 7, No. 1, 1988.

Prieto J: *The Effects of the Uruguay Round Agreement on Agriculture on Access to Sugar Markets*, ISO MECAS(95)9, London 1995.

Timoshenko V P and Swerling B C: *The World's Sugar–Progress and Policy*, Stanford University Press, Stanford, 1957.

UNCTAD: *Handbook of International Trade and Development Statistics*, various issue; *Monthly Commodity Price Bulletin*, various issues, Geneva.

Van Hook A: *Sugar – Its Production, Technology and Uses*, The Ronald Press Company, New York, 1949.

Waggoner P: 'How Much Land Can Ten Billion People Spare for Nature?' *Task Force Report*, No. 127, Council of Agricultural Sciences and Technology, Ames, 1994.

World Bank: *The World Bank Atlas, 1994*, Washington, 1993.

Index